THE
WILD BUNCH

XII   WIND AND SMOKE   *189*
          Snakes Alive!   *189*
          Signs and Superstitions   *194*

XIII STORMY ROADS   *199*
          Seat of Justice   *199*
          Gallant Outlawry   *202*
          Bully of the Town   *206*

XIV   LORE AND LEGEND   *211*
          The Fighting Parson   *211*
          Treasure Trove   *214*
          Indian Footprints   *216*
          Fact and Fable   *222*

XV   MEN OF THE MOUNTAINS   *229*
          Backhill Hermit   *229*
          Hideaway Bent   *233*

XVI   TRAITS AND TRENDS   *243*
          The Woman Who Waits   *243*
          Economic Drift   *246*

      Notes to the Text   *249*

INTRODUCTION

"Who will lament these simple mountaineers?" begins the first of half a dozen sonnets that compose Dennis Murphy's *Doomed Race*, a native son's elegy to a people "trampled by science and betrayed by man / And all but disinherited of earth." The answer to Murphy's question—a lament of its own—was a list of names longer than he might have expected, especially in the Year of the Ozarks. When it was issued as the 225th volume in the Contemporary Poets of Dorrance series by a Philadelphia publisher in 1941, *Doomed Race* had to get in line to tell the world about the Ozarks. At the very moment that Murphy's book hit shelves across the country, an obscure wanderer and self-taught artist in Missouri was putting the finishing touches on *Pioneers of the Ozarks*, a sort of *Doomed Race* in visual form. Lennis Leonard Broadfoot's amateurish but oddly compelling charcoal character studies lamented the coming extinction of the true Ozarkers, the woodcutters and farmers and crafters and musicians of the backroads neighborhoods that Route 66 and the modern world had long since bypassed. Gaze upon their weathered faces, Broadfoot implored the reader, for these are surely the last of their kind. It was a sentiment after Murphy's own heart.[1]

Broadfoot's *Pioneers of the Ozarks* would not see the light of day until 1944, even though his introduction indicates that he finished his part of the process in 1941. It would have been fitting for his publisher to have rushed the book into print—for it truly seemed to be the Year of the Ozarks—before more than 350 Japanese fighters and bombers transformed 1941 into the year of something else entirely. Just two of many works of art and entertainment focusing on the Ozarks produced that year, Broadfoot's *Pioneers of the Ozarks* and Murphy's *Doomed Race* captured the urgency with which people of various stripes approached the task of telling the story of the region and its people. It turns out that Murphy and Broadfoot were far from the only ones lamenting these simple mountaineers.

The Ozarks shone brightly in popular culture in 1941. Devotees of Harold Bell Wright's classic novel *The Shepherd of the Hills* bristled over the Hollywoodization of the plot, but moviegoers still flocked to see John Wayne in the Technicolor film version. Anyone interested in more authentic Ozarks accents could catch *Arkansas Judge* (costarring a young Roy Rogers), *Mountain Moonlight*, or *Tuxedo Junction*, three pictures starring the southwestern Missouri musical-comedy trio known as the Weaver Brothers and Elviry. On radio Arkansan Bob Burns—Bing Crosby's former comedic sidekick—launched *The Arkansas Traveler* in 1941 and anchored the show with outrageous stories of Aunt Doody, Uncle Fud, and other fictional relatives from the southern slope of the Ozarks. Elsewhere in Southern California, young actors Gloria Grahame and Robert Mitchum played the leads in a bawdy *Tobacco Road* knock-off called *Maid in the Ozarks*. After titillating Angelenos, it would find months of success in Chicago before continuing a cross-country tour that culminated in a Broadway debut after the war. Even the national pastime felt the region's imprint. In a season that saw Ted Williams top the .400 mark and Joe DiMaggio hit safely in a record fifty-six consecutive games, it was Ozarker Mickey Owen who made the most memorable (and infamous) play of 1941. When Brooklyn's all-star catcher mishandled strike three on what would have been the final out of the fourth game of the World Series, the error opened the door for a Yankees comeback victory. The demoralized Dodgers went on to lose the series and had to wait fourteen more years before capturing their first championship.[2]

The bibliophiles of Flatbush found little reason to celebrate the Ozarks, but 1941 was a bonanza year for other readers enamored of this mid-American highland region. Publishers offered a trio of nonfiction books, each attempting to explain whatever it was that made the Ozarks so unique and irresistible at the tail end of the Depression. Marguerite

Lyon in *Take to the Hills* and Catherine S. Barker in *Yesterday Today* seemed to be describing two very different regions—the first Ozarks filtered through the romantic lens of a Chicago back-to-the-lander, the second through the clinical and critical observations of a New Deal social worker. As the Year of the Ozarks drew to its close, readers caught their first glimpse of the most ambitious of the three, Otto Ernest Rayburn's unapologetically romantic *Ozark Country*, the fourth title in the American Folkways Series from New York's Duell, Sloan and Pearce. "Unbiased interpreters are needed to tell the romantic story of the Ozarks," Rayburn gushed without the slightest hint of irony. He was, of course, no freer of bias than were Broadfoot, Murphy, and just about anyone else chronicling the Ozarks. Like them—and like his friend Vance Randolph—Rayburn was drawn to the quaint and anachronistic, primitive survivals in a modern world. His Ozarkers may have provided "a firm cultural bridge between the worlds of yesterday and tomorrow," but it was clearly the region's strong scent of yesterday that lured Rayburn and kindred souls to the hills and hollers.[3]

It is telling that it was Wright's *The Shepherd of the Hills* that first introduced young Rayburn to the region that would become his lifelong obsession. He latched on to Wright's almost mystical view of the Ozarks and its "seclusion in the very heart of a continent steeped in commercialism and flushed with progress." Like so many romantics, Rayburn was trying to elude modernity, and he found in the backwoods Ozarker "a colorful personality 'lost' in isolation."

. . . . . .

Rayburn may have been a stranger to the rocky hillsides and deep hollers when he first arrived in the Ozarks, but he was no neophyte to rural living. Born in 1891 on a farm in southeastern Iowa, Otto Ernest Rayburn moved with his family to a farm in southeastern Kansas shortly after the turn of the twentieth century. In 1909 he enrolled in the preparatory academy at Marionville College, a tiny Methodist school in southwestern Missouri—"without realizing that I was in the Ozarks," he recalled years later. Returning home after nine months to begin a teaching career,

Rayburn continued his formal education a few years later when he moved to Baldwin City, Kansas, and entered another small Methodist college, Baker University. There he finished his preparatory degree and enrolled in the freshman class of 1916 at the grand old age of twenty-five. It was at Baker that Rayburn first read *The Shepherd of the Hills*, and so enamored of Wright's Ozarks did he become that he took the train to southwestern Missouri in the spring of 1917—"The hills called and I answered"—and purchased a forty-acre plot of land near the town of Reeds Spring, just a few miles from the setting of the beloved novel. Service in World War I brought a halt to Rayburn's first Ozark sojourn. Discharged in the spring of 1919, after almost two years in the army, he returned to Kansas to teach and spent his summers camping out in the Ozarks.[4]

Rayburn finally made the move to his adopted home region in 1922. An avid reader of Henry David Thoreau, John Burroughs, and other chroniclers of a life lived close to nature, Rayburn gave up teaching to build a cabin (Hideaway Lodge) on his own Walden Pond, a forty-acre homestead in the White River country of southwestern Missouri. Supporting himself with the cash he received from selling timber rights and the few dollars he made peddling candy to workers building a new highway through his neighborhood, Rayburn fished, floated the James Fork of the White River, hunted, trapped, and typed out his first musings on the Ozarks. Convincing a local to help him build a houseboat on the White River and float it to New Orleans, he and his friend journeyed as far as Cotter, Arkansas, in the fall of 1923. The friend's decision to take the train back home seemed to snap Rayburn out of his Huckleberry daze, but instead of returning to Hideaway Lodge, he found work as a one-room school teacher in rural Baxter County, Arkansas.[5]

Northern Arkansas was Rayburn's home for the next eight years, during which he worked mostly as a teacher and superintendent at a Presbyterian mountain mission school in the remote Madison County hamlet of Kingston. There Rayburn attempted to emulate another of his heroes, Elbert Hubbard, when he established the Kingscraft Press. Operating out of a room in the mission school, the press specialized in fine printing and published Rayburn's first book—a volume of poetry

entitled *The Inward Real, or an Ozarker Looks at Life*—but Kingscraft
proved "a struggle and a financial loss, from the start." It was also during
his time at Kingston that Rayburn began writing Ozark-themed columns for Little Rock's *Arkansas Gazette* and the *Tulsa Tribune* and made
his initial foray into "wildcat journalism," launching his first magazine,
Ozark Life. Coedited with another midwesterner and World War I veteran, Ted Richmond, the magazine reflected Rayburn's penchant for
boosterism and his deep interest in anything and everything Ozarks—
from folk songs and folktales to dialect and home remedies. And he
approached all of it in an earnest and eager manner, as if he had discovered the most wonderful and unbelievable place on Earth.[6]

The longtime bachelor tied the knot while teaching at Kingston. His
bride, Lutie Beatrice Day—a Texan sixteen years his junior—gave birth
to both of their children (Gloria Juivon, called Glovon, and Billy Joaquin)
in the latter half of the 1920s. An inveterate joiner and founder—and
apparently possessed of boundless energy as well—Rayburn took an
active role in the American Legion and the Kingston Presbyterian
Church and found the time to create three different organizations in the
late 1920s. Two of those, not surprisingly, were focused on his adopted
region: the Ozark Wildlife Association and the Ozarkians. Only the
last survived for more than a meeting or two. The Ozarkians, a covey
of regional writers and enthusiasts, reflected Rayburn's lifelong desire to
surround himself with kindred spirits, and its membership list grew to
include native and adopted Ozarkers from various walks of life, including
Vance Randolph, writers Charles J. Finger, Rosa Zagnoni Marinoni,
and Bernie Babcock, Missouri Congressman Dewey Short, lyceum
entertainer Thomas Elmore Lucy, tourism entrepreneur and booster
William H. "Coin" Harvey, and Springfield newspaper and radio personality May Kennedy McCord—"Queen of the Hillbillies."[7]

Believing—erroneously, as it turned out—that he was due a paid
sabbatical, Rayburn left Kingston at the conclusion of the school year in
1930 and moved his family and printing press fifty miles to the southwest, where he set up shop on the crest of the Boston Mountains in the
little railroad burg of Winslow. It was a typically impulsive move for

the peripatetic romantic—and led to typically disappointing financial results. At the end of 1931—the Depression deepening and debts piling up—Rayburn sold *Ozark Life*, left his printing press behind, and packed his young family off to the other side of the Ozarks, settling in the small town of Eminence in the rugged Current River country of southeastern Missouri. There he launched another modest magazine, the *Arcadian*—and two more organizations, the Arcadians and Hillcrofters—but the magazine folded after a year and a half. Spending the next six months at a tourist camp on the James Fork below Galena, Missouri, where he forged a friendship with Vance Randolph, Rayburn reluctantly abandoned the Ozarks in January 1933. Moving Lutie Beatrice and the kids to Texas, he settled near his wife's family in rural Hopkins County and took a job as a school principal.[8]

"Publishing an Ozark magazine is like going on a snipe hunt and holding the sack," Rayburn reminisced late in life. "For most people, once is enough. But not for me." The heart of the Depression found him hundreds of miles from his beloved Ozarks, but Rayburn kept the booster flame burning for the region to which he longed to return—and he did so largely through the publication of his third magazine. *Arcadian Life*, which he started just a few days after arriving in Texas, did not break his string of unsuccessful periodicals. It may have been his biggest money loser yet. *Arcadian Life* seemed headed for the grave until Rayburn's fortunes turned in the middle of the decade. He was forty-five years old when Congress passed a bill mandating payment of bonuses for World War I veterans in 1936 instead of the original date of 1945. It was, he recalled, "the largest sum of money I had ever received." The bonus provided Rayburn the financial wherewithal to make his way back to the Arkansas highlands—only this time it was the Ouachita Mountains that beckoned. Settling his family in the little village of Caddo Gap in southwestern Arkansas, Rayburn found work as superintendent of the local rural consolidated school district. He continued to publish *Arcadian Life*, on rare occasions ending the month in the black, and found a small Arkansas printer to publish a cheap "booklet of philosophical prose" that he called *Roadside Chats*. It was during this sojourn in the Ouachitas that he made his most enduring contribution to the study and celebration of the Ozarks—the book that you now hold. Learning of Duell, Sloan and Pearce's intention to commission a book on the Ozarks for its American Folkways Series, Rayburn mailed samples of his work to editor Erskine Caldwell in the spring of 1940. "I am completely sold on you because your writing is different," Caldwell wrote back, and Rayburn relinquished his superintendent's job for a part-time teaching position in the fall to concentrate on writing.[9]

By the time *Ozark Country* was released, six days before the bombing of Pearl Harbor, the author was back in the education business, having assumed the superintendency of the little Rural Dale School in Garland County, Arkansas. *Arcadian Life* enjoyed its largest readership to date, but Rayburn's busy schedule forced him to stop publication just a few months after his book came out. The magazine bug bit again before long, and the summer of 1943 bore witness to the first issue of *Rayburn's Ozark Guide*, his fourth and final effort. It was his first profitable publishing venture. Suffering frayed nerves and a bout of ill health—a rarity for the robust outdoorsman—Rayburn resigned his job at Rural Dale in December 1943 and went into business as a real estate broker. But the Ozarks continued to beckon. As World War II drew to a close, Rayburn looked to move back to the hills about which he had been writing for twenty years. He took a shine to West Plains, Missouri, but found it "short on folklore." His search ended 150 miles to the west, where he found a small town that "seemed to have everything I needed." Confident that Eureka Springs, Arkansas, "could be made the folklore capital of the nation," Rayburn packed up his wife and son—Glovon had recently married—and headed for the old resort town in 1946. He was joined by Randolph two years later.[10]

Capitalizing on the booming postwar travel and tourism market, he reached an ever-expanding national audience with *Rayburn's Ozark Guide*, which eventually grew to a fat eighty pages in length. Though the chamber of commerce and town leaders shot down his grand vision of "Pioneer Village"—a sort of nineteenth-century Ozarks version of Colonial Williamsburg—Rayburn had otherwise found his elusive arcadia and the financial security to enjoy it. He would spend the rest of his life in Eureka Springs, the only time in his rambling adult existence that he tarried more than half a dozen years in one place. Penning colorful stories of the backwoods, peddling real estate, running a bookshop, and guiding tours of his unique new hometown, Rayburn invited readers to come experience the fleeting old days in the Ozarks. At the center of an eclectic coterie of writers, artists, and Ozarks enthusiasts, he coordinated the annual Ozark Folk Festival and played a leading role in the creation of the Arkansas Folklore Society. Rayburn's years of boosterism and promotion brought him recognition in the 1950s, including a distinguished service award from the Ozark Playgrounds Association and the honorary titles of Arkansas Traveler and Ambassador of Arkansas from governor Orval Faubus. And the prolific Rayburn continued to find time for writing outside his work on the magazine, finishing his autobiography and a history of Eureka Springs, all while amassing a forty-foot-long shelf of notes and files that he called the Ozark Folk Encyclopedia.[11]

He was still dutifully adding to this collection when he died at the age of sixty-nine on October 30, 1960. At the time of his death, Otto Ernest Rayburn had certainly made himself one of the leading voices of the Ozarks, contributing more to the understanding—and mythologizing —of the region than anyone not named Vance Randolph. No one did more to promote the Ozarks to tourists, readers, and home seekers, and no one—not even Randolph—developed a deeper admiration for the region and its people. Per his wishes, the Ozark Folk Encyclopedia— which Rayburn considered his "major contribution to culture and to the Ozarks"—eventually found its way to the special collections of the University of Arkansas Libraries in Fayetteville. It remains at the university today, as does the most complete collection of surviving issues of Rayburn's magazines. For researchers, the Ozark Folk Encyclopedia is an amazing grab bag of all things Ozarks, as esoteric as it is encyclopedic. Some six decades since his death, however, Rayburn's most enduring and accessible contribution to his adopted region is *Ozark Country*.[12]

. . . . . .

Ozark Country was the third nonfiction book on the region released to a national audience in the last half of 1941. Rayburn's romantic spirit matched that of Marguerite Lyon, whose *Take to the Hills* was the first of the trio to emerge. A copywriter for a Chicago advertising agency, Lyon and her husband had bought a farm near Mountain View, Missouri, during the Depression. While Mr. Lyon went back to the land full-time, Marge spent weekends and holidays in rural southern Missouri and began writing about the couple's experiences and colorful neighbors in "Marge of Sunrise Mountain Farm" features for the *Chicago Tribune* in 1939. Largely made up of these features, Lyon's *Take to the Hills* proved a hit with its target audience: city folk with a nostalgic jonesing for an imagined, idealized rural life.

The book published between the release of *Take to the Hills* and *Ozark Country*, however, set a very different tone. Despite its romantic title, *Yesterday Today* was the yin to *Ozark Country*'s yang. The author, Catherine S. Barker, was an educated newcomer to the region who accompanied her academician husband to northern Arkansas and then found herself traveling backroads through the hills and hollers of the Ozarks as a New Deal social worker. Spending her time with the region's most destitute and desperate residents, her account of the Ozarks was a critical one, more condemnatory than celebratory.

Rayburn was well aware of the side of Ozark life that the chambers of commerce and boosters generally ignored—unsanitary homes with no outhouses or wells, illnesses resulting from insufficient diets, substandard schools, grinding poverty—all things chronicled by Barker. But it wasn't in his nature to dwell on such negatives. After all, it was his romantic attachment to a fictionalized Ozarks that lured him to the region. He remained committed to perpetuating this idealized and nostalgic image of his adopted home throughout his thirty-five years of chronicling the Ozarks. This commitment was nowhere on better display than in *Ozark Country*, which, like Lyon's book, contained a number of anecdotes and stories previously published as newspaper features.[13]

Reinforcing his sepia-toned vision of the Ozarks, Rayburn introduces readers to his region through the people and customs of fictional

Woodville, Missouri, a whitewashed (and seemingly whites-only) utopian composite of the many small towns and rural places he had called home. His decision to introduce each chapter with a Woodville vignette reflects the seamless melding of truth and fiction, reality and legend, in Rayburn's Ozarks. "It is not my business to draw the line between fact and fallacy," he claims in *Ozark Country*, and he made good on the promise. The book contains snippets of history—albeit history riddled with inaccuracies— but its primary focus is the subject of its series, folkways. Consequently, Rayburn covers much of the same ground cultivated by Randolph ten years earlier in *The Ozarks: An American Survival of Primitive Society*. He does so, however, without Randolph's fascination with the darker, seamier side of their adopted region or his more consciously anthropological approach. Rayburn also lacks Randolph's flair for sophisticated yet accessible wordsmanship that better endures the ravages of time and changes in taste. Modern readers will likely struggle through Rayburn's slavish recreations of thick Ozarks dialect and repeated references to the "redman" and "redskins," among other terms now considered offensive. The supposedly pure northern European racial heritage celebrated in the book's second chapter serves as another reminder that *Ozark Country* and its author were products of a less inclusive era.

Rayburn's style blended elements of folklore, travel writing, and regional boosterism—"readable Americana" was the politely dismissive phrase one reviewer employed. Looking back at *Ozark Country* sixteen years after its publication, Rayburn admitted to writing the book in "the spirit of romanticism." "I was looking at the Ozarks through rose colored glasses," he recalled. "I saw only what I wanted to see."[14] What Rayburn saw was an Ozarks where country folk carried the undiluted blood of their Anglo-Saxon ancestors and spoke a dialect little changed in more than three centuries, a land of old-timey mountain music, granny women, tall tales, and superstitions. In Rayburn's Ozarks it was still worthwhile to talk about black bears, water-powered gristmills, and backroom spinning wheels, even if they were rarer than airports by midcentury.

Ozark Country had the misfortune of being released at the moment the Year of the Ozarks was transformed into the year the United States entered World War II. With one exception, Rayburn's book received little national promotion from reviewers—but that exception was a big one. On January 18, 1942, the *New York Times* gave *Ozark Country* full-page treatment on the front page of its book review section. Under the headline "The Ozarks, Deep in America," reviewer R. L. Duffus admitted that "if you are looking for folkways you can hardly do better than turn to the Ozarks." Given the recent barrage of Ozark folksiness in books and popular culture, the statement was probably more a message of surrender at that point. Duffus, a middle-aged, Stanford-educated New Englander with a list of erudite books to his credit, was polite, even though he recognized *Ozark Country* for the overwrought celebration that it was. "Page Messrs. Rousseau and Chateaubriand!" he declared after quoting one particularly romantic passage lauding the unspoiled solitude of the hill people. Beneath the placid surface of Rayburn's storybook Ozarks, Duffus sensed a more realistic and less idealized existence, especially for one half of the population. "This seems to be a man's world," the reviewer noted of an account slanted heavily toward the male perspective. "One suspects a good many wives are overworked in this Ozark Arcadia. The men do the hunting and fishing—it is, indeed, their duty. The women, as is also their duty, cook, clean house, sew and look after the children." All things considered, Duffus found Rayburn's Ozarks too good to be true. "The present reviewer doesn't for a moment believe that the Ozarks are as picturesque and as Arcadian as Mr. Rayburn says they are," he concluded. "A good part of the Arcadia is in Mr. Rayburn's head. But that is the way with most Arcadias, and the one Mr. Rayburn describes is a pleasant one to visit." Duffus may have written his review with one decidedly arched brow, but he was not immune to the guileless charms of a veteran promoter. "Maybe we wouldn't like to live in the Ozarks," he confessed, "but it is agreeable to visit them in Mr. Rayburn's company. Mr. Rayburn is just ingenuous enough, by art or artlessness, to be the best of guides."[15]

Indeed he was, and more than a few people were guided to and through the Ozarks by Rayburn's magazines or *Ozark Country*. Despite initially disappointing sales, by the time Rayburn self-published his autobiographical *Forty Years in the Ozarks* in 1957, *Ozark Country* was in its fourth printing. More than a few readers must have agreed with Duffus's recommendation of the book as a pleasant diversion to "take one's mind off the war."[16] In the postwar years, *Ozark Country* continued to appeal to people who believed the modern world was wiping out an existence that once was comforting and nourishing, a style of life more tranquil than volatile, more dogtrot than rat race. The passage of time continuously replenishes this population, each generation convinced that something fundamental, something vital to humanity's understanding of itself, withers as the physical and cultural markers of its youth pass from the scene. All of us reach this understanding if given enough time. Rayburn simply got there quicker than most. He was one of those rare souls born with a powerful sense of loss, even before losing a thing. In his bones he knew the Ozarks flickered with the embers of a lost world. The arcadia in his mind fanned those embers into a roaring *Ozark Country*.

· · · · · ·

The romanticism and primitivism that motivated Rayburn were very much in line with the spirit flowing through most other Ozarks works of the age and the fascination with the region in general. Whether outsiders like Rayburn, Randolph, and Lyon, or natives like Broadfoot and Murphy, the chroniclers of the Ozarks shared with other seekers of anachronism a primitivist streak, a romantic's desire to discover in a rural and marginal region the survival of an authentic premodernism. For the traditionalist disillusioned with the seeming failure of America's brand of modernism, the Ozarks was about projection and protection. It was a region upon which the hopes and desires of disenchanted observers could be projected, a place whose allegedly premodern residents should be protected against the harmful and irreversible effects of the modernizing world.

The Ozarks had come of age by 1941, its image fully formed in the American consciousness. It is fitting, then, that a fellow who contributed so much to that regional social construct had the last word on the Ozarks that same year. So, in the inviting spirit of Otto Ernest Rayburn, I welcome you back to an age of fascination with regional distinctiveness. Welcome back to the Year of the Ozarks. Welcome back to *Ozark Country*.

Brooks Blevins

NOTES

1. Dennis Murphy, *Doomed Race* (Philadelphia, PA: Dorrance and Company Publishers, 1941), 13; Lennis L. Broadfoot, *Pioneers of the Ozarks* (Caldwell, ID: Caxton Printers, 1944).

2. See chapter 3 of Brooks Blevins, *Arkansas/Arkansaw: How Bear Hunters, Hillbillies, and Good Ol' Boys Defined a State* (Fayetteville: University of Arkansas Press, 2009); Lee Server, *Robert Mitchum: "Baby, I Don't Care"* (New York: St. Martin's Press, 2001), 51; Jeffrey Marlett, "Mickey Owen," https://sabr.org/bioproj/person/mickey-owen/, accessed August 3, 2020.

3. Marguerite Lyon, *Take to the Hills: A Chronicle of the Ozarks* (Indianapolis, IN: Bobbs-Merrill Company, 1941); Catherine S. Barker, *Yesterday Today: Life in the Ozarks* (Caldwell, ID: Caxton Printers, 1941); Otto Ernest Rayburn, *Ozark Country* (New York: Duell, Sloan & Pearce, 1941), 32, 34.

4. Ethel C. Simpson, "Otto Ernest Rayburn," *Encyclopedia of Arkansas History & Culture*, www.encyclopediaofarkansas.net, accessed March 13, 2018; "Marionville Collegiate Institute," www.lostcolleges.com/marionville -college, accessed March 13, 2018; Otto Ernest Rayburn, *Forty Years in the Ozarks* (Eureka Springs, AR: Ozark Guide Press, 1957), 4, 18–19, 50; Brooks Blevins, *Hill Folks: A History of Arkansas Ozarkers and Their Image* (Chapel Hill: University of North Carolina Press, 2002), 142–43. Information on Rayburn's stay at Baker University courtesy of Baker University archivist Sara DeCaro, via email to Blevins, March 13, 2018. See also Simpson, "Otto Ernest Rayburn, An Early Promoter of the Ozarks," *Arkansas Historical Quarterly* 58 (Summer 1999): 160–179.

5. Rayburn, *Forty Years*, 7, 28–44.

6. Simpson, "Otto Ernest Rayburn"; Rayburn, *Forty Years*, 45–51.

7. Rayburn, *Forty Years*, 52–55.

8. Rayburn, *Forty Years*, 59–72.

9. Rayburn, *Forty Years*, 50, 74–79.

10. Rayburn, *Forty Years*, 79–85.

11. Rayburn, *Forty Years*, 86–97.

12. Rayburn, *Forty Years*, 86–97.

13. Rayburn, *Forty Years*, 8.

14. Edith H. Crowell, "Review of Ozark Country," *Library Journal*, November 15, 1941, 999; Rayburn, *Forty Years*, 8.

15. R. L. Duffus, "The Ozarks, Deep in America," *New York Times*, January 18, 1942, 6: 1.

16. Duffus, "Ozarks, Deep," 6: 1.

EDITOR'S NOTE

To improve the readability of *Ozark Country*, this reissue includes minor adjustments to formatting and punctuation. It also includes corrections of misspelled words and other small errors contained in the original version, such as incorrectly identified newspaper or book titles. Otherwise, the style and language of the original, including words and phrases considered offensive today, appear as they did in 1941.

OZARK COUNTRY

AUTHOR'S FOREWORD

The characters in the first sketch of each chapter of this book are fictional and do not refer to actual persons, living or dead.

Some parts of this book have appeared in the *Arkansas Gazette*, the *Arkansas Democrat*, *Ozark Life*, *Arcadian Magazine*, and *Arcadian Life*. I have drawn upon several books and periodicals for basic historical facts, notably Fred Allsopp's *Folklore of Romantic Arkansas*, Vance Randolph's *Ozark Mountain Folks* and other works on the Ozarks, and May Kennedy McCord's "Hillbilly Heartbeats" in the Springfield *News and Leader*.

I am indebted to innumerable persons for assistance in the folklore research necessary for this work, but I cannot hope to list all their names here. Thanks are due in a large measure also to June Denby, Vance Randolph, and Arthur H. Estabrook for reading first drafts of the manuscript and offering suggestions.

Otto Ernest Rayburn
Caddo Gap, Arkansas

CHAPTER I

A World Apart

. . . .

Loafer's Glory

Woodville is an Ozark community nestled in the elbow of contentment. A quarter of a century ago, this backhill village had no roads for motor convenience, and no inclination among its citizens to build them. The utopian complexion of the neighborhood was freckled with squatty cabins and scarred with broken-down rail fences. The atmosphere of the place was charged with wholesome laziness and tranquil indifference. Beyond the hills, a machine age was being ushered in and the commercial world throbbed with expectancy. But all was quiet as a stark calm at Woodville in the Missouri Ozarks. There was no dominant urge to chase industrial phantoms, no quest for sophisticated culture. Life moved along in its commonplace way with the customs of the fathers acceptable to the children, even to the fourth generation. The hillsman had learned to polish his jewels of consistency with arcadian simplicity and was satisfied with things as he found them.

I sat on the counter in Tart Tuttle's general store satisfied with life. The open prune box by my side offered the maximum of opportunity and I helped myself. Lazily I ate the fruit and flipped the seeds at the old cat drowsing contentedly on a sack of dried apples by the salt barrel. Tart was occupied with reading the postal cards that had arrived on the twice-a-week mail. He gave me and the prunes no attention at all. What matter a few prunes, thought the merchant, if the goodwill of a customer is retained.

It was high noon in the quiet hills. Within an hour or two the "store-porch jury" would assemble to sprawl in the welcome shade, discuss current topics, pass judgment, and whittle time into nothingness. I had arrived at the store an hour early to read my mail before the crowd gathered. My appetite for prunes satisfied, I stretched myself the full length of the counter and watched a mouse inspect the butter tub and shy away. Surely, I thought, this is the ideal place to loiter and recuperate, to harness life's forces against evil days that follow civilization's excesses. It was the laziest place I had found in the drowsy Ozarks since leaving my home in a neighboring state and burning the bridges behind me.

Tuttle's store hung on the brow of a knoll in a little valley that bordered a tumbling river. The ramshackle building was shaded by a large tree known in the neighborhood as the Old Drunk Walnut. Many years before a pioneer had built a distillery by the tree and dumped the mash waste out the door. The effect of the seepage was miraculous. The tree got hilariously drunk and never sobered up. The leaves on the tipsy limbs curled like a hillbilly's trigger finger. But the old walnut appeared to be endowed with good nature and did not grow any nuts to drop on loafers' heads. It seemed to wink approval at everything we said and did.

A general store in the Ozarks is a conglomeration of almost everything hillsmen eat, wear, and use. Tuttle's place of business was a jumble of contradictions. Stick candy kept company with plug tobacco, and bolts of calico sometimes got too familiar with the vinegar barrel. Boots and shoes out of boxes lay tangled on the open counter where the merchant or customer had tossed them. Hats and overalls covered with dust were piled on a shelf propped with a scantling. There was snuff for pleasure and pills for pain in a flyspecked showcase patched with cardboard. Everything was topsy-turvy from the front to the rear of the store. The post office in the corner was about the only orderly arrangement in the entire building. Tart, upon being commissioned postmaster, had taken a large dry goods box and built a dozen pigeonholes in it for the mail.

This was placed on the top of another large box and centered by a small opening through which stamps were sold and deliveries made.

The bookkeeping in the store was in line with the merchant's general habits. He owned a daybook but seldom took the trouble to use it. A charge account might be penciled on the salt barrel or marked on the lid of a shoebox, but even that was not considered necessary. Tart Tuttle had an almost infallible memory. "Just carried everything in his head," the neighbors told me. And his extension of credit was very nearly universal. Once a stranger in a covered wagon pulled up at the store. "Hey, there," he bellowed, "bring me out a pair of number ten brogans." Tart produced the shoes and the traveler tried them on. "Pay you this fall if the boll weevils don't catch up with me," he said as he headed his team toward the Arkansas cotton fields. Believe it or not, he did return and make payment.

It was the thirteenth day of the month, and a Friday to boot, but I am not superstitious in such matters and gave it no thought. But it did make a difference with Ed Bullock who lived "a whoop and a holler" down the trail from the store. Ed was cautious as a tomcat on a milk shelf. He had not neglected rubbing a little charcoal in his matted hair that morning. He knew that the footlog across Clabber Creek would be slippery after the freshet the day before, and his new boots were not trustworthy. Superstition says that charcoal in the hair is good luck insurance.

Tobe Mullins, sometimes reticent, sometimes talkative, but always philosophical, realized the cultural value of the store-porch session, and nothing short of a feud or a funeral would have kept him away. Dinner over, he made excuse to his thrifty spouse that he had seen some young squirrels in the clearing and, gun on shoulder, dog at heels, sauntered off into the hollow below the cabin. He planned his course to reach the store in the nick of time to open the discussion.

Hite Lindsey, shiftless but likable, had shingles to rive and repairs to make on his shanty, but the opportunity for rich social intercourse with his fellows called him to the store. He sat on a cracker box next to Lem Logan, chewing homegrown tobacco and whittling out a toy from a block of cedar. Lizzie, his overworked wife, had urged him to remain at home that evening and spend the time at such monotonous labor as mending holes in the roof. She had stood in the door with one baby nursing from a skinny breast and another, about a year older, astraddle her hip as she begged her man to give some consideration to his family. But Hite didn't push the collar like his father before him and could see no need for such strenuous labor when the rabbits were out in the open and everything pointed to a spell of dry weather. Anyway, shingles might curl if put on in the light of the moon. "No call t' rip his britches over it."

Other representative citizens of the Woodville community were present to air their views, stretch their sentiments, and tune in on the lore and logic of the day. It was a distant echo of the old New England town meeting, with a peculiar hillbilly slant, resurrected in the backhills of the Ozarks.

The meeting opened informally with refreshment from Tart Tuttle's hospitable jug. As yet the limb of the law had not stepped in to threaten the community with prohibition of liquid corn. The mountaineers could sell the product by bushel or barrel as they preferred. Each man tipped the jug as a matter of course and thought nothing about it. Random remarks drifted with the lazy tobacco smoke from clay and corncob pipes. Weather is a prime topic for conversation on such occasions. Naturally, it is a thing of first importance to men who depend upon rain and sun to grow the crops they neglect to cultivate.

· · · · · ·

Signs of change in the weather are common knowledge to every hillsman. A rainy Monday means that it will be a rainy week. A rain on the first Sunday of the month is a certain sign that showers will come on the three Sundays following. The old couplet "Rain before seven, shine before eleven" is an esteemed adage of the hill country. When the blue of the sky is thickly studded with stars, it is a sign that rain will be falling soon. When there is a circle around the moon, the number of stars in the circle tells how many days before the next rain. When horses refuse to drink, or the rain crow squawks, it portends a break in dry weather. A new moon is wet or dry, depending upon its position in the heavens. Shooting stars foretell unsettled weather. When the sunrise is red, rain is almost sure to follow. If it rains on the twentieth day of June all the grapes will fall off the vines. A storm is expected when rabbits seek security in protected places, and when chickens go to roost earlier than usual or stand with ruffled feathers, tails to the wind. The cock, which hillsmen call rooster in ordinary conversation, is considered to be one of nature's best forecasters. His persistent crowing before nightfall is a certain sign that a freshet will come before morning. Ordinarily, if the sun sets clear, the next day will be fair. But for some unknown reason, Tuesday is an exception in certain sections of the Ozarks. A clear sunset on Tuesday means a rain before Friday.

In addition to this traditional weather lore, these men at Tuttle's store knew all the popular signs connected with the moon and zodiac. The almanac is a favorite textbook in the hills and its teachings are taken seriously. But there is a strange divergence of belief and practice among hillsmen. By all known signs it was an ideal day to kill tree sprouts that were spreading into the fields and almost every farmer in the community had sprouts to kill, but, just the same, ten or twelve men occupied kegs and benches on the store porch under the old walnut with no inclination to swing ax or grubbing hoe. Folk life is like that. Wholesome laziness is as essential in flavoring the personality as fatback is in seasoning turnip greens. Of course, these men worked on occasion, and worked hard, but the call of companionship could not be denied and Tart's store was the only place in the neighborhood suited to such pastime. Of course, the womenfolks dropped in occasionally to swap their butter and eggs for such commodities as are not produced on their small farms, but it was not fitting they should loiter after their business was transacted.

. . . . . .

Tobe Mullins approached the main topic of the afternoon with exasperating cautiousness. Eleven pair of eyes were on him, including my own, impatiently waiting for the information he had to deliver. Only the day before he had returned from the county seat where he had "set" on the jury during the three-day session of circuit court. He had things of importance to divulge.

"I'll be gol-durned if'n that Luke Walter's hawg-stealin' case didn't turn out jist like I calculated it would," began Tobe as he reached for Tart's ever-flowing jug, threw back his head and, like a thirsty chicken, let the "talk-water" slip down, scarcely moving a throat muscle.

Silence hung like heavy vapor in the shade of the friendly old walnut tree. Eleven pair of ears were alert but none of us betrayed any undue curiosity. Tobe stroked his drooping tobacco-stained mustache thoughtfully as he let the import of his statement sink in. He loved the limelight, and in his own unique way never failed to dramatize a commonplace occurrence.

Tobe's dialect was typical of the hillsman who butchers his English with discrimination. His "hit" for "it" was a stroke of emphasis. He changed vowels and dropped consonants in true hillbilly fashion. Basically a speech with illiterate phrasing, it carried a wealth of lingual survivals. I especially enjoyed the fluency with which he used Elizabethan words and phrases.

This colorful Ozarkian dialect is rapidly passing. The influence of schoolteachers and radio is having its effect. Only a few old-timers use the picturesque dialect that was carried to the Ozarks by their Anglo-Saxon forebears.

"I don't begredge a feller a little hawg meat once in a while but I like t' see him git it honest-like," continued Tobe. "If'n a man's up agin it, I'll go right into my smokehouse an' share what I got with him. But this here stealin's gittin' fur too common in th' county. Th' jedge thought so, too, an' he wus aimin' on puttin' a stop t' hit. We'uns knowed he had his back up right frum th' time he rapped fur order in th' courthouse. He had a turrible sourcastic look on his face when th' high sheriff brought Luke in."

"'Air ye goin' t' plead guilty?' asked th' jedge.

"Luke wus as fidgety as a turkey gobbler tied t' a choppin' block even if he did have th' dried gizzard of a hoot owl tied 'round his neck fer good luck. He swallered hard an' shook his head. Said he wouldn't since he'd already give a lawyer feller five dollars to defend him.

"'Moight as well,' said th' jedge, 'yer guilty or ye wouldn't be hyar.'"

Ed Bullock passed his store tobacco and Tobe took a chew. Ed's new boots were giving him the third degree. He had filled them with soaked corn the night before to swell them but the result was far from satisfactory. He sympathized with Luke in his "pinched" condition. Tobe chewed his quid of tobacco a few seconds, closed one eye, and taking careful aim at a grasshopper sunning itself on a nearby jimsonweed, let loose a stream of "ambeer" that knocked the insect into the dust. Pleased with his skillful marksmanship, he went on with his story.

"Hit wus a hard nut fer ol' Ben Blakely, th' distric' attorney, t' crack. Pears like he jist couldn't get nary a thing 'ceptin' hearsay stuff agin Luke. Of course ever'body knowed he wus guilty as a suck-egg houn' dog, but knowin' air one thing an' provin' air another'n. Luke tried t' put up an alibi, sayin' he wus tomcattin' down on Bull Crick at th' time th' hawg wus stole. He up an' tole all about hit right thar in th' courthouse. 'Cordin' t' my notion, a feller that'll handle that sort o' talk with decent womenfolks right in th' room orter be tarred an' feathered an' rid on a lye-soaked rail clean t' th' Arkansas line."

Hite Lindsey, eyes swimming in corn liquor, nodded his approval.

"An', by cracky, he had two witnesses to back 'im up. Both of 'em got on th' stand an' swore they had seen Luke in th' Bull Crick settlement that very day. An' that thar lawyer of Luke's shore wus a slick one. His voice gurgled like long sweet'nin' pourin' out'n a jug. I snuck a look at th' other fellers on th' jury an' ever' last one of 'em wus a drizzlin' an' wipin' their noses on their sleeves.

"All of a suttent I reckon th' jedge got his belly full o' sich whimperin' talk. He took his mallet an' banged so hard th' winders fairly rattled, an' bellered out that th' time fer pleadin' wus all took up. Then he instructed us an' he didn't beat 'round th' bush about hit. He jist as plain as told us not t' come back frum th' jury room till we found Luke Walters guilty in th' worst degree.

"Luke had gone t' sleep by this time, a-settin' in th' big cheer by th' lawyer's table. Th' sheriff walked over an' give 'im a kick on th' shinbone an' he jumped up an' grabbed his laig an' went hoppin' 'round th' room like a one-laigged shite-poke. Hit ort t' be contempt o' court t' go t' sleep right under th' jedge's whiskers.

"Wal, we went t' th' room th' sheriff had fixed up fer us back o' th' jailhouse an' after playin' a couple o' games o' pitch cards t' sorta steady our nerves, we elected a foreman an' begin t' ballot. But never did all vote alike. Th' count wus 'leven t' one an' thar we stuck.

"After 'bout three-four hours th' jedge got turrible restless with us settin' back thar drinkin' spring water an' playin' cards, an' takin' votes on Luke between games. Th' sheriff said he chawed up a ten-cent plug o' store tobacker while waitin' fer us t' come t' a decision. After a while, his patience got plumb wore out an' he jist couldn't stand hit no longer. He ordered us brought in t' th' courtroom. We lined up in front o' His Honor an' he asked th' foreman if we had reached a verdict. 'No,' said Sam Willis, th' feller we had elected, 'th' count is 'leven t' one.' Ye ort t' heerd that jedge rave.

"'Who is that thar one man?' roared th' jedge. 'Pint 'im out t' me!' Sam pinted t' me as th' contrary one.

"'What!' bellowed th' jedge. 'Ye would dare hold out agin 'leven good an' true men sich as these? What d'ye mean by refusin' t' uphold th' laws o' th' state?'

"I tried t' speak but my voice hung in my throat. Anyhow, th' jedge didn't give me a chance t' say nary a word. Sich a lambastin' as I got! Th' sheriff stood handy like as if t' take me t' jail if'n th' jedge ordered him to. At last His Honor jist had t' stop talkin' t' ketch his breath.

"'Yer Honor,' I says, havin' sorta got control o' myself, '*I wus th' only one on your side!*'"

The climax of Tobe's story brought hearty laughter all around, and Lem Logan was reminded of a somewhat similar incident that occurred during court week in Taney County.

· · · · · ·

The day was almost gone and the doves in the pine thicket mourned its going. The shadows shifted in and out through the cornfield in the valley like mice playing hide-and-seek in a barn loft. But juicy yarns and dry tobacco continued to make the rounds with the store-porch assembly until the sound of a supper bell in Goose Neck Hollow caused an adjournment. Scattering like quail in a barrage, each man sought his home. An hour after sundown an owl hooted on Smackover Ridge, but no one heard it except the two Logan boys who were on their way to a pie supper at the Bug Tussle schoolhouse. "Tired Nature's sweet restorer, balmy sleep" had come to Woodville.

Location and Names

Some Ozark horse breeders think they can produce a colt of a certain hue by waving a cloth of the desired color in front of the mare at the time of breeding. This defies the Mendelian laws, but not many hillsmen have heard of Mendel and the rules of dominant and recessive traits are not common knowledge in the hills. Perhaps a break with science is pardonable if the purpose is achieved.

I break with literary tradition in this book by mixing fiction with fact. The first section of each chapter is colored with fictitious names and incidents as a prelude to the matter-of-fact material that follows. From atmosphere and patterns we go to actual lore and history. Each has its part in depicting the flavor and individuality of this region.

. . . . . .

The Ozark Country is an egg-shaped uplift sprawling in the mammoth bed of the Mississippi Valley. It is a highland region which occupies the southern half of Missouri, the northwestern part of Arkansas, and a few counties in eastern Oklahoma. Some geographers include the southeastern nook of Kansas, the southwestern part of Illinois, and even a portion of western Tennessee. But I prefer to restrict the Ozark Country to the first three states. This expansive empire of hills and valleys, and occasional stretches of rolling prairie, occupies an area equal to that of the state of Georgia—approximately 60,000 square miles. The greatest length from the cloud-pillowed peaks of the Ouachitas (pronounced Washitas) in western Arkansas to the junction of the Missouri and Mississippi Rivers is a little more than 300 miles. The average width of the region, including the foothills, is about 200 miles. Comparatively speaking, the Ozarks contain no mountains at all. Just folds of little green hills with occasional peaks protruding from them. The highest of these peaks is in the Ouachita Range where Mount Magazine reaches a height of 2,823 feet above sea level. The country is marked with deep, rugged hollows, large subterranean caverns, and the largest flowing springs on the continent.

Some scientists and historians do not consider the Ouachita uplift to be a part of the Ozark region. They give the highlands south of the Arkansas River a separate geographical status. This theory of separation is based upon the geology, flora, and fauna of the area, which are said to be typical of the southern Alleghenies. But we are not greatly concerned with geological, botanical, and zoological lines here. It is the story of a people belonging to a given culture that interests us. My association with hillfolks in the two regions during the past twenty-five years leads me to believe that they have a common ancestral background, and that their underlying traditions are the same. There are slight distinctions in dialect but they are scarcely noticeable to the average traveler.[1]

· · · · · ·

The name Ozarks is cradled in folklore. It is the abbreviated corruption of a French term first applied to the region by French-Canadian trappers or by adventurers who mined lead in the mountains of southeastern Missouri. Some historians say that the word is derived from *bois aux arcs* which means "wood for bows." They explain it in this way: The Osage Indians occupied a large part of this highland area at the time of the French occupation. These natives hunted and fought with bows and arrows, and the wood of the *bois d'arc* was used in making the bows. The trappers learned that the Indians were using this wood and from that fact called the region Bois Aux Arcs. The term was later shortened to Aux Arcs but even this was too much of a tongue-twister for the English. They joined the two words, substituted letters, and Ozarks was the final outcome.

Another name origin is presented by students who disregard the Aux Arcs theory. During the days of French occupation, lead mines were opened in the mountains west of the Mississippi River. A German scientist, Abraham Gottlob Werner (1750–1817), had written a book on geology which was popular with students of the subject about the time of our Revolutionary War. Werner made two divisions of the rock formations of the earth: aqueous rock formed by the action of water and containing fossils, and azoic rock formed by fire and showing no traces of organic life. Some of the pioneering French had read this book and when they discovered the large granite rocks in southeastern Missouri, they called them azoic. These rocks form a rough circle fifty or sixty miles in diameter, and the best lead mines were located in the segment or arc in the northeastern portion of the circle. The name Azoic Arc was applied to this particular region. When enterprising English colonists pushed into Missouri following the Revolutionary War they found this name applied to the granite uplift in the southeastern part of the state. Later, it was associated with all the hill country of both Missouri and Arkansas as far south as the Arkansas River. Folk linguists clipped and coupled the name so that Azoic Arc became Ozark.[2]

Ouachita is a French modification of a word of Indian origin and is thought to have been the name of an extinct Indian tribe which once occupied the highlands of western Arkansas. A fanciful legend says that the name was applied to an Indian chief and means Speeding Deer. Here is the colorful story that tradition has given us:

For years the land of the Ouachitas in Arkansas has been one of dreams and visions. In this region a long time ago, nature dropped a link from a mountain chain. This link runs east and west for fifty miles and is called the Cross Mountains. Nature was in a kind mood and created a passageway for wagons which were later to wend their way to and fro upon the earth in their unceasing quest for that better place.

Centuries before the white man visited the new world, there dwelt a mighty nation whose chief was Ouachita, the Speeding Deer. This nation was blest of Manitou; the rivers teemed with fish and the forests were full of game and honey. The people but willed it and it rained.

The Great Spirit vowed to Chief Ouachita that he should live and reign forever if he broke no moral law, and that each faithful redman should for many, many years abide in the Valley of Vapors and no blessing would be denied him. The secret of the waters, where the old were said to regain their youth, was imparted to the chieftain. A truce was formed by all the tribes for use of the healing waters, which the Great Spirit had warmed, and peace was in this neutral land of the redman.

The tribe of the Ouachitas prospered and grew like magic until one day there came a White God, fair of form and pale of face, making friendly offers. The chief of the tribe thought he saw in the stranger a successor to himself so he slew his pale-faced brother, breaking the tribal vow to Manitou and bringing vengeance upon his people. Mountains spewed forth molten lava until the valleys and plains were a seething sea of brimstone; rocks were crushed and covered and twisted, with precious stones in their pockets. The famous tribe of the Ouachitas was destroyed, but it was decreed that the spirits of these tribesmen sigh, ever sigh, for a plunge into the fountain of healing waters.

A far more probable explanation of the origin of Ouachita is found in the lore of the Choctaw Indians. In the language of this tribe *owa chita* means "big hunt." According to the records of certain French explorers, these Indian hunters sometimes crossed the Mississippi River and penetrated westward as far as the Ouachita River in their quest for the buffalo. This region was "the land of the big hunt." It is reasonable to believe that both the river and the region secured the name, Ouachita, from these famous owa chitas.[3]

. . . . . .

To Henry Schoolcraft, historian and explorer, should go a great deal of credit for popularizing the name Ozarks. He preceded the large bulk of sturdy pioneers who came early in the nineteenth century to make their homes here. Schoolcraft began his Ozark observations in 1818.

He recorded information about hills and valleys, springs and streams, soils and minerals, cliffs and caves, ways of life of the early settlers, and the lore of the native Indians and of the wildlife that sustained them. He gathered this valuable information into books which were published both in England and America. The person who possesses one of those treasured volumes is fortunate indeed.[4]

Pioneer Ingenuity

Stories of pioneer methods in meeting the issues of life in the wilderness read like fiction, but investigation reveals hard lines of fact written in the lives of the stalwart men and women who pioneered. The Ozarkian book of experience is no fairy tale. Frontiersmen had to have food, clothing, and shelter, and it was the business of the men to provide these essentials in the face of adverse circumstances. Women went alongside their men, sharing privations, bearing children, and managing the household. Crude situations in the early days inspired creative genius and instilled crafty business acumen. Life had to be taken at face value and frequently had to be reduced to its lowest terms in order that men could survive.

The first settlers in the Ozarks were pioneers of the first water, baptized in hardship and depending largely upon the bounties of nature for sustenance. Wild game flourished in the woods and the streams were full of fish but, to secure these bounties, hunting weapons had to be manufactured and ammunition supplied. Give a man a flintlock musket or Hawkins rifle, a horn of powder, a pouch of bullets, and a hunting knife, and he was master of the wilderness situation. Many of the early Ozarkians were expert gunsmiths. Others made knives of high quality. The famous Bowie knives made by a blacksmith at Washington, Arkansas, have never been excelled in quality or workmanship. Gunpowder was manufactured in crude mills operated by water power. Lead was provided for bullets from various diggings in the hill country. Even in the days of earliest settlement, when each little neighborhood had its parcel of families, there was a division of labor. Some men were expert in boring rifles, others in shoeing horses. Gristmills were built and operated by men who knew the milling trade. Liquors were made by men who understood the intricacies of distilling. Women carded wool and cotton, operated spinning wheels, and manufactured clothing on homemade looms. Crude cotton gins and saw rigs were set up to help provide the necessities and occasional luxuries of pioneer life.

· · · · · ·

One of the first powder mills west of the Mississippi was established by John B. Williams in Stone County, Missouri, soon after his arrival from Kentucky in 1835. Williams settled on Flat Creek about a mile above its conjunction with the James River, and set about building a village that became a trading center for a radius of fifty miles. A powder mill was considered to be of vital importance to this section; the outposts of civilization were hundreds of miles away and the difficulties of transportation made the cost of importation excessive. Springfield had been established in 1830, but as a town it was still in its swaddling clothes.

The Flat Creek mill was a crude affair. Williams built a heavy log frame in the watercourse, with a huge sycamore log as a crossbeam. In the middle of the log a depression was hewn to the depth of two feet and was used as a mortar for mixing. Working in the mortar was a wooden pestle. To withstand the pressure of pounding and crushing, it was made of the hardest wood obtainable. An undershot waterwheel provided the power. Pins driven into the pestle worked against similar pins in the wheel shaft so that when the water, running under the wheel, turned the shaft it caused the pestle to be lifted and dropped into the mortar, mixing the saltpeter, sulphur, and charcoal into gunpowder. The sulphur had to be imported from the outside world but the other two ingredients were Ozark products. The charcoal was made from soft wood such as linn and box elder and was prepared in a kiln near the mill. Large quantities of saltpeter were secured at Bear Den Cave across James River. The dirt bearing the chemical had to be given special treatment before it was ready for the mortar. It was handled in much the same manner as ashes are treated for making lye soap. The Williams mill made three grades of powder—a coarse musket powder, a medium grain for shotguns (after this bore was introduced into the Ozarks), and a very fine powder for squirrel rifles. To make the finer powder it was necessary to hammer it a little more with the pestle. Drying sheds were provided to allow moisture to evaporate from the mixture.

Most of the old-time Ozarkers manufactured their own bullets in molds made at home or by local blacksmiths. In communities where the earth did not provide an easily accessible store of lead, the bluish-white metal was secured from traders. The balls varied in size with the bore of the gun to be used. The caliber of the old smooth-bore flintlocks was comparatively large, but the popular Kentucky squirrel rifle took a ball weighing about one-half ounce, approximately .50 caliber. Many Ozark hunters had their rifles rebored annually if a capable gunsmith could be found to do the work. This caused a gradual enlargement of the bore, sometimes to .60 caliber. It is said that the muzzle-loading rifles of these early settlers varied in bore from .38 to .60 and were adequate weapons for both large and small game, and for protection against Indians.

Wadding material had to be provided to separate the powder from the bullet and to keep the ball in place until the discharge was made. Paper was scarce in the early days and hunters frequently turned to nature for this material. The paperlike substance used by hornets in making their nests was found suited to this purpose. But it was impossible to convince the pugnacious insects that they should cooperate in supplying this commodity.

The nest of the hornet is a cone-shaped affair made from the soft inner bark of trees and hung on a tree or bush sometimes within reach of human hands. The insect's instinctive confidence in its protective powers provides adequate protection for the domicile. The inner side of the nest contains horizontal layers of comb hung together by columns. The single opening at the bottom of the nest is about one inch in diameter.

Various methods were used in capturing nests inhabited by the fierce insects. A venturesome woodsman might try to cover the cone-shaped habitation with a sack at nighttime, or build a smudge and smoke the hornets from their home. One old-timer told me that he once tried to plug the hole in the nest with a corncob. Early one morning he filled a pocket with cobs and went to the woods to risk combat. The nest he found hung low and was easily reached from the ground. Carefully, he inserted a cob to plug the nest but a sudden blow on the head told him that something was wrong. The cob was too small for the opening and a guard had made fight. Hasty retreat saved him.

Hornets desert their swinging nests in autumn and pass the winter in deep holes they have excavated in decayed trees. The coarse, gray paperlike material of their nests was then available for the hunter's use.

. . . . . .

"Cash money" was a scarce article in the early Ozarks and it was sometimes necessary to make substitution for the gold and silver that carried the government imprint. The pioneers had need of a medium of exchange in dealing with visiting traders and among themselves. One of the strangest stories of Ozarkian ingenuity is that of the "Yocum Dollar."

The Yocums were pioneers in the backhill country, entering Missouri and Arkansas in the early part of the nineteenth century. It was a Yocum who fed Henry Schoolcraft and his companions roast beaver tail in the White River country in 1819. Other Yocums moved in from Illinois a few years later. A group of five or six families of them crossed the Mississippi and headed their linchpin wagons, pulled by sturdy oxen, toward the Springfield settlement. This was the last outpost on the frontier and consisted of a trading post and two or three houses. Leaving Springfield behind them, they headed southwest into the James–White River country, cutting their way through a virgin forest. They stopped for a year or two at a place now called Yocum Pond and then made permanent settlement near the mouth of Kings River.

The Yocums were almost completely isolated from civilization, and their social and industrial life was largely with friendly Indians and scattered hunters, trappers, and fur traders. Legend says they secured a silver mine from the Indians and worked it for a number of years. The legendary location of this mine is on White River somewhere between the Kings and James tributaries. According to the stories, silver taken from this mine was used in making a trade coin called the Yocum dollar. It is said to have been used for several years as a medium of exchange in that section. Descendants of the Yocum pioneers claim to have seen the molds in which the coins were made.

All went well with this emergency exchange until one of the settlers tried to pay the proof fee on his claim with Yocum dollars. He presented the trade coins at the Springfield office and, although they were refused, the government agent is said to have sent one of the coins to Washington for examination. It was found to contain more grains of pure silver than the United States dollar. It was uniform in size with the regulation government coin, but no attempt was made at imitation. It had just two words stamped on it, "Yocum Dollar."

In 1848, news of the discovery of gold at Sutter's Mill in California reached the Ozarks. The Yocums who owned the secret mine were adventurers and decided to try their fortunes in the West. The story goes that they plugged up the mine and refused to disclose its location even to relatives. They expected to return and work it later, but these Yocums never came back to the White River country. Some of the molds used in manufacturing the coins were left with a relative who operated a gristmill in the Kimberling settlement on White River. But this equipment is now lost and the silver mine has become an Ozark legend.[5]

· · · · · ·

Years later, another experiment with trade money was made in this same section of the Ozarks when B. F. Carney of Crane, Missouri, issued his own currency and circulated it in several states. This happened during the Bank Holiday, soon after Franklin D. Roosevelt became president in 1933. Carney issued a quantity of one-dollar emergency exchange notes. The paper had this statement printed on it:

B. F. Carney will pay the bearer one dollar when this note is presented to him with proper endorsement therein, proving its commercial negotiation at least fifty times, with payment by the bearer to B. F. Carney the sum of two per cent of the face value hereof at each such negotiation. Payable at my office in Crane, Missouri.

   (*Signed*) B. F. CARNEY.

   Seven hundred of the emergency notes were given out and about four hundred of them were properly endorsed by fifty or more signatures and redeemed at face value. Some of them were cleared in banks as far away as St. Louis and Kansas City. Three hundred of the notes never returned for redemption. The Chase National Bank of New York City has six of them in its permanent collection of monies of the world.

· · · · · ·

Tales of Ozark ingenuity are legion, and they testify to the foresight and business acumen of the hillsman. Pioneer ways were sometimes strange ways and not always tempered with justice, but they gave assurance of economic survival without outside assistance. Sometimes the people rebelled against crafty methods that usurped their rights or disturbed their frontier freedom. Stock laws have always been a nemesis to hillsmen, and even today tourists must drive with caution in the backhills to avoid striking livestock on the highways. The making of illegal liquor is still a bone of contention between Ozark natives and federal authorities. Many law-abiding citizens wink at the idea of liquor enforcement in the backhills, and "revenuers" are as unpopular with hillsmen as ticks with tourists. Methods of gain are not always approved by Ozark communities, and many a man has carried on a legalized business against the wishes of his neighbors. Take the case of M. M. Chandler and his famous "toll bridge" on Caddo River.

   In the Ouachita highlands of Montgomery County, Arkansas, a mile below the village of Caddo Gap, the Caddo River tumbles over stones in a rock-lined passage called the Narrows. Solid walls hedge the crystal waters into a churning channel where perch and bass play hide-and-seek among boulders that have fallen from the cliffs in ages past. It is a scenic spot and many tourists go there to loiter in sun and shade and listen to the music of the waters. Fly fishermen pause to tempt the cunning bass with their lure. It is a good place to stretch one's sentiments, to weave colored threads in the tapestry of one's dreams. But the Narrows has not always been an arcadian paradise with a contented twinkle in its eyes. Time was when silver clinked within its walls and tragedy stalked in the offing. Old-timers tell of the sojourn of Cole Younger, the famous outlaw, at the Gap and how he posed as an eye doctor under the name of Dr. Shrewsberry. Many a native, never suspecting the man's true identity, called on the "Doc" for relief from eye afflictions. The James gang sometimes used this pass as a shortcut into the hills.

About the fourth decade of the nineteenth century a wagon trail was built through the Caddo River Narrows. It became an important trailway for wagons and horsemen between Fort Smith on the north and Hot Springs and Arkadelphia to the south. In the early days this mountain gap was a tight squeeze for traffic. There was barely room for a wagon to pass between the overhanging cliff and the tumbling river. High water was a big problem and the road was sometimes closed for days at a time. In 1870, M. M. Chandler took charge of the gristmill and cotton gin which were operated by water power a short distance below the pass. It was a popular milling and ginning center for natives within a radius of twenty or thirty miles. Chandler saw the need for a better passageway through the Narrows and applied for a charter from the State of Arkansas to build a toll bridge "lengthwise with the river" for a distance of 345 feet through the pass. The charter was granted for a period of thirty years and the county in which the bridge was built set the price of toll. The rates were scheduled at one dollar for a wagon and team, fifty cents for a man on horseback, and twenty cents for a footman. But Chandler charged only half these prices and citizens of Montgomery County were permitted free passage.

Chandler had difficulty keeping the bridge in place. Floods came and the structure was washed away. The 345-foot wooden bridge was then replaced with one 225 feet in length, and the ends were filled in with rock and dirt. But this second bridge was also washed out. The third one was only 160 feet in length; when it was carried away, the old pioneer decided to construct a pike through the entire passage. But the county officials objected to this, pointing out that it could not be classed as a bridge and that the collection of toll would be prohibited. To get around this objection, Chandler built a dirt pike, ribbed with rock, leaving a 12-foot gap in the center. In this space, he constructed a log pen, ten by twelve feet, filled with rocks and covered with boards. This met the requirements of the contract and he continued collecting toll.

Many difficulties were met in making collections from travelers. Once a cowman from Texas rode up to the pass and asked that the chains be lowered for his passage. Chandler refused to do so until the fee was paid. The Texan dismounted from his horse and asked Chandler to have a drink with him. He unlaced a saddlebag but brought out a Colt revolver instead of a bottle. The chains were lowered at the point of the gun and the bridge owner lost his fee. But Chandler was not easily bluffed and kept a shotgun handy to enforce collections when necessary.

County authorities tried to put Chandler out of business. They secured an injunction against him in circuit court, but the old pioneer took it to the supreme court of the state and the decision of the lower court was reversed. The county paid Chandler $1,000 damages and he continued operating the bridge until 1884 when he sold his mills and moved away. Early in the twentieth century, a railroad was built through the Gap and, a little later, a state highway. To make room for them, the overhanging cliff was blown away and the site of the old toll bridge buried underneath a mass of dirt and boulders. A few willows and tramp birch have squeezed their way through the debris, but there is nothing left to indicate where the old bridge stood. It was one of the few toll bridges in the world built "lengthwise with the river."

. . . . . .

The long isolation period, beginning shortly after the purchase of the Louisiana Territory in 1803, and lasting until the advent of motor transportation a hundred years later, has made the backhills of the Ozarks a world apart in American life. It was an interesting epoch, resplendent with heroic deeds, but for several decades the hillsman had no way of communication, except through the mails, and few came to interpret his way of life to the outside world. In more recent years much unreliable publicity has been given the Ozark world in books and periodicals, and on stage, screen, and radio. Slapstick comedy has ridiculed the native of the hills almost beyond redemption. Unbiased interpreters are needed to tell the romantic story of Ozarkland.

. . . . . .

Justice is sometimes slanted in a peculiar manner in the backhills. Things move from the sublime to the ridiculous in a singular way. Take the "bull trial" of the eighties. Old-timers continue to talk and shake their heads over this famous trial held more than fifty years ago in the Boston Mountains of Arkansas. It is not a tall tale from the windy hilltops but can be verified by persons still living.

A mountain farmer owned a bull that was no respecter of fences or persons. He was monarch of his domain, and the best stake-and-rider fence in the country was no barrier to his invasions. Even the most modern fence on the more up-to-date farms was only a slight inconvenience to his migrations. He was the terror of the community and even his owner despaired of controlling him. Finally, the bull invaded one too many cornfields. The enraged farmer, whose crop had been destroyed, swore out a warrant and had the animal arrested. The law brought his bellowing majesty to the shade of a large oak tree where the trial was held. The case against the bull was plain enough but the proceedings lasted almost all day. Lawyers threw aside their coats and pleaded for or against the aggressor. Witnesses swore, natives cursed, and the bull bellowed his displeasure. After careful deliberation, the jury found the animal guilty in a degree deserving punishment. The verdict rendered, the justice of the peace assessed fine and costs. Then came the puzzling question of payment. After considering the problem from all angles, the judge decided to butcher the animal and use the meat as payment. A barbecue followed with judge, jury, lawyers, witnesses, and the general public taking part. It was a festive occasion and long remembered by those present, but the old-timers to this day shake their heads and say it was not a fair trial. They point out that the judge neglected to appoint an interpreter for the bull.

· · · · · ·

A day of better understanding is now dawning. The public at large is beginning to appreciate the humor and character of the Ozarkian. Vance Randolph has led the way in folklore with a dozen books. Charles Morrow Wilson and Wayman Hogue have featured the hill country, and its interesting folkways, in works of fact and fiction. Rose Wilder Lane, Nancy Clemens, and Thomas Hart Benton deserve special mention for their vivid portrayals of Ozarkian life. On the platform and in her newspaper column, "Hillbilly Heartbeats," May Kennedy McCord preserves and defends the lore of the hillsman. Charlie May Simon gives many of her juvenile stories an Ozarkian background. Mary Elizabeth Mahnkey interprets the true spirit of the hills in poetry and prose. On screen, stage, and radio, Bob Burns, "Lum and Abner," "Mirandy," and the Weaver Brothers and Elviry portray the hill people with wit that gurgles like cider from a hillbilly's jug. We are beginning to recognize the heritage of the Ozark hillsman as a firm cultural bridge between the worlds of yesterday and tomorrow.[6]

CHAPTER II

Anglo-Saxon Seed Bed

. . . .

Salt of the Earth

A late evening sun winked over the bald portion of Breadtray Mountain. The old ridge road from Woodville to White River was crystallized with age, the wagon ruts washed into miniature gullies. Verdant layers of moss cushioned the giant boulders by the roadside. Below tumbled a swift mountain stream, fresh from the bowels of the earth, its clear icy waters caressed by weeping willows and guarded by ragged birch which stood like sentinels along its borders. Oaks and cedars interlaced with vines dotted the hillsides in comely confusion. The varicolored hills around me, with arms extended to the advancing twilight, added the touch of halcyon repose to complete the scene.

The call of the open road had led me to the scenic White River country of the Missouri Ozarks. Leaving my baggage at the boarding house in Woodville, I had gone in quest of adventure, following the old ridge road southward to the river. I walked and enjoyed myself, with no thought of the approaching darkness. My Ozarkian quest had become more than just following a will-o'-the-wisp. I was seeking the lore of a people reputed by sociologists to be the seed bed of Anglo-Saxonism in the United States and the last survival of Elizabethan culture in the Western world.[1] Harold Bell Wright had told about the region in his

romantic novel *The Shepherd of the Hills,* picturing the Ozarker as a colorful personality "lost" in isolation. This seclusion in the very heart of a
continent steeped in commercialism and flushed with progress appealed
to me as a fact endowed with paradoxical appeal, and one worthy of
investigation.

Darkness came rapidly upon the heels of twilight, and walking on
the mountain trail became more and more difficult. I suddenly realized
that a man who had trekked through the hills all day should have a place
to lay his head at night. I began to wonder what I would do for bed and
board in this sparsely settled region. But luck was mine and opened for
me the gate to a new world. A gentle breeze from the river carried with
it the odor of frying bacon. A dog barked and I knew that a house was
not far away. At Woodville, I had heard much of White River hospitality.
I decided that now was the right time to pull the latchstring.

A dim light showed through a clump of trees. I approached it with
caution. Half a dozen potlicker dogs howled warning as I turned from
the trail and climbed a fence that did not offer the convenience of a gate.
I stopped at a respectable distance.

"Hello," I called through cupped hands.

There was no answer except that the dogs increased their chorus
of howling disapproval and one of the braver ones approached uncom-
fortably near. Then a door of the house opened and the head of a man
appeared. I explained that I was a stranger in the hill country and asked
shelter for the night. The man quieted the dogs and invited me in. That
was the beginning of my acquaintance with the Freemans—with Big
Dan and his veteran father, Uncle Henry. It was an acquaintance that
ripened into real friendship.

Dan Freeman had taken life in the rough and made it pay dividends.
He had that virility which, added to native intelligence, makes the house
of the soul a pleasant habitation. He could work all day on the farm or in
the woods and then dance or foxhunt all night without apparently tiring.
Although in the middle forties, he had not lost that quick wit and wholesome humor that were parts of his youthful nature. Big Dan, as everybody
called him, was always ready to join in a prank but was also equally willing

to lend a hand in time of need. Everybody liked Daniel Freeman and respected his opinions even when they did not agree with them.

"Clever folks live down on White River," Lem Logan, the Woodville blacksmith, had told me. "Mighty clever folks an' white clean through. Last fall me an' Hite Lindsey went down across th' river t' look fer a stray steer, an' come back by th' Freeman settlement. They wus butcherin' some hawgs that day an' Abe Howell from over on Bull Crick wus helpin' 'em. We had et a turrible sorry dinner at that eatin' house on th' state line, but with Big Dan an' Uncle Henry hit wus different. That tenderline meat an' flour gravy an' hot biscuits wus sure invitin'. Abe is a right good eater an' hit wus a sight th' way he took t' them vittles. An' Hite an' me kept him purty good company. No better folks anywhere than them thar Freemans. Not fine-haired a-tall, even if Emily has been away t' high school, an' they own most of th' good river land clean up t' th' mouth of th' James."

Henry Freeman, eighty-year-old hillsman, lived with his son, Dan, on the old Freeman place near the ferry. He was known for miles around because of his prowess as a hunter and his integrity as a citizen. He was an old-line Ozarker of the old school, with the map of England on his face and Elizabethan traditions in his blood. His language had a smack of Shakespearean flavor to it. It is true that his words were strange vagabonds long strayed from their native soil but they carried a charm that captivated me. Uncle Henry could say "hope" for help, and "whup" for whip in such a musical way that the ear could not refuse the delightful cadence of pronunciation. With him it was "spile" for spoil, "hist" for hoist, and "bile" for boil. His blue eyes sparkled as he talked of the good old days when each home had "its taper to cheer the vale with hospitable ray."

Uncle Henry liked to talk of old times. Life was rich in contentment in those pioneer days, according to the old man. The theory that generosity means much in the life of a people was thoroughly tested and found good. It was an age of hunting and fishing, church-going, Sunday visiting, logrollings, barn raisings, quiltings, husking bees, play parties, square dancing, horse trading, going to mill, and singing and visiting by the fireside. Each man knew his neighbor, understood his needs, and stood ready to help him in solving pioneer problems. Farmers traded work during the busy season, and little cash money changed hands. The undercurrent of friendliness led to understanding and, for the most part, the community life was peaceful. Whatever the hillsman's intellectual deficiencies and social shortcomings may have been, his wholehearted generosity made up for them. It was always considered discourteous in that day to accept payment from a stranger for bed and board except in the established lodging houses. It was a day of chivalry in Ozarkian life. Of course, many of these traditional practices have survived to the twentieth century, but the old-timers could already feel the influence of the machine and its corresponding commercialism, and could sense the meaning.

Flashing eyes told me that Henry Freeman had an active mind and an intuitive fitness given him by nature in reward for obedience to her laws. He had spent practically his entire life in the Missouri Ozarks, emigrating from Kentucky with his parents when he was a lad. He had known the day of the oxcart and the tarpole wagon and had lived to see the beginning of motor transportation. As a young man he had hunted and fished and searched for buried treasure in many sections of the Ozark Country. He had sought the lost Slater Copper Mine along the Current River, hunted bear, deer, turkey, and smaller game in the Boston Mountains and the canebrakes of Arkansas, floated streams, explored caves, living his youthful years fully and freely. The one dark chapter of his life was the Civil War of the sixties and he was reluctant to talk about it. He had taken but little interest in the opposite sex until at the age of thirty he met Mary Austin of Woodville. He courted her in true Ozark fashion and, in due time, they married and settled on a part of the land homesteaded by his father a quarter of a century before. Aunt Mary, as folks called her, had been dead nearly ten years when I arrived on the Ozark scene. Uncle Henry now lived with Dan and his family in the big double log house which the pioneer Freemans had built just after the War Between the States. There was plenty of room for the old man as Dan's family was small. It had been twenty years since the marriage of Daniel Freeman and Sally Evans and, contrary to the custom of the hills, they had but one child. That was Emily, an attractive girl of seventeen. This young woman impressed me immediately with her radiant personality. Surely, I thought, these Freemans were the salt of the earth.

Supper with this Ozark family made an indelible impression on my mind. I had arrived, an unexpected guest, a short half hour before meal-time but there was no scarcity of food, no framed apologies. The table was loaded with good things to eat. Crisp bacon was served with delicious crackling corn bread. There was yellow butter from which the moisture had been all "whacked out" by a cedar paddle. Baked beans, brown and savory, were dished from a blue crock. A pitcher of cold buttermilk from the springhouse sat alongside a platter of lettuce, radishes, and onions from the garden. There was fluffy wheat bread, baked at home, with apple jelly if one cared for it. For dessert we had ginger cake and dried peaches that had simmered in their syrup through the long afternoon. To partake of such wholesome food in such a pleasant environment was to slip back into the Elizabethan age of old England. I decided that Lem Logan was right. These Freemans were "mighty clever." They belonged to an aristocracy of brains and honor with a pedigree that isolation could not weaken. Later on I came to know many such old-line families in the backhill country of the Ozarks.

After supper we retired to the parlor to enjoy an hour or two of conversation and music. It has been said that nowhere in the world are the old tunes rendered with greater fervor than here where the Ozarks thrust up their rugged flintrock shoulders against the sky, sheltering their primitive people from a civilization ever rushing westward. Dan Freeman was a fiddler and Emily accompanied him on the guitar. Eli Bradshaw, a young hillbilly employed as hired man, played the banjo. He worked by the "dry month," Dan said, and had plenty of time on rainy days to play music. Dan and Eli played at country dances throughout the White River country but Emily seldom went with them. Sally Freeman drew the line for her daughter's social activities and the ungoverned dances of the community were excluded. With Big Dan it made no difference. He was a friend to everyone and at home in any crowd. Many a time when the boys got "lickered up" and trouble brewed, Dan stepped in to pacify the situation and avert trouble. His good humor and interest in his fellow men made him a kind of moral balance wheel in the neighborhood.

I called for music which was characteristic of the mountains and for more than an hour the walnut logs of the old house reverberated to such romantic melodies as "Leather Britches," "Sally Goodin," "Sourwood Mountain," and "The Arkansaw Traveler." Then they sang old ballads that had been brought over from England and Scotland and transplanted in Ozarkland. Some of Dan's favorites were "Barbara Allen," "The House Carpenter," "The Jealous Lover," "The Blind Girl," and that ripping old play-party song, "Old Joe Clark." One song the hired man sang impressed me strangely. He called it "The Lily of Arkansas" and said it was a pop-ular ditty throughout the "Lapland" region. (Lapland is the territory of southern Missouri where, as they say, "Arkansas laps over into the Show Me State.") Here is the song as Eli sang it:

> My father built the bow, the ship that sailed the sea,
>   With four and twenty seamen to keep him company;
> The waves and winds are beating, while sailing on the sea,
>   Lie low, the *Lily of Arkansas* has parted you and me.
>
> I fear my love has drownded, I fear my love's been slain,
>   I fear my love's been drownded on his way to France and Spain;
> The waves and winds are beating, while sailing on the sea,
>   Lie low, the *Lily of Arkansas* has parted you and me.
>
> There's girls enough in Texas, I know there's one for me,
>   But my own dear and lonely one is far away from me;
> The waves and winds are beating, while sailing on the sea,
>   Lie low, the *Lily of Arkansas* has parted you and me.

The Freemans ran cattle and had several hundred on the range at the time I visited them. Dan would make occasional trips into Arkansas to add to his herd. He liked to tell stories of these trips and enjoyed teasing his wife who was a native of the Wonder State.

"Talk about that book, *Three Years in Arkansas*, insulting the state," said Dan. "I can tell one that actually happened and it just about equals the hens roosting on the meal barrel, and the old cat and kittens in the stump table."

Dan had a pleasing bass drawl and his English was comparatively good. Sometimes he dropped an *s* or slid into a quaint Chaucerian vernacular but he did not butcher the King's English in the usual hillbilly fashion. Just as in England the Yorkshire dialect differs from that of Dorset, so does the folk speech of the Ozarks vary with class and locality.

"A few years ago," continued Dan, "Dad and me took a long trip into the Boston Mountains buying cattle. Night came on us in the Big Buffalo country and we put up at Albert Heffner's place. Al was a bachelor and as clever a man as lived in that country, and he fed pretty good. We had one objection, though, to his method of housekeeping. That one thing, in our estimation, was enough to offset all the good qualifications of the household. Al had a pet pig he was very fond of and he let the critter have the run of the cabin. It must have weighed close to ninety pounds and was a right pert shoat. It was an antic brute and during supper it ran between our legs and squole and took on terrible. Al finally quieted the pig by pouring some flour gravy into the stove hearth that he used for a trough. The pig et his supper with relish and then laid down in the corner and went to sleep. When it came time to go to bed, Dad and me found that we was quartered in the same room with the shoat. It seemed to be a friendly sort but we didn't take any chances with our clothes. We rolled them up, put them under our heads and slept on them. We forgot our shoes, though, and had to pay for our neglect. That blame pig chewed the strings out of all four of them."

Dan's wife was a turkey raiser and her flock of bronze birds, roosting on the stake-and-rider fence that cross-stitched the barn lot, was a sight to behold. She explained to me that when the fowls were young she "poked a grain of black pepper into each one's throat and made it swallow it" as an inoculation against disease. In the late fall, the great flocks of turkeys were herded to the market place at Springfield like so many sheep or cattle.

Uncle Henry told me how he took eggs to market when he operated a country store near the ferry. They were packed in clean straw in a wagon bed, a layer of straw alternating with a layer of eggs to the top of the bed. Boards were placed over the top and clamped down to keep the eggs from shaking and breaking. At Springfield they were put into crates and shipped by train. Freighters had skillets and coffeepots tied to the sides of their wagons as they camped out going and coming. It took a week to make the round trip of about eighty miles.

Stories and music and repartee made the evening pass too speedily. I had found an Anglo-Saxon seed bed in the fat marrow land of the Ozarks and was reluctant to leave it. But hillfolks do not keep late hours, and at ten o'clock Dan took a lamp and lighted me to my room. I sank into a bed of soft feathers and immediately went to sleep. A visit like this is an experience to tell one's grandchildren.

Backgrounds and Movements

Half a century before the Civil War, folks from the Appalachian Mountains began trekking westward, pushing across the Mississippi River and settling the highland regions of Missouri and Arkansas. With slow ox teams and boat-shaped wagons they followed the Indian trails and the crooked streams to the land which destiny seemed to have reserved for them. Here they built homes and institutions which carried the pioneer spirit to the fourth decade of the twentieth century.

A Spanish philosopher said: "The native Briton carries his English weather in his heart wherever he goes. It becomes a cool spot in the desert, and a steady and sane oracle in all the deliriums of mankind." The old regime in the Ozarks in its way exemplified British character, which had been planted first on the Atlantic seaboard, then moved west into the Appalachians, and later transplanted in the Ozarks. These people have retained much of their racial purity to the present day. When the great tides of immigration swept westward to the Pacific, the backhill sections of the Ozarks were passed by. Left alone, it was natural for the hillsman to preserve the traditions and continue the customs and beliefs of his ancestors. There was no melting pot in the hills. Communities were "kinned-up" with first cousins and "last cousins" without end. For more than half a century there was little marriage with outsiders. This practice is considered to be a genetic evil, if carried too far, but in the Ozarks it resulted in a remarkable purity of the race. Two things have contributed to this: first, the rough contour of the country which provided a measure of geographical isolation; second, the staunch character of the men and women who settled it.

The movement westward from the Atlantic seaboard to the fertile valleys of the wilderness beyond the crest of the Appalachians began as early as 1765, but the migration did not reach its peak until the years following the Revolutionary War. In 1763, King George III drew a line along the ridge of the Alleghenies and prohibited settlement beyond it, but that did not keep hardy frontiersmen from filtering through. Daniel Boone left his home in North Carolina in 1769 to risk settlement in "the dark and bloody ground" beyond the mountains. There were several hundred settlers beyond the Appalachian ridges when the Revolution broke out in 1775. The greatest influx of settlers came in the early part of the nineteenth century. From 1800 to 1820 there was a population gain of over 320 percent in Kentucky, Ohio, and Tennessee.

Stories of the Wilderness Trail have become a vital part of our history. From the thirteen original states, settlers pushed westward along the Mohawk River or through southwestern Virginia and into the valley of the Tennessee River. There were various feeders to these roads from the east and the south. Wagon trains moved up the James River in Virginia and up the Yadkin in North Carolina. At Kingsport, in the upper Tennessee Valley, the trail divided. The right fork went through the mountains at Cumberland Gap and into Kentucky. The left route proceeded to Knoxville where it was joined by a road from the south, then on to Nashville where the level land began. From these strategic points the travel movement spread out like fans, catching in its folds the Bluegrass region of Kentucky, the hills of western Tennessee, the prairies of Indiana and Illinois, and the Ozark and Ouachita highlands

west of the Mississippi. The Wilderness Trail was followed by thousands
of families during the half century that followed the Revolutionary War.
Another route to the Ozarks was down the Ohio River from Pittsburgh
or up the Father of Waters from New Orleans. Even before the Louisiana
Purchase of 1803, St. Louis was an important gateway for thousands who
traveled the river route.

The French were the first white men to enter the Mississippi Valley
and to put their mark upon the land. Some of them pushed into the
eastern Ozarks, to work in the lead and salt mines of that region, and
became permanent settlers. Numerous place names attest to this. French-
Canadian trappers combed the hills and streams for beaver and other
fur-bearing animals. This French influence is remarkable because of its
tenacity. In a recent study of the descendants of these pioneers in one
community, Professor Joseph Carrière said, "The habits and customs of
the villagers have changed but little since their forefathers founded the
community in the eighteenth century." The dialect of this Gallic people
is unintelligible to the average American.

In the early eighteen hundreds economic conditions in Europe sent
thousands of settlers of sturdy rural stock to the Western world. In the
year 1827, a total of 22,000 Irish and Germans came across. Some of
these people caught the western craze immediately and followed the
Wilderness Road into the mountains. A small portion found the way to
the Ozarks. But the imprints of these peoples are comparatively insig-
nificant. The mark of the Briton predominates.

Arthur H. Estabrook, in a study of the population of the Ozarks,
makes the following statement concerning the early settlement of the
Missouri and Arkansas hill country:

> A large part of the population of the Ozarks in 1820 to 1840 was
> derived from the migration out of the Southern Appalachians.
> The story of this migration, its duration, and the original sources
> of the migrants, is partially told in the 1840 and 1850 United
> States census records of the Ozark Mountain counties. The
> birthplace of each member in a family is recorded in these cen-

sus records. The movement of any given family can be traced. The record of one family in Newton County, Arkansas, in 1850, selected at random, gives the picture of this migration. William Lewis was born in 1801 in Virginia. His wife was born in 1805 in Tennessee. They had children born in Kentucky in 1825, 1827, 1829, 1832, 1834 and 1836. Their next child was born in Newton County, Arkansas, in 1838. Thereafter, five children were born in Arkansas. Many such examples could be cited from the records. A few of the older members of the family groups were recorded as having been born in some European country, especially England, Wales, and Scotland. For the most part, however, their birthplaces were given as Pennsylvania, Maryland, Virginia, or the Carolinas. A small percentage of the general population of the Ozarks at this time came from Georgia, Alabama and Mississippi. Only a few had come from the northeastern states.

The Ozarks, like other sections of the country, had a continuous migration from the first years of settlement. In the third decade of the nineteenth century, Texas was opened to settlers from the United States and many Ozarkers followed Stephen F. Austin to settle the lucrative prairies of that virgin land. Countless Ozark families helped compose the wagon trains of the forty-niners and later migrations to the west. The Mountain Meadows Massacre of Arkansas emigrants in 1857 was a tragic incident of these migrations. Others went to the fertile level lands of Oklahoma and Kansas and the prairie states farther north. Since 1890 there has been a shift of the rural population of the hill country to Midwest industrial centers such as St. Louis, Kansas City, Joplin, Springfield, Tulsa, Oklahoma City, Memphis, and Little Rock. But regardless of these movements a large portion of the population remained locked in the hills.

The natives of the Ozark Country may be divided roughly into two classes. First, the old-line Ozarker who came early and established himself permanently in the hills. He is usually a fundamentalist in his thinking and determinedly unprogressive in the eyes of the outside world. His speech and mannerisms are true to the mold of his ancestry. He was schooled in hardship and nourished with patriotic fervor, and is one of our best examples of the conservative American. His sons and daughters of recent generations have taken places of trust and responsibility throughout the country as business and professional workers.

On the other hand, there is an undesirable class in the Ozarks just as in other parts of the country. Many of them are modern nomads, seeking green pastures wherever they may be found. Some are faulty branches of good ancestral trees. The low economic level of these people has contributed to their moral delinquency. It is from this type that the outside world gets its prevailing impression of the hillbilly. Imaginative writers, speakers, and actors have played up this element as typical of the highlands, much to the discredit of the old-line Ozarkers. From all sides the hillsman has been shot with ridicule and stabbed with criticism. He has been accused of living in a state of culture lower than the Indians we dispossessed. He has been labeled as a descendant of "the white trash of the lush midlands who fled to the hills for sanctuary during the Civil War, when the quality folks were fighting for La Belle Confederacy." He is said to wallow in squalor and ignorance, and it is alleged that meanness crops up in him like bristles on a razorback hog. These libels are based upon free use of the imagination, faulty observation, or downright ignorance.

The hillsman is not the long-whiskered, tobacco-chewing illiterate the movies picture him to be. He differs from the average American because of his century of isolation, but good roads, improved methods of transportation, and better schools have almost completely leveled this inequality. The hillsman is losing his distinctive traits and is becoming a drab, standardized American. Once the transformation is complete, the romantic Ozarks will live only in song and story. The average Ozarkian does not realize the value of his heritage to himself and to the world, and is making no serious attempt to guard it against the inroads of twentieth-century civilization. The chief attraction of the Ozarks is the integrity and independence of its citizens, and it is discouraging to see conventionalism wiping out this priceless heritage of freedom.

Of course, we have an undesirable class in the Ozarks but it is a mistake to think of this group as composed entirely of people of low economic level. Many of them have made money and gained power and prestige in their communities. They drift into politics and help rot the core of the body politic. All through the years there has been a slow transfusion of blood from undesirable sources into the veins of some of the old-line Ozark families, and it has left its mark. Such infusions must be considered to get a true idea of Ozarkian character. Some of the finest old-line families have petty traits that reveal a mixed inheritance. People here are good and bad, shiftless and thrifty, as in other sections of the country.

The population of the vast Ozark mountain region, including the foothills, is approximately one million people, and it is spread over one hundred counties in three states. Sociologists have divided the people roughly into three groups. The first group lives in the cities and larger towns such as Springfield, Joplin, Fort Smith, Fayetteville, Harrison, Monett, and West Plains. Here economic, educational, and social conditions are on a level with the country as a whole. The rural population is divided into two groups: first, those living in privileged conditions in the smaller towns and villages and in the favored rural sections where the land is productive and modern methods of farming and marketing have been introduced; second, the folks of the underprivileged sections where low economic, social, and educational levels prevail. Much of the soil in these regions is too poor for profitable farming and the one important resource, timber, is nearing depletion. Probably one-fifth of the total Ozark population is now centered in the cities and larger towns. An equal number lives in the favored rural sections. That leaves approximately 600,000 people in the Ozark and Ouachita areas who must struggle for a livelihood against adverse economic conditions.

Regardless of the contrasts and inequalities of the Ozark Country, I have found it to be a modern arcadia where one may enjoy simple happiness, innocent pleasures, and untroubled quiet. It is true that the old ways of living are disappearing rapidly and the shifting of the gears of custom adds bewilderment to the hillsman's problems. But it is still possible in some sections of this romantic land to turn back the clock and listen to the hum of the spinning wheel, the creak of the loom, the groan of the waterwheel at the mill, the rhythmic poetry of the cradle in its golden sea of grain, and to enjoy the generosity that springs from every true hillsman's heart. This is the background of a people nurtured in solitude and unspoiled by the workaday commercial world.[2]

CHAPTER III

Hillsman's Harvest

. . . .

Toothsome Treasures

I'll go up on th' mountain top
　　An' grow me a patch o' cane.
I'll make a jug o' molasses, too,
　　Fer t' sweeten Liza Jane.

Poor little Liza,
　　Little Liza Jane,
Poor little Liza,
　　She died on th' train.

I went t' see my Liza Jane,
　　She was standin' at th' door,
Her shoes an' stockin's in her hand,
　　Her feet all over th' floor.

Poor little Liza,
　　Little Liza Jane.

Lem Logan sang as he pounded the anvil in his blacksmith shop at Woodville. Attracted by the sound of his voice and the clang of steel on steel, I turned aside from the main trail. I knew what it meant when Lem sang "Liza Jane" in a reckless sort of way. Business was dull and he was just killing time. In his lucid mind were visions of fishing adventures and bee hunting.

Arriving at the shop, I found Lem making nails, forging them on the end of the anvil which was made for that purpose. Yes, business was dull. Lem Logan never made nails when he had anything else to do. Forty years ago he had worked with his father on this same spot making nails. Old Joe Logan was one of the best nailsmiths in the Ozark Country. But this honorable trade had had its day. Lem could make five hundred nails in a twelve-hour day but a machine in St. Louis could turn out the same number, polished and sharpened, in less than two minutes. No use competing against the impossible. But this thrifty smith still made a few nails for his own use and sometimes he sold a handful to a tourist who was interested in relics of bygone days.

My entry into the shop caused Lem to lay down his hammer and stop his singing. I could see from the faraway look in his eyes that he had something on his mind.

"Yer jist th' feller I've been wantin' t' see," spoke the blacksmith as he reached for his snuffbox and laid a quantity of the dust behind his lower lip. "Remember me tellin' ye 'bout that thar bee tree I found last week on Smackover Ridge? Wal, today is a good a day as any t' cut it. What d'ye say we give 'er th' works?"

I knew little of woodcraft and had never helped cut a bee tree, but anxious to learn folkways firsthand, I agreed to help him. Within ten minutes we were headed for the ridge with ax, cross-cut saw, smoke bellows, and four tin pails to take care of the honey.

Wild honey is a gift of the gods to the lover of sweets in the backhills. It is a source of sweetening of great importance, a toothsome treasure to relieve the monotony of a coarse diet of corn bread, sow belly, and pinto beans. Almost every man of the more isolated sections of the Ozark Country is an expert bee hunter and he seldom fails to bring home the honey. An average tree contains forty or fifty pounds of this wildflower concoction, and occasional rich ones produce twice that amount.

In the old days when a frontiersman found a bee tree he usually killed a deer, skinned it, and sewed up the salvaged honey inside the animal's skin. That was before the age of tin containers. Tubs and buckets were made of wood and were none too plentiful in pioneer homes. The woods were full of deer and it was an easy matter to make a kill. The deerskin, properly stitched with buckskin thread, made an excellent sack for the honey.

The life of a bee hunter is an adventurous one, but it has strict requirements. It is no child's play to "course" a bee through the woods to its homing tree. Bee hunting has its highly specialized technique. As Lem Logan explained, the insect must first be properly baited, and the coursing process that follows is done in a scientific manner. It requires a keen eye and a peculiar natural aptitude.

Lem Logan was an experienced bee hunter and seldom did he fail to find a tree when a bee sampled his bait. As we walked up Goose Neck Hollow en route to Smackover Ridge, he told me how he did it.

"'Bout all a feller needs t' go bee huntin'," he said, "is a can of water an' sugar mixed purty thick t' use fer bait. I soak a corncob in th' sweet'nin' overnight an' then lay hit on a stump or th' top of a rail fence where I have seen bees a-workin'. Purty soon a yaller bee'll come buzzin' along an' load up on th' sugar. Hit takes on all it can carry an' then makes two or three circles above th' bait 'fore hit goes bee-line fer th' tree. A feller's got t' have a good eye t' keep up with th' critter while it's makin' them circles. When I git th' direction it goes, I don't lose no time gittin' through the woods. If'n I know th' country, I have a purty good idey where the tree is fer bees have a way o' flyin' that lets a feller know 'bout how fur they're goin'. Sometimes I set a second bait 'bout fifty steps away frum th' first one an' let a bee take off frum thar. Hardly ever have t' set more'n two baits t' git th' right direction. But even then it ain't easy t' find th' tree. I keep my eyes peeled fer a big holler oak. When I git close enough I can hear th' buzzin', an' if th' wind is jist right, I can smell th' honey, too.

"When I sight th' tree I walk 'round till I see th' hole they're usin', then I cut a big X deep through th' bark with my barlow. A tree that's marked can't be teched by nary other bee hunter. 'Tis sort of a unwritten law of th' woods, this marked-tree business. Ever'body knows what it means. Nobody but a low-down skunk would cut a marked tree in these here hills. Even if it is on th' other man's land don't make no difference.

"I usually chop or saw th' tree purty soon after I find hit, sometimes on th' same day if it ain't too late. Lots o' mornin's I'm out a hour by sun waitin' with my bait an' that gives me time t' do all th' work in one day. Most of my bee huntin' is done on Sunday since pap died an' I had t' take over th' runnin' of th' shop.

"One time when I wus a kid of a boy, pap found a bee tree right at th' head o' this here holler. We wus needin' some sweet'nin' purty bad, so he took his rifle gun an' went up on th' ridge an' killed a buck deer. He brought it home an' skinned it an' hung th' meat in th' smokehouse. He got a feller who lived down on th' crick t' go with him t' cut th' tree. Hit wus shore a rich one and they sewed up close t' eighty pounds o' honey in the deerskin. Jist as they wus ready t' start home a couple o' wild turkeys flew over an' lit about a quarter up th' holler. Pap an' th' feller with him had their guns along so they decided t' foller th' turkeys. They wus a big holler stump 'bout seven feet high standin' close by an' pap drapped th' skin o' honey into it. They wus gone a couple o' hours and brought back a big gobbler. When they got t' whar they had cut th' bee tree, they heerd a awful noise inside that stump they had left th' honey in. Sich scratchin' an' takin' on ye never heerd. They slipped up t' th' stump an' pap swung hisself up an' looked in. What d'ye think, a half-grown bar wus in that thar stump after th' sweet'nin'! Hit had clumb up th' outside an' drapped in, but after loadin' up on th' honey, hit couldn't climb out. Thar hit wus all stuck up frum ears t' tail an' takin' on turrible. But pap soon put it out o' misery. He clumb a tree an' shot th' critter between th' eyes. Th' honey wus mostly ruint but we had plenty o' meat at our house fer quite a spell."

By this time we had arrived at the tree, which was on Hite Lindsey's land at a point where the ridge dips into the hollow. After sawing and felling the tree, Lem quickly cleared away the limbs that would interfere with our progress. He had instructed me to use the smoke bellows while he chopped a hole in the trunk for the removal of the honey. The fun began. I puffed smoke and fought bees for all I was worth. Lem chopped vigorously and soon had an opening through which to remove the treasure. After filling the four pails to the brim with the golden liquid and comb, we started homeward. Of course, we had gotten a few stings during our encounter with the bees, but we pulled out the stingers and rubbed honey on the spots to stop the swelling. We stopped at Hite Lindsey's place long enough to tell his wife, Lizzie, to take a bucket and get the rest of the honey.

"Sometimes th' bees don't use th' holler of th' tree a-tall but stick th' honey on th' outside," explained my companion as we walked down the hollow. "This don't happen often though fer bees is smart an' know not t' leave their honey out in th' weather unless they can't do no better."

The tree-cutting and honey-salvage experience is one which hills-men enjoy many times each year. Wild honey is "long sweet'nin'" much to be desired and no native need be without it.

That afternoon at the store Tobe Mullins enlightened me upon the sweetening lore of the backhills. Back in the early days when highways were unknown in the Ozarks, crude wagon trails served as the only out-lets. Transportation was difficult and expensive. Natives off in these hills learned to dispense with practically all luxuries. Even the necessities of life were limited and home products were substituted whenever pos-sible. Refined sugar, often called "short sweet'nin'," was a rarity on the hillsman's board. The country merchant always had a barrel of it on hand which he was eager to sell for cash or swap for prime coonskins or for roots of the goldenseal. But it was almost prohibitive in price and was used sparingly. In a few neighborhoods the sap of the hard maple was made into sugar and used as a table delicacy. This sweetening from the hillsman's woodlot was exceedingly toothsome. But most of the sugar requirements were met by wild honey and sorghum syrup, commonly called molasses. There might be a little refined sugar in the gourd to set out when company came, but for the most part this costly product, like candy, nuts, and oranges, was for Christmas, birthdays, weddings, picnics, and other special occasions.

"Four or five years ago," said Tobe, "I went with Ed Bullock an' Hite Lindsey t' round up a herd o' hawgs that had strayed t' th' Bull Crick settlement. We stopped at Abe Howell's place fer dinner. When Abe's woman, Susie, poured th' black, scaldin' coffee, she asked us which we would have, long or short sweet'nin'. Ed took 'long' since he wus use t' hit at home. Susie took a jug o' sorghum an' poured a couple o' spoonsful into Ed's cup. Hite figured he would take th' 'short' product. Not havin' any white sugar, Abe got up frum th' table an' took down a leather bag that wus hangin' on a peg by th' kitchen stove. He pulled out a cake o' maple sugar, bit off a chunk as big as a hicker nut, an' laid hit in Hite's sasser. I drunk my coffee without no sweet'nin'."

Folks in the White River country like to tell of the time when Uncle Abe got liberal and treated his entire family, except two of the older boys, to all the precious cane sugar they could eat. It is reported that Abe needed only one or two drinks of corn whiskey to open his heart and touch his pocketbook. The fact that he went through the year without getting a haircut, or without even currying his long, grotesque whiskers, and that he wore a homespun suit colored with red oak bark, shirt outside his pants, in preference to store clothes, was no real indication that he was stingy. He preferred yellow whiskers tucked in his shirt and hair that warmed his neck against the cold winds of winter. And the thought of store clothes never entered his mind. But to get back to the story.

It happened when the Howell family went to the bottoms in Arkansas one fall to pick cotton. But let Abe tell it in his own peculiar way as reported to me by an old settler.

"Wal, s'r, I fetched th' hull dang bunch of 'em into one uv them thar big stores in town, an' I sez, sez I, 'See hayer, mister, if ye'll let these here youngens an' their mammy eat all th' short sweet'nin' they want out'n that thar bar'l, I'll pay ye a silver dollar!' Wal, he let 'em do hit an' they shore dug their fingers into that thar sugar an' nearly strangled gettin' hit down. After they got their bellies full, I went an' looked in th' bar'l. An' I'll be dumfuzzled if they had et enough so you could miss hit, an' me already havin' paid th' feller th' dollar. Course they wus only seven of 'em as Lum and Ezra had stayed at home t' take care o' things an' t' look after Nate Watkins' still while he went t' th' county seat t' set on th' jury."

. . . . . .

At one time the hard maple was common in many sections of the Ozarks, but civilization has taken a heavy toll of this beautiful, productive sugar tree. The closely grained wood is valuable for furniture making and furnishings in houses. It is durable and takes a high polish. It is also serviceable to the shoemaker for pegs and lasts. This demand has thinned the Ozark forests of this flaming torch of autumn and sweet wooer of spring, but one may still find an occasional "sugar orchard" in the backhills.

With the first thaw of late winter, the harvester visits the maple groves and taps the trees with an auger. Wooden pegs or spouts are driven into the trunks, and wooden troughs are provided to carry the dripping sap to suitable receptacles. When a sufficient amount of the watery fluid is collected, it is boiled in flat sorghum pans over a slow fire. The sticky syrup must be of just the right consistency before it is drawn off and put into another vessel, usually a copper kettle, for the crystallizing of the sugar. When the liquid starts sugaring, it is beaten with a paddle to give it a firm grain. It is then removed to small muffin or cake pans and cooled. The cakes weigh about a quarter of a pound and sell in the country stores at five or ten cents each, the price being regulated by the supply and the tourist demand. Large producers sometimes sell the sugar in the bulk for as much as fifty cents a pound. This sugar may be returned to its liquid form by boiling with a little water. Spread on corn or wheat cakes over a thick layer of country butter, it makes a dish to set before the king.

Molasses made from sorghum cane is one of the most popular hill products. Sorghum making is a time of festivity in the backhills, seasoning the autumn days with gaiety even as maple-sugar time seasons the spring. The native Ozarker is an artist in making syrup. During my sojourn in the Woodville neighborhood, almost every farmer had his patch of cane which he stripped, cut, and hauled to mill. Most of the syrup was made at Ed Bullock's mill where the toll was one third of the sorghum or a dime a gallon.

Sorghum cane is not particular about the type of soil in which it grows and it requires but little cultivation. These factors, not to mention the hillsman's sweet tooth, account for the numerous cane fields. Boys and girls usually do the stripping. It is a real adventure to attack a cane field with a paddle in each hand. It recalls Don Quixote and his windmills.

I spent several days at Bullock's mill where the stalks of green cane were crushed in a crude horsepower contraption and the watery juice transported to a long flat cooking pan. Ed's old mule, Jude, was hitched to a long pole which operated the cane press. 'Round and 'round the circle poked Jude through the molasses-making season of autumn. This old mule had spent ten years in the milling business and had learned to take his time. The pan was set upon a roughly built furnace of rock under which burned a slow hickory fire. Ed was an expert at sorghum making and was known far and near for his skill. He knew just how to regulate the fire in order to turn the whitish liquid into reddish gold of the proper thickness. Too much heat scorches the sorghum; too little makes it strong and of dark color. In either case the product is ruined for commercial purposes.

The atmosphere was filled with the spicy tang of the boiling sorghum as Ed stirred the liquid and skimmed off the greenish scum. Neighboring children stood by, dipping pieces of cane stalks into the boiling molasses to form suckers. Late in the evening the liquid was drawn off and stored in a barrel. That night the young folks had a taffy pulling around a bonfire. The molasses was boiled in an iron kettle until of the right consistency to make into taffy. Then it was pulled into long white strands and eaten by the young people.

It has been said that one touch of nature makes the whole world kin. The sweet tooth of mankind is universal and never ceases to ache. And whether it be soothed by the refined sugar of agriculture and chemistry, or by the natural long sweetening of the backhills, matters little. The long and the short of it is to have the sweetening.

Bounties of Nature

The harvest of the hills is not limited to one or two short seasons each year. Every sign of the zodiac offers the alert Ozarker opportunity to profit from nature. With the approach of Groundhog Day in February, state laws close the hunting and trapping season and the numerous Nimrods stack their guns and store their traps for other hill activities. Catfish get hungry after the first spring rise, and wily bass jump for flies in the clear streams. There are delicious wild fruits and berries to be picked from bush, twig, and vine in summer and early fall, and nuts to be gathered and sacked for the market or home consumption. As the autumn season comes on the harvest of wild herbs and roots with medicinal properties offers profit to the hillsman who knows the alphabet in the book of nature.

Wild ginseng, goldenseal, and mayapple all grow in the Ozarks and are still quite plentiful in the pockets of the mountains where the lumber camps have not denuded the forest of its larger trees. These plants, especially ginseng and goldenseal, grow in the shaded areas of the wooded hills and require several years to reach a stage of maturity. They do not flourish in cut-over lands where the monarchs of the forest have been removed. The Indians and early settlers knew the worth of these plants in making simple medicines, but there was little commercial demand for them until about the year 1860.

Ginseng and goldenseal have been grown in the Ozarks as commercial crops since 1901. Gardens of less than two acres have produced $10,000 worth of seed and medicinal roots in a four-year period. The juices extracted from these plants are used in compounding medicines both for internal and external use. Most of the ginseng produced in Arkansas is shipped to China where the Orientals use the drug in great quantities. But the war in that country has greatly retarded the trade in this commodity. More attention is now being devoted to the culture of goldenseal which, properly dried, brings about three dollars a pound. The seed is also utilized and sold at a high price.

Mayapple, also known by the names mandrake, hog apple, wild lemon, and raccoon berry, is prolific and patches of it dot the valleys and rich uplands. The root of this plant has strong cathartic properties and was highly prized by old-timers as a liver medicine. It is not difficult to recognize this plant with its palmate, yellowish-green leaves and its solitary white flower in the fork of the stem. The roots are dark brown and about the size of a man's little finger. It is very fibrous and shrinks considerably when dried. It has a commercial value and is dug after the fruit matures in autumn.

Numerous other herbs are dug, dried, and marketed and, though the compensation is small, it provides pocket money for the family. Dandelion, horsemint, nightshade, boneset, buckhorn brake, peppermint, goldenrod, black root, blue flag, crowfoot, sundew, wild clover, and many others supply ingredients of commercial value from root, leaf, or seed. Bark is stripped from the trunk or roots of the slippery elm, dogwood, white walnut, sumac, white pine, and wild cherry and carried to market.

But not all the herbs and wood products collected in the Ozarks are laid upon the scales at the country store or shipped to urban markets. Many of them are used for home consumption—in compounding salves, making teas, or as substitutes for store products that cost money. Take the toothbrush as an example. No need of spending a dime for the manufactured article when nature provides it free. Of course, the younger folks now get their brushes at the store and spread them with highly advertised pastes and powders, but many of the old-timers still prefer nature's product and show full sets of natural teeth to attest to its efficiency.

My introduction to the hillsman's toothbrush came in 1922. That was the year Tomp Turner and I built a houseboat and took a 300-mile float-trip down White River. At Cotter, Arkansas, we sold our boat and parted company. Being penniless and with winter coming on, I took the job of teaching a three-month school in the Baxter County hills. Soon after the opening of the term, I noticed that my pupils (there were sixty of them) had the habit of cutting short twigs from certain trees on the school ground, and chewing on them. The twigs were about the length of a pipestem and, at first, I thought it was slippery elm bark they were after, or some succulent wood with which I was unacquainted. Upon inquiry, I learned that these twigs were used as toothbrushes and that they served the purpose well. Later I tried this custom myself and discovered that a twig or root from the elm or hackberry makes a good instrument for mouth sanitation. Many natives have improved upon this practice by making the twig a "mop" for snuff. This is not to be confused with the dipping of snuff. The latter practice consists of pouring a quantity of the powdered tobacco behind the lower lip, after which it is placed by the tongue.

The use of the twig toothbrush is an old, old custom and dates back to 1700 B.C. when the practice was a religious rite in southern Europe. Ancient lore says that the priests made out a schedule for the people to follow in brushing their teeth. On certain days of the week, the rite was performed in a definite way. On other days it was omitted entirely and the mouth was cleansed by rinsing with twelve mouthfuls of water. The priests said prayers before and after the toothbrushing rite.

Hackberry and redbud roots make the ideal mountain toothbrushes, and folks in the backhills are always looking for these succulent woods. Since a brush can be used only once, it takes a quantity of them to supply a family.

. . . . . .

The trapping season in the Ozarks begins around the first of December and lasts two months. Thousands of pelts are secured by the men and boys who comb the watercourses for their prey. There are raccoon, opossum, skunk, mink, muskrat, red and gray fox, and an occasional timber wolf to test the trapper's skill. The pelts secured are slipped around boards or stretched open on the side of a building until they dry. They are then sold to local buyers or shipped direct to nearby cities. Thousands of dollars are brought into the Ozark region annually through the sale of pelts.

The opossum has become a regional emblem in western Arkansas. Each December, when the frost is on the persimmon, the Polk County Possum Club holds its annual banquet and funfest at Mena. The club was organized in 1913 and now has thousands of members. A few weeks before this gala event, a call goes out for bids on the supply of opossums for the banquet. All animals sacrificed at the festive board must be Polk County products and less than two years old. The requirements usually state that the opossums must be fed on a fattening menu of persimmons for four or five days preceding date of delivery. Folks come from far and near to sit at the long tables in the banquet hall and partake of baked 'possum and sweet potatoes. Funsters and fast music make the occasion an outstanding annual frolic in the Ouachita hills.

The bounties of nature are not restricted to the land. The clear streams that twist through the hills in shimmering silver have abundant riches in their churning waters. Dressed catfish bring fifteen cents a pound, and the blue cat is a giant in his old age, sometimes reaching one hundred pounds in weight. Buffalo fish in the rough sell from seven cents to ten cents per pound and they are caught in abundance at certain seasons. Suckers are grabbed at shoaling time, catfish are noodled in summer and gigged in winter, game fish are caught with hook and line. Fishing is both a sport and a business in the backhills.

In late summer when the rainy season is past, and the streams are clear, the hillsmen who follow the rivers know that it is mussel time. Early and late, boats are in the stream transporting shells. Many tons of them, worth thousands of dollars, are harvested from Ozark streams each year. A few valuable pearls are found in the shells each season, and this feature of the quest adds a spice of adventure to what would otherwise be classed as monotonous work. Not every mussel digger finds a pearl, but hope leads him on and tomorrow the big find may come and enrich the worker beyond his fondest dreams.

The mussel harvest may begin at any time after the spring rains are over and the rivers reach a normal level. The digger can accomplish little when the streams are high and muddy. For ideal shell digging, the water must be as clear as a mirror.

An Ozark stream is no place for a tenderfoot. I recall the first time I tried to paddle a johnboat across White River. The stream was high and swift and I was inexperienced. I did not know how to take advantage of the current and consequently I landed several hundred yards downstream. It took me several weeks to learn how to feather the paddle and send the boat where I wanted it to go. Mussel digging requires skill in boating and a knowledge of the anatomy, quality of shell, pearl-forming traits, and habits of life of the bivalve clam. The work is an art that requires diligence and perseverance. The digger must be hardened to all kinds of weather and accustomed to life in the water. The industrious worker is up with the sun and continues his work until twilight shadows darken the water.

There are several methods used by mussel diggers in getting the clams from the bed of the river. The two most commonly used in the White and Black Rivers are scooping and sticking.

When the clams have been permitted to grow and reproduce without being disturbed for several years, they collect in the mud and gravel of the river bottom. In shallow places near the shoals, these bivalves may be scooped into boats with a wide fork. Two good workers with a boat between them often scoop a ton a day. Sticking is a much slower method, but it is sometimes necessary where the clams are scattered. The tool, called the sticker, is a long stick sharpened on the end or reinforced with a rigid wire. The worker knows that unless a mussel has been disturbed it will always be found in the mud at the bottom of the stream, with the top crack of the shell, or eye, sticking up. When this opening is located in the clear water, the sticker is quietly and expertly inserted at just the right place so that the shell clamps down and holds until the hand of the worker lifts it into the boat. This is slow, tedious work, but by keeping steadily at it a worker may harvest several hundred pounds in a day and earn a living wage.

The diggers have a dumping ground near their camp or houseboat where the clams are piled for sorting. After the day's work in the river, the men sort the shells, sometimes working far into the night by the light of a lantern. The expert can tell at a glance which shells are marketable and which are not. After sorting, the bivalves which have shells of commercial value are tossed into a huge kettle or pan and boiled to loosen the meat from the shell and make opening easier. After they have been boiled sufficiently to kill the shellfish, the shells are pulled from the soft flesh and tossed to the drying pile. The worker keeps an eye open for pearls during the shelling process. I have heard hillsmen say that only the male bivalves have pearls in them but I take this statement with a grain of salt.

After the shells are dried, they are piled on trucks and transported to nearby railroad points where they are loaded on flatcars. They go to factories to be made into buttons, knife handles, manicure sets, keys, and frets for musical instruments, and numerous other objects. The price the digger receives for his shells varies from twenty to sixty dollars a ton. Quality as much as supply and demand determines the value of the product. A license or permit from the state is usually required to carry on this work.

It is in the larger streams of the Ozark Country that the shell and pearl industries are most profitable. White River is perhaps the most productive stream, with Black River, its tributary, a close second. Many diggers live with their families in houseboats while harvesting the aquatic crop.

· · · · · ·

The greatest source of revenue in the backhill regions is the timber industry. In 1826 the first steam sawmill in Arkansas was built at Helena on the Mississippi River. Since that time fully 20,000,000 acres of the state's forestlands have been cut over. Experts estimate that about 1,500,000 acres of virgin timber remain in the state. In Missouri a similar depletion of forestlands has occurred. The Ozarks offer a diversity of trees for timber and there are few lumber requirements that the area cannot meet. Out of about two hundred species of native trees, at least thirty supply products for the lumber industry. Pine ranks first, followed by red oak, white oak, and red gum. A great variety of forest products go for special purposes. Walnut and hard maple make durable furniture. Thousands of small cedars are cut and sold each year for Christmas trees. Mistletoe is cut from its host tree and marketed for Yuletide decoration. Willows are twisted into rustic furniture and baskets. The wood of the downy hawthorn, or red haw, is whittled into shuttles for looms. Dogwood is popular for parts of machines in fabric mills. Pine billets are cut by the millions and transformed into paper products in milling towns adjacent to the Ozarks. Cedar poles are cut from the mountainsides, nailed together to form rafts, and floated by river to market. Crossties are hewed with the broadax from oak and pine.

When crops are poor on the hillside farms, hillsmen turn to the woods for a livelihood. Tie hacking is hard work but it offers a source of revenue when other means fail. To hew, or hack, a crosstie with a broadax requires skill and industry. Usually two men work together, sawing the timber in proper lengths and then carving the ties with the ax. Sometimes a man goes at it alone, cutting the lengths and smoothing the ends with great skill. On Saturday he loads a few ties on his wagon and goes to town. Buyers for railroad companies pay him a fair price for his product, but it is a hard living at best.

Nature's bounties have been the succor of many thousands in the Ozarks for more than a century, but the depletion of forests and the harnessing of streams for flood control and electric power are death knells to the old way of life. The building of power dams may be a commercial necessity, but it is difficult for the hillsman to understand and appreciate the modern stoppage of his streams with concrete. In his mind, "damn," not "dam," is the proper word to use.

CHAPTER IV

Necessities of Life

· · · · · · · · · · ·

Hillcroft "Vittles"

It was in the Big Springs country of the Missouri Ozarks that I discovered a backhill home which appealed to me as a perfect example of rural independence. I had left the broad highway and was walking along trails that were clean and pungent, crossing streams that mirrored the coquettish curves of the hills, traveling perhaps ten miles into the very heart of the forest. Suddenly, I dropped from the rim of a lean ridge into a garden of paradise. In a fertile cup of the hills lay a farm. The closely cropped meadow presented a strange contrast to the forest through which I had traveled. The fields, lush with grain, seemed an Eden in the forest primeval. I walked toward a group of buildings surrounded by trees in the center of a little valley. There I found a large two-story house with a spacious veranda and a cozy fireplace. Giant trees, green grass, and a gurgling spring made the lawn an actual oasis. Contented cows, symbols of arcadia, stood knee-deep in lusty grass in a pasture near the barn. Hens dusted themselves with earth and sang in joyous discord. Talkative geese swam in the clear stream below the spring. The family consisted of a plain-spoken, middle-aged father, a cultured young mother, and two boys whose eyes sparkled with the joy of living. There was a dog stretched at its master's feet and cats lying lazily in the noonday sun. With this rural family I ate a dinner of vittles from the well-flavored earth: corn bread and untreated milk, vegetables cooked in their own juices, dried apple pies fried to a rich golden brown in pure lard, fruits with the sun in them.

It all seems a beautiful dream as I retrace this adventure in memory. Here was the "folklure" of the hillcrofter in its most complete simplicity. The stress of modern life with its tragic conflicts was not felt in this valley of contentment. Men might envy and hate and struggle over possessions in the outside world, but here were sweetness and light that almost defied description.

A croft is a small farm, or tract of land, and a crofter is the one who cultivates it. Hillcrofters are tenants of the land who live the simple life close to nature. They are guardians of tradition and folklore in the backhills. This family in the Big Springs country belonged to the landed aristocracy of backwoods America. The Anglo-Saxon tradition was their heritage. They were content with the living the earth provided.

In these modern days, standardized foods, in tin cans or cellophane, are gradually replacing the hillbilly's homegrown vittles. It is refreshing to find crofters who continue to dry and can fruits and vegetables, make preserves and jellies, butcher their own hogs and cure the meat in the old-fashioned way, bake delicious bread made from burr-mill meal, and spread the table with the vitalized foods of the good earth.

Tucked away in the backhills is a style of cookery which produces dishes to rival the cuisine of the Old South—perhaps a two-year-old, home-cured ham with soda biscuits and ham gravy, or a side of pork ribs roasted before an open fire and basted with the drippings, or hog jowl cooked with lye hominy, or spicy molasses cake.

In the recipe book of the hill country it is just one turn from the sublime to the ridiculous. Take the old hillbilly formula for making "vinegar." A jar is filled with water and sweetened. Some grains of corn are named after the meanest people in the neighborhood and dropped into the water. It is then sealed and set up to let nature do its peculiar work. That is vinegar with a mean punch.

Ozark sugar-cured ham is a favorite mountain delicacy. The farmer does his own butchering and treats the meat with a preparation made from brown sugar, pepper, and saltpeter. The meat is hung in the smokehouse and smoked with hickory chips. Experts say there is a mystery in the curing of a ham that even scientists do not understand.

Sausage is flavored with sage and stuffed into muslin bags. Fish are rolled in meal and floated in hog fat. 'Possum is baked or parboiled with red pepper seasoning on a mat of sassafras twigs to give it flavor; it is served with candied sweet potatoes.

The fame of sweet potatoes roasted on a clean hearth in front of an open fireplace is widespread. The hillsman knows this technique thoroughly. He sweeps the hearth rocks clean and spreads a layer of hot ashes on them. In the ashes he lays the potatoes, not quite touching each other. These are covered with a layer of ashes and topped with a bed of hot coals. Sometimes a cup of water is sprinkled on the ashes just before the coals are spread on. In about thirty minutes the potatoes are raked out of the ashes and eaten without seasoning or ceremony.

In the old days all the cooking was done on the open fireplace in skillets, pots, and movable ovens. Sometimes a board was heated, spread with dough, and set before the fire at the proper distance and angle to bake johnnycake. Ash cakes were baked from cornmeal batter on the hot rocks of the hearth, the paste being spread on cabbage leaves or corn shucks.

Pork has been the principal meat in the Ozarks since wild game became scarce. The hogs are seldom corn-fed but fatten upon the acorn mast of the forest. The meat is salted or sugar-cured and then smoked. In the old days, venison was cut into small strips and jerked. The meat was hung on poles or scaffolds about three feet from the ground and coals of fire were laid beneath. It took from two to three hours to do this jerking.

Corn bread is the Ozark staff of life. It is baked in various forms such as corn dodger, hoecake, johnnycake, cracklin' bread, mush, scrabble, and plain corn bread. The most simple forms use only three ingredients—meal, salt, and boiling water.

Cracklin' bread is made by putting the meal in a bowl and mixing a small amount of salt and soda with it. A hole is made in the center of the meal and a handful of meat cracklings is dropped in. A small amount of boiling water is poured over it and allowed to stand. The next step is to add enough sour milk to make a rather thick batter. The hillswoman uses her hands to divide the dough into two or three parts, then she shapes it by passing it from hand to hand and patting it. It is placed on a hot griddle to bake. The golden-brown cakes, baked from burr-mill meal, would make an epicure smack his lips.

A number of wild plants are used for greens in the backhills, among them being watercress, dandelion, plantain, dock, lamb's-quarter, and poke sallet. The last three may be cooked together and they make a tasty dish. They are first boiled for half an hour and then fried in grease which has been prepared by frying slices of fatback rolled in flour. Slices of hard-boiled eggs are added and the dish is served with green onions and corn bread.

Watercress is plentiful in the spring branches and many a hill family goes traipsing with tin pail and garden rake to get a mess of this green stuff. At meals it is served wilted, like lettuce, with bacon grease and vinegar.

Not all hillbilly cooking is tasty and digestible. The skillet is used overtime in preparing meals. White biscuits are sometimes half baked and milk is not always plentiful. Biscuit bread, sorghum molasses, and perhaps a piece of fat meat compose the breakfast menu for many hillsmen. The dinner and supper contain heavy foods such as working men require, but there is frequently a shortage of fruits, vegetables, and salads. Corn bread, with or without cracklings, "case-knife" beans, or whip-poor-will peas make up a big part of the daily rations. On Sunday, there may be fried chicken served with mashed potatoes and cream gravy, especially if the preacher is to be present at dinner. Many families, formerly denied a balanced ration, now get their vitamins from the grapefruit and oranges supplied to them by the relief office.

Some writers claim that the women of the backhills are notorious for their bad cooking, but it all depends upon the type of home you visit. The old-line Ozarkers have a style of cookery which rivals the best in the land. They have plenty to eat and know how to prepare it. But only a part of the backhill population belongs to this class. Shiftless people everywhere are noted for their bad cooking, and the Ozark region is no exception.

Raccoon are plentiful in the backwoods and yearling coon is considered good eating during the winter season. The first step in preparing a coon for the pot is to take off the hide and remove the kernels from the legs. If these kernels are left in, the meat may be very bitter. After the insides are removed, the meat is usually soaked overnight in saltwater with one-half cup of salt to eight or ten quarts of water. The fat is then taken off and the meat is parboiled in one-half milk and one-half water. The dressing is made as for chicken, put inside, and sewed up. Slices of bacon are spread on the meat and it is baked slowly for three hours.

In pioneer times, coffee came from the store in the bean and was ground at home in small hand mills. Before the introduction of these grinders, it had to be mashed up in a rag. The coffee was boiled in pots and served scalding hot. There were no percolators.

The hillswoman is always on the lookout for wild fruit and berries. Wild plums, blackberries, and huckleberries are picked both for market and home canning. Beets, turnips, apples, and potatoes are holed up and covered with hay and boards to prevent freezing in winter. Apples and peaches are peeled and sliced and dried on the house roof.

With Tobe Mullins, a mess of good vittles is the apple of a man's eye. But his apologetic attitude is amusing. He will ask you to "come in and have a dirty bite" when he well knows that Mandy, his wife, is one of the best and cleanest cooks in the backhill country. The table may be loaded with tempting viands, but Tobe will dramatize his excuses for not providing in a better way. It is just a way of the hills and does not in the least interfere with Mandy's cooking.

Art Crafts and Skills

The fireside industries of the backhills, such as spinning, weaving, and numerous other skills, have lost their traditional atmosphere and have gone to town for profit. The folklorist seeks unspoiled crafts which were developed in that self-sustaining folk age of the past. But it is difficult to find them in their natural settings even in the isolated sections of the Ozarks. Spinning wheels may be found, but not many of them are operated in the old way. Dusty with age, they are stored in smokehouse or attic. Looms, which once groaned under the tread of thrifty housewives, have been destroyed or set up as tourist attractions. A modern sewing machine hums in the cabin; the old cradle is rusting in the shed, outdone by reapers; the muzzle-loading rifle, made with deliberate care by a local gunsmith, is a relic of yesteryear crowded out by modern firearms. The machine age has played havoc with the old handicrafts of the Ozarks. The revival of these industries at the present time has a commercial slant which was unknown in the old days. Only a few scattered remnants of the old ways remain to remind us of the hillsman's opposition to change.

As late as forty years ago Ozark hillfolks were solving their economic problems in a satisfactory manner without outside aid. The farmer made his land supply not only food for the table but material for making shoes, clothing, and various other household and farm necessities. He usually raised a few sheep and cultivated a patch of cotton, hemp, or flax. This supplied necessary raw materials for the women who were expert in making various kinds of cloth.

Sheep-shearing time was in early spring but quite often the wool would be tied into bundles and stored until winter. Then it was brought out to be cleaned and carded. The wool was washed thoroughly with soap and water and sometimes greased to make it handle better. Carding is the separating and straightening of the fibers of the wool or cotton in preparation for spinning. The fibers, thoroughly dry after washing, are drawn between two brushes called cards which are made of fine wire set into leather with a wooden background and provided with wooden handles. Carding was pretty much of a chore for the womenfolks in the old days. The expert carder knew how to test the material between her fingers and when she found the fibers smooth and straight, gave the upper card a skillful movement that turned out a small roll of the wool or cotton ready for the spinning wheel.

The spinning was done on a homemade wheel which produced a coarse yarn for the loom. An expert spinner sits by her wheel, foot on the treadle, the carded wool in her lap. She feeds the wool or cotton slowly to the wheel with her hands, twisting each bit with a deft movement of her fingers as it is drawn into the mechanism. The material must be supplied evenly to get best results. The thread of yarn is wrapped around a spindle and later tied up in bundles called skeins. It is used for knitting socks, mittens, and sweaters and for weaving into cloth.

The cloth called linsey-woolsey was in much demand by the old settlers, who fashioned it into winter clothing for the women. The material was woven on handmade looms and consisted of woof or filler of wool. The warp or cross-threads were of linen or cotton, depending upon the material available. The clothing popular with menfolks was a garment called jeans. It was of wool with a cotton chain.

Thread was made from cotton because the woolen yarn was too coarse for ordinary sewing. It required an immense amount of labor to produce the same amount of thread that can now be purchased at five cents a spool. First, the cotton had to be picked and hand-seeded, if no gin was available. Then it was cleaned and carded for the wheel. The fibers were twisted into threads and wound on wooden spindles.

Myrtle Lain of Camden County, Missouri, tells me that when the country stores began to carry unbleached muslin at a price not altogether prohibitive, the hill women would buy the material, tear it lengthwise, and use the warp for thread. The ravelings were twisted to give them sewing strength.

"We sometimes criticize elderly women for being 'stingy' with sewing thread," said Miss Lain, "but, when we consider the scarcity of the article in the early days, we can hardly blame them for conserving the short lengths that we would toss into the wastebasket.

"My grandmother used to save the basting threads from a finished garment," continued Miss Lain. "She would use scraps of thread to piece quilts or to patch torn garments. She had learned the value of the thread 'when thread was thread.'"

An important step in the process of cloth making was that of adding the color. Some of the homespun cloth was not dyed, because it was used in making towels and blankets and did not need color. But cloth to be made into wearing apparel was colored to suit the whim of the wearer. The dyeing art is passing rapidly with the older generation. Cheap synthetic dyes are now available at every country store and the use of natural products is almost a lost art. Pioneer Ozark women had few manufactured dyes, but they knew how to get the colors they wanted from leaves and bark. Woolen yarn laid in a kettle between layers of walnut leaves and soaked with water produced a beautiful shade of brown. Sometimes walnut hulls were used. Peach leaves—if pulled in midsummer—or the inner bark of the peach tree made a brilliant yellow. Sumac berries provided black. A few articles such as indigo, alum, and copperas were bought at the store. Green was produced by dipping yellow cloth into weak indigo. The root of the madder produced a red dye of a different hue from that of pokeberry. It was more permanent and would not wash out. Faint blue could be produced from cedar but it took store-bought indigo to make a really worthwhile blue. The colors were set into the cloth with alum or copperas and many of them have held their brilliancy for more than a century.

Sometimes the color was dyed in the wool, that is, put in before the wool was carded. This was especially true in making blue jeans. But in most cases the yarn was dyed after the spinning and sometimes the cloth was colored after it came from the loom.

"Warping the chain" is an old-time phrase that means getting the warp threads into shape for the loom. It is important that these fibers be straight in order to run smoothly through the harness eyes of the loom. This was done by stringing the fibers on wooden pegs usually driven into the logs of a building.

Looms for weaving cloth, carpets, and rugs in the old days were hewn from white oak or other durable wood and were made with such care that some of them are still usable after a century of service. Weaving nomenclature, including such words as woof, warp, shuttle, harness, and sley, is almost unknown to the younger generation. Pioneer women really worked at their looms. A good weaver could do four yards of cloth in a day and experts have done as much as fifteen yards of carpet.

A pioneer achievement recorded in the memory of an aged woman in the Arkansas Ozarks is worth telling. The father of the family made a sudden decision one Saturday evening to take a trip to a distant state the following Monday. His wardrobe did not contain a suitable pair of trousers for the trip. On the following morning, before the sun was up, the womenfolks began carding and spinning wool. By noon it was ready for the loom and the weaving began. Late Sunday night, the work was completed, everything done by hand, even to the buttons which were whittled from wood and covered with cloth to match the jeans.

The weaving art is not lost in the Ozarks. With the coming of tourists it has been revived and carried on as an important fireside industry. But the weaving is not of cloth for homespun garments for general wear. Attention is now given to rugs, coverlets, and counterpanes. Some Ozark women have become expert in copying designs from postcards, newspaper clippings, and other sources, and produce artistic articles of rare beauty. One design called Turkey Tracks has an interesting superstition connected with it. It is said that brides-to-be hesitate to put such quilts into their hope chests as they instill a desire to wander. And Ozark girls do not fancy husbands who stray away from home.

In the old days rags were saved and washed and cut into narrow strips called carpet rags. These were sewed or "tacked" together and woven into colorful rag carpets. Coral Almy Wilson of Boone County, Arkansas, gives the following version of a rag-tacking bee in a backhill home.

"Lorene, ye kin git th' rags out an' start sortin' 'em over. We'll start on that rag carpet this mornin'. We got t' color a lot o' tham old things fer we ain't got no red hardly. Bud, yo' ketch ol' Beck an' go t' th' store an' git th' red colorin'. I kin make all th' yaller I need 'ith copperas, an' walnut hulls 'ill do a purty brown. Sumac makes a good black an' Sis Bolen done promised me all her ol' green linsey. I aim t' pay her fer hit by cardin' cottin this winter. Tham dutch shirts an' dresses 'ill be blue enough.

"Arizony, yo' can cut th' buttons an' seams an' rip th' hems. Be keerful an' don't waste a scrap that'll do t' make strings. Be shore t' cut 'em even, jist about a half inch wide. I do hate a bumpy carpet. Don't use that thar store thread. Hyar's plenty o' homespun. Save th' backs o' all them skirts fer quilt pieces. Bud, stop an' borry Emmelett's shears so I can help cut.

"Jist a pound t' a ball an' a ball an' a half t' a yard, that's th' way I figger. Twenty-five yards 'ill cover th' big room. Make haste now, chillen, an' don't waste a thing."

Homecrafts in the old days included the tanning of leather and the making of shoes for the family. Women made bonnets from gingham or calico for everyday wear and fancy high-backed ones of chambray for Sunday and special occasions. There were slat, poke, and dude bonnets, with and without ruffles, and colored to match the dress. Men shod their horses and repaired harness and farm implements. They molded bullets and made sights for their guns. Local blacksmiths and gunsmiths did special repair work that could not be done at home.

Women were skillful in many kinds of needlework. "Lamp mats were crocheted in a double treble," says Mary Elizabeth Mahnkey, "going in with your needle again and again in one place, until a very ruffly effect was achieved."

Girls wore charm strings around the neck, with buttons substituted for beads. Buttons were collected and traded and each girl tried to outdo her friends in this pastime. When a girl secured 999 buttons she stopped collecting as the thousandth button was to be given her by the man she married.

Woodcarving is both an art and a pastime in the Ozarks. Mountain men are expert whittlers and always keep their pocketknives sharp and shiny. A dull knife is a disgrace in hillbilly circles. Carving in wood has always been associated with folk life. As early as 4000 B.C. men enjoyed cutting designs with sharp instruments, and excavations in Egypt and Babylon show that the people of that age were skillful in the art. Whittling and loafing go well together and the hillsman is proficient in both. A whittler, sitting on a nail keg at the country store, creates a tranquil atmosphere that defies all disrupting tendencies. Whittling has its place as a psychological buffer. Watch the shavings fall as Tobe maneuvers his wits in a horse trade. He whittles so nonchalantly that all motives of concern are blotted out. Anxiety needs a legitimate shield and whittling does the trick.

Woodcarving talent is turned to good account on long winter evenings. Ax handles are carved from white oak which grew on the north side of a rocky hill. Churns are made from cedar, perfectly joined, and finished with sandpaper. Boats and paddles, furniture for the home, and many other wooden products are manufactured by isolated hillsmen. Baskets are made from hickory, willow, and buckbrush. Cedar is a popular wood with carvers because it is easy to work and the supply is plentiful. In pioneer times farmers made harness hames from crooked limbs of elm trees, wooden rakes and pitchforks, moldboards for plows; solid wagon wheels were sawed from the ends of large logs. But that type of farm equipment was discarded long ago and supplanted with factory-made products.

The manufacture of homemade dolls is a new industry in the Ozarks, and a promising one. Naoma Clark of Winslow, Arkansas, originated the Hillbilly Doll which is now widely known throughout the country. She carves her dolls from native cedar and dresses them in hillbilly fashion with Mother Hubbards or jeans as the sex decrees. Flour sack is used for underclothing and a slat bonnet or perhaps a "duck nest" stiff hat covers the head. Other popular Arkansas dolls are the Bob Burns' Kinsfolks group designed by Anne Park of Van Buren and the homemade products of Lulu Scott (Aunt Boo) at Mountainburg. Two of Aunt Boo's famous character dolls are Uncle Matt and Aunt Mollie of *Shepherd of the Hills* fame. First honors in doll artistry, of course, go to that eminent Ozarkian Rose O'Neill, designer of the famous Kewpie doll. Her art has been widely acclaimed throughout the world. The hillbilly types are not so elegant as the distinguished Kewpie, but they are cleverly done and attract much attention. They are popular with visitors to the region.

The art crafts of the Ozarks were at their best when necessity set strict requirements. With the necessities of life dependent upon the dexterity of fingers, there was an urge for completeness that made artisans into artists. The handicraft age is a colorful chapter in the book of Ozarkian life and worthy of highest consideration and due respect.

Socialized Labor

The average Ozark hillsman has never made the acquaintance of social-
ism as a political doctrine but he is quite adept in cooperating with his
neighbors in "socialized" labor. Certain activities of the hill country such
as logrollings, house- and barn raisings, cornhuskings, quiltings, and various other "workings," are managed in a way to reduce the cost to the
minimum, and to enrich the social life of the community. It is an old
mountain custom to work together in enterprises which require mass
labor to get the thing done.

In pioneer times, logrolling was one of the best examples of fraternal
assistance and economic interdependence. When the first settlers entered
the Ozarks, most of the land suited to farming was covered with a heavy
growth of virgin timber. The land had to be cleared and made ready for
the plow. The trees were felled with ax or saw and the wood cut into
lengths varying from eight to twelve feet. Then word was given out that
a rolling would take place on a certain date. Early on the morning of the
appointed day, the men went into action. Each worker was equipped with
a stick or pole called a handspike. This tool was shaved from hickory sap-
lings or split hickory trees, slightly tapered, and sharpened at both ends. It
was five or six feet long and two or three inches in diameter at the center.

Two of the strongest men in the group were selected to "make daylight" by running their handspikes under a log and lifting it high enough
for other workers to shove their sticks under. Two by two the men took
their places alongside the log until a sufficient number was present to
"tote" it to the heap. Seven large logs comprised a heap. Smaller limbs
and branches were usually placed in separate piles. The farmer would do
his own burning and "chunking up" until the wood was reduced to ashes.
Millions of feet of high-grade timber were destroyed in this manner.
Sawmills were few in the sparsely settled country and it was imperative
that the logs be removed in order to till the land. Sometimes the trees
were "deadened" with the ax and let stand a year or two before removal.
In recent years poison chemicals have been introduced for use in killing
the trees.

While the men rolled logs, the womenfolks were busy preparing dinner. At the sound of horn or bell, the workers assembled at the house, washed the dirt and grime from their hands and faces in wooden tubs provided for that purpose, and seated themselves at the long table. The festive board was laden with boiled ham, fried chicken, and perhaps plates of beef and mutton, or venison and wild turkey if in the early days, for the Ozarkers are meat eaters like their English forebears. There were boiled potatoes, corn bread, turnip greens, lye hominy, and biscuits so soft and fluffy that, when they were pulled apart, one thought of picking cotton in Dixie. The feasters tapered off with cake, custards, and half-moon dried-apple pies. The meal was washed down with black coffee or buttermilk.

When the day's work was over, a dance-frolic was sometimes held to complete the occasion. The dancers stepped to the rollicking music of fiddle, guitar, and banjo until they were near exhaustion before returning to their respective homes. The farmer's farewell to his guests usually took the form of "Much obliged until you're better paid."

Barn- and house-raisings were conducted in much the same manner as the logrolling. The preparatory work was done by the owner, assisted by members of his family or hired hands. Then the neighbors came in for the raising and the work was usually accomplished in one day.

The old hewed-log houses of the Ozarks are fast tumbling down and will soon exist only in the land of memory. They were the first houses of the pioneers and the only kind that could be built at that time. Few sawmills had been opened in the back country and lumberyards were unknown. But these log structures were real castles to the early settlers. The country was covered with the finest of timber, and about all the tools the pioneer brought with him from his native country were a chopping ax, broadax, a handsaw, crosscut saw, hammer, hatchet, and a few augers. With these tools and a few dull-pointed cut nails, he built his first house. W. S. White of Polk County, Missouri, explained to me how the building was done.

The first step in the housing program was to go to the forest with axes, crosscut saw, and a chalk line, fell the trees, and hew the logs.

Straight trees, usually oak or walnut, that carried a good size for fifteen or twenty feet, were selected. After the tree was felled and the limbs cleared away, the saw was used to square the trunk at the butt. Then the trunk was sawed into logs of proper length for the building. The woodsman then took his chopping ax and scaled the bark off a narrow strip the full length of the log. The chalk line snapped a straight line down the place that had been scaled as a guide for the hewing. The man then mounted the log with his chopping ax and scored it from one end to the other, sinking the blade to the depth of the chalk line. He did the hewing with his broadax which is a short-handled tool with a blade ten or twelve inches in width and the handle bent slightly away from the center to keep from skinning the hands.

The hewing of timbers is an art almost as old as the human race. The Ozark pioneers were skillful workers in wood. They hewed to the line from one end of the log to the other. The process was repeated on the other side and the log was ready for the building.

With oxen or horses the logs were dragged, or loaded on the running gears of a linchpin wagon and hauled, to the building site. Then the neighbors came in for the raising. A definite procedure was followed in erecting the building.

The corners of the house were properly squared and the walls raised by an improvised plumb line of twine string weighted with a piece of lead. Four "corner men" carried up the corners and the balance of the workers were left on the ground to lift the logs into place. The first two logs were flattened to rest on the foundation stones and "saddle notches" cut near the ends of each of them. The top logs were notched to fit the saddles of the lower ones. This process was continued as the walls of logs rose higher and higher, carried up by the plumb line to the height desired. If the wall became too high for the men on the ground to push the logs into place, ropes and push-poles were used to elevate the timbers.

The workers prepared for the roof by pulling the logs in on two sides and shortening and sloping the ends of the ones on the other two sides until the last log became the ridgepole of the roof. Sometimes pole rafters flattened on top and bottom were used, but this plan called for lumber to plank up the gables. These poles were notched to fit the edge of the top logs of the wall and slanted on the other ends to fit together at the top.

Boards for doors, windows, boxing, and sheeting were a big problem before the coming of the sawmills. A whipsaw operated by two men was sometimes used to divide the timber lengthwise and make crude lumber. Most of the early cabins had puncheon floors. A puncheon is nothing more than a slab of heavy split timber with the face cut smooth with an adz. The round side was flattened to fit the sleepers underneath. Doors were made of hand-sawed lumber and hung with wooden hinges. Wooden shutters were made to slide back and forth in front of the windows. Glass had to be imported and it was seldom seen in the early days. Some cabins were built without windows and the ones that had openings used oiled paper as a substitute for glass.

When the building was ready for the roof, a straight-grained oak or pine tree was selected and cut into twenty-four-, thirty-, or thirty-six-inch lengths and worked into eight-sided blocks for the making of clapboard shingles. The shingles or boards were split from each of the eight sides, working toward the center of the block, with a sharp tool called a rive. These boards were lapped about half and half on the boards or poles of the roof, and fastened with dull-pointed cut nails.

The cracks between the logs in the first houses were chinked with clay, but this process was improved upon in later years by filling the spaces with short pieces of split timber and chinking around them with lime and sand mortar. Many of the houses had the logs fastened together at the corners with large wooden pegs driven through auger holes.

The simplest cabins were built square with a saddle roof, and a lean-to kitchen in the rear. But a more elaborate architecture was used in constructing the better homes. The double house was popular with Ozarkers who could afford it. It was built in two sections with an open hallway or "gallery" between, and covered with a common roof. Pegs were driven into the logs in this hallway and hung with onions, peppers, and other products of garden and farm. It made a convenient shelter for the hound dogs, home from the hunt, and was a storehouse for harness, fish gigs, boat paddles, and odds and ends of every description. Coonskins were stretched on the walls and 'possum and mink hides swung from the rafters during the trapping season.

To complete the log house, one or more fireplaces were needed. The fireplace and chimney as a single unit originated in England nearly five hundred years ago. It was a great improvement over the open fire in the center of the room with the smoke escaping through the rooftree. This Anglo-Saxon idea migrated to America with the earliest settlers and became the popular heating and cooking contrivance wherever wood was plentiful. All the old Ozark homes had chimneys of one type or another. Chimneys of cut stone were built into the better houses, but the poorer people were content with crude rock structure or one of the stick-and-clay variety.

When the hillsman decides to build a mud chimney (natives say "chimley") neighbors gather in to help him with the work. They dig some good "chimley dirt" of clay and dump it into a pit or barrel along with some straw, or fodder from last year's cornfield. Water is poured over this and the mixture is stirred and churned until it forms a mortar. This mortar is in turn made into large mud balls with some straw wrapped around the ball, forming what is called a "mud cat."

The frame for the chimney is shaped like a square-shouldered, long-necked bottle. It is constructed of rough timbers with small pieces running crisscross in "pigpen" fashion. This makes a foundation for the "cats" which are laid on firmly. After the chimney reaches a height beyond a man's reach it is necessary to "sling the cats" to the men who are working on the scaffold higher up. "Stray cats" fall on the workers until they are covered with mud from head to foot. But showers of mud cannot diminish the enthusiasm of the merry, bantering crowd. Chimney building carries with it an atmosphere of goodwill and merriment, characteristic of all old-time activities.

CHAPTER V

Fun and Frolic

. . . .

Swing Your Partner

"You can talk 'bout your fox chases and camp meetin's," said Tobe Mullins, "but a dancin' frolic beats 'em all fer a good time. Hit may be a sin t' say it, but I feel nigher Paradise when callin' a square dance than at any other time. That thar fiddle music eats right in t' my bones an' makes me cut capers I wouldn't think o' doin' nowhar else. Course a leetle dram o' corn licker helps put a feller in shape fer callin'. Church folks says dancin' is a turrible sin but I jist can't think of hit that way."

I had received an invitation to a play party at the home of Daniel Freeman and was hesitating about going. I knew that the fountain of Freeman hospitality would be full to the brim and overflowing but being a stranger in the hill country, I had made it a practice not to attend country dances.

"This here frolic won't be a real dance," explained Tobe, "an' they won't be no drinkin' or tomcattin' goin' on 'round th' place. They'll play old singin' games without th' fiddle music. Church folks don't object t' this kind of a frolic. Like as not, th' preacher's daughter 'ill be thar."

Borrowing Tobe's saddle mule I rode with Tip Logan to the party. When we entered the house, the players were already on the floor and in full swing. They were singing a song that went something like this:

Coffee grows on the white oak tree;
The river flows sweet brandy-o;
Now choose the one to roam with you,
As sweet as sugar in the candy-o.

Two in the center and you'd better get about,
Two in the center and you'd better get about,
Two in the center and you'd better get about,
And swing that lady 'round.

Twenty high-spirited young people were in the living room of
Dan Freeman's double log house, polishing the planks of the floor with
their stout shoes and apparently enjoying life fully and freely. Tip and
I squeezed in at the door and watched the fun. The players were in an
irregular formation, standing around the walls of the room in the sem-
blance of a circle. The first stanza of the coffee song was being sung as
we entered the room, and one young man was skipping around inside
the circle, apparently looking for a partner. Just as the singers reached the
line, "As sweet as sugar in the candy-o," the boy grabbed a winsome girl
by both arms and gave her a violent spin around the circle. He did just
as the singers told him to do—"And swing that lady 'round."

Then the first stanza of the song was repeated and the girl in the
ring chose a boy from the group around her. This young man selected
a girl for his partner as he stepped to the inner circle. Without losing a
step, the two couples traced a figure eight on the floor and were in their
proper places in the center of the room when "candy-o" was reached by
the wayside troubadours. Then came the order from a dozen throats:

Four in the center and you'd better get about,
Four in the center and you'd better get about,
Four in the center and you'd better get about,
And swing them ladies 'round.

Then the fun really began. Everybody seemed to catch the spirit of
the occasion and showed enthusiasm by clapping hands and stomping
feet. Acorns peppered the roof above our heads as an overhanging oak

joined the celebration. A few gay young swains cut capers on the sidelines as an extra attraction. If the gods frown upon such gaiety surely they were all on a vacation at that moment. The two couples in the center of the room were following the traditional scheme of the old game to the letter. The first couple quickly took positions facing each other some four or five feet apart. The second boy took a position a few feet behind the first young man and the second girl took a relative position behind the first girl. Then boy number one took his girl's hand and passed her on the right. They circled so as to meet and pass in about the same spot, followed by the second couple, and tracing a figure eight on the floor. Then came the coffee verse again and the last couple coming in selected another couple to join them. Now three couples were in the center and the crowd sang accordingly:

> Six in the center and you'd better get about,
> Six in the center and you'd better get about,
> Six in the center and you'd better get about,
> And swing them ladies 'round.

The figure eight on the floor now became a whirling mass of skirts and stomping feet as the boys in line each took a girl by the hand, right and left alternately, weaving among them and circling back into place.

I had attended numerous play parties while growing up on the Kansas prairies but this game was a new one to me. I saw that it was difficult of execution, but the young folks of the White River country knew it so well they moved through the intricate figures almost automatically. I had almost given up hope of trying to follow the dancers in the serpentine course they were taking, when, to my surprise, Emily Freeman chose me as her partner and half dragged me into the circle. I felt awkward as a bull in a china shop. We were the fourth couple to join the whirling group in the center and before I knew what it was all about, I was being pushed and pulled into the required positions. I tried to double-shuffle Ozark style, but it seemed that my feet were tied. Emily was a good teacher, however, and I soon forgot my embarrassment sufficiently to get about in a fairly acceptable manner.

When the fifth couple had been initiated into the ceremony, we began an elimination process. With each stanza, a couple would drop out, beginning with the boy and girl who first entered the game. The song now went like this:

> Ten in the center and two step out,
> Ten in the center and two step out,
> Ten in the center and two step out,
> And swing them ladies 'round.

After a while just one couple was left inside the circle and, as the final stanza of the song closed, this boy and girl took positions with us around the walls of the room. Then came a recess period with the boys filing out of the room to chew tobacco, roll and smoke cigarettes, and attend to other important matters. They took turns with the old gourd dipper at the spring and laughed and joked over trivial matters. The vernacular was pitted with some obscenity and a few racy stories were told, but there was no overflow of vulgarity. Liquor was entirely absent but two or three of the young men spoke of being as dry as a fish out of water. Tobe Mullins had told me there would be no drinking at the Freeman party and his words proved true. Had it been a dance, almost every man would have carried a pint in his bottle-pocket.

The girls, excepting half a dozen who went to the spring, remained seated on the crude benches Dan Freeman had built to accommodate his guests. They waited patiently for the return of their "lords of creation" in order that the frolic might continue.

The next game we played (I was now one of the bunch) was "Down the O-hi-o." I had been brought up on the Virginia reel and as this game was merely a variant of it, I had no difficulties as in the coffee song mix-up. We took our positions in parallel lines, facing our partners across the room. Tip Logan and Emily Freeman started the ball rolling. There was neither fiddle nor guitar to inspire us but we didn't really need them. A score of voices sang:

> The river is up, the channel is deep,
> The waves are steady and strong.

The river is up, the channel is deep,
As we go marching along.
Down the river, oh, down the river,
Oh, down the river we go, oh-o,
Down the river, oh, down the river,
Oh, down the O-hi-o.

At the beginning of the song, Tip advanced to the center to meet the girl from the foot of the opposite line. Emily went through the same procedure with the boy at the foot of our line. Then Tip swung Emily with the waist swing and proceeded to give each girl in the line a right-hand swing, alternately swinging his own partner with the left. Then, hand in hand, they skipped down the room and took positions at the foot of their respective lines. The second couple then started "Down the O-hi-o." There were eleven couples in all and the one stanza was getting monotonous before half of us had taken our turn. But the Ozarkers knew their "O-hi-o" and added a stanza.

The water is dark and lapping the shore,
The wind blows steady and strong,
The water is deep and lapping the shore
As we go marching along.
Down the river, oh, down the river,
Oh, down the river we go, oh-o,
Down the river, oh, down the river,
Oh, down the O-hi-o.

Many other fine old-time swinging games were played on that October night at the Freeman party. A few that I recall are: "Buffalo Girls," "Old Brass Wagon," "Skip t' My Lou," "Pig in the Parlor," "Miller Boy," "Carrie Nation," "Going to Boston," "Four Hands Up to Rowser," "Shoot the Buffalo," "Josie," "Three Little Girls A-Skating They Went," "Old Dan Tucker," "The Girl I Left Behind Me," "Across the Hall," "Sally Goodin," and "Weevily Wheat." Some of these are "cheating games" in which a boy cuts in when the changes are being made. "Pig in the Parlor" is a game of this type.

> My father and mother were Irish,
> My father and mother were Irish,
> My father and mother were Irish,
> And I was Irish, too.

> It's right unto your partner,
> And left unto your neighbor;
> Back unto your partner,
> And all promenade.

Another stanza runs like this with the same chorus.

> We've got a new pig in the parlor,
> We've got a new pig in the parlor,
> We've got a new pig in the parlor,
> And he is Irish, too.

In this game, the players form a circle with girls on the right. They circle left while the stanza part of the song is sung. Then comes a right and left and "back to your partner" as in the square dance. It is during these changes that the extra boys (the "pigs") in the center of the circle try to get partners. The boys left without partners at the time of promenading become the new "pigs."

I enjoyed myself immensely at the Freeman party and could not realize the lateness of the hour when the clock struck twelve, informing us that it was Sunday and time for frolics to cease. As I walked with Tip Logan to where we had tethered our mules, I stepped lightly to the tune of the song we were singing when midnight came to disrupt the party. The spirit of the party's gaiety had captured me and I was a happy, contented prisoner. As we rode toward Woodville, our mules pushed to a trot by the homing instinct, I visualized a lifetime lease on the hills with a cottage built for two. A stanza from "Weevily Wheat" kept ringing in my mind.

Don't you think she's a pretty little miss,
And don't you think she's clever,
And don't you think that she and I
Would make a match forever?

In the years that followed, I learned that the play party with its sing-ing-swinging games is an important social institution in the Ozarks. Like the plain life of the hills, these games are simple in execution but with a catchy rhythm that does not fail in its intended effect. Where the play party originated and what people first chose it as an innocent pastime is not known. Of this much we are sure, it harks back to the seventeenth century in England and probably goes far beyond. Some think these tunes began in the nursery and later found their way into the parlor as pastime for adults, but we have no data to prove this.

Radio artists give these games added color with musical accompani-ment. This naturally adds zest to the playing, but it must be remembered that these are singing games and became popular with a certain class of people because of the superstition that "the devil's in the fiddle" and brings evil influences to the dance. Of course, the Ozarks have always had an abundance of string music. But in almost every community there are people with religious or moral convictions who oppose the dance. The young people of this group had to have recreation and they substituted the play party. Even the minister's daughter could dance to the tune of "Skip t' My Lou" without becoming the subject of gossip. It can be said to the credit of the play party that it is traditionally dry, while the little brown jug is closely associated with the dance. Folk attitudes toward dancing provide an abundance of interesting folklore.[1]

On with the Dance!

The square dance is faster, gayer, and more complicated than the play-party games. Stringed instruments, such as fiddle, guitar, banjo, and mandolin, set the tempo for this romantic pastime and create an urge to stomp and caper that is almost irresistible. To dance to an old fiddle tune, guided by a skillful caller, is to find happy release and forget the cares of isolation and poverty. Even the good deacon of the "deep-water" church may be pardoned for patting his foot when "The Eighth of January" is played. The square dance helps heal the wounds of privation that pioneer life is heir to. It is an important balance wheel of rural life, an outlet for pent-up streams of emotion.

The church has always been the enemy of this type of dancing, and with good reason. The public dance is usually accompanied by drinking and fighting and probably has its share of responsibility for illicit relations between the sexes. Most hillsmen who attend dances think that liquor is needed to enliven the occasion. The age-old tradition of "the devil in the fiddle" is reinforced by the charges of immorality that have given the public dance a shady reputation. But, good or bad, the institution continues to be a favorite social pastime in and out of the hills. A logrolling or a barn raising without a square dance to follow would be like serving a formal dinner without dessert.

Dances are frequently held as the culminating event of various workings that call folks together in the hills. Or the frolic may be given to honor some visiting friend, or as a farewell party to someone who is moving to Texas or California. Sometimes the occasion is worked up by local musicians who want to make a little extra cash with their playing. Or some enterprising young man in the neighborhood may get up a dance just to have a good time. Of course, the established dance halls in the villages and the platforms at picnics are strictly commercial affairs and are planned to make money for the managers.

No invitation is necessary to attend a country dance in the Ozarks. The news is "norated 'round" by word of mouth and everybody is urged to attend. Naturally, the rakings of the hills turn out in full force and frequently bring discord to an otherwise pleasant gathering. If trouble is brewing in the neighborhood, the dance is the place to climax the event and get even. Menfolks in the backhills carry pocketknives whetted to a keen edge and do not hesitate to use them when the occasion demands. Almost every hillsman owns a shooting iron and usually conceals it on his person when attending a dance. Preparedness for emergencies is not overlooked.

A few years ago while I was teaching school in the backhills I had difficulty in persuading my larger boys that they should not carry their pistols on basketball trips. Once when my team was warming up for a game in a neighboring town, a pistol dropped from the bottle-pocket of one of my players. But it was out of sight in a flash and nothing was said about it. On numerous occasions I have attended dances where the men would go outside between sets and fire their guns into the air. "Jist t' raise a little hell."

If the dance is a public affair and arranged for profit, numbers written on pieces of cardboard are sold to the men who wish to dance. If it is a home affair, twenty-five cents usually pays for the right "to dance all night 'til the broad daylight." At the picnic and town frolics, round dancing is sometimes alternated with the sets, and the customary price is ten cents for each dance. The average home dance brings in three or four dollars and most of it goes to the fiddler and his accompanists. At the larger dances, two or three sets are run at one time and the promoter makes a good profit. Sometimes supper is served and an additional charge is made for it.

When everything is set for the start, the manager calls out, "Numbers 1, 2, 3, and 4, take the floor." The young men who hold these numbers secure feminine partners and take their positions with ladies on the right. One of the dancers may call the set or it may be an outside caller. The fiddler tests the strings of his instrument with the bow, and the guitar pickers complete the final tuning. A nod from the caller puts things to work. The catchy music weaves a magic spell, the caller sets his hat on the back of his head and shouts, "All join hands and circle eight."

The eight dancers take hold of hands and circle to the left, stomping and capering as the mood impels. This is the initial movement in the square dance and is followed by directions that depend upon the call being used. If it is a "pep-up" set, "Across the Hall" is a good example. This is the way I learned to dance it in the Ozarks.

"Circle eight."

"Half around, turn right back go pat 'er down."

This preliminary circling, left and right, is a "warmer-upper" for figures to follow.

> Balance eight 'til you get straight,
> You swing Sue and I'll swing Kate,
> Swing 'em 'round like swingin' on a gate.

To balance means to move toward a person or couple opposite, then back. The swinging technique varies somewhat in different sections of the country. The traditional square dance does not call for the waist swing with its hugging propensities. The man grasps the lady by the arms and gives her a violent spin, the dancers stepping to the music in a sort of lame-duck fashion. In the early days certain taboos were strictly adhered to but looseness of decorum has crept in recently. Sometimes the girls would lift their arms slightly as if inviting the waist swing but drew them in quickly if it were attempted. A young swain might succeed in getting his arm into the coveted position but it was the exception rather than the rule. For a stranger to take such familiarities would be a gross insult to the lady and might have fatal results. I have seen men knocked down on the dance floor for attempting this unconventional swing.

> Once and a half, a cow and a calf,
> Twice six bits makes a dollar and a half.

Each man swings the girls in turn with a whirl that goes once around and then breaking at the halfway point in order to meet the next girl at the proper place. This differs from the "grand right and left" where the men take the girls' hands as they weave in and out around the circle.

The "once and a half" figure takes a little time and gives the caller opportunity to put in some original wit. He may call out something like this:

> Irish potatoes tops and all,
> Swing her now or wait 'til fall.

Or:

> Pullet in a cage, coon on the ground,
> Swing them gals as you go 'round.

The "once and a half" over, the couples are in their original places facing the center. The caller shouts:

> First two gents cross the hall,
> Right-hand swing.
> Back to your partner and do the same.
> Cross the hall and a two-hand swing,
> Home again—do the same old thing,
> Cross the hall and do-si-do—
> Don't swing at all.
> Partners the same.
> With the left-hand lady promenade the ring.

These directions are almost self-explanatory. The figures are danced by two couples only with the remaining four dancers waiting their turn. "Do-si-do" means to dance around each other without touching. The promenade with the lady on the left gives the men new partners for the next whirl.

> Same two gents with brand-new girls,
> Cross the hall with the same old whirl.

The directions continue as before and so on until the last girls go through. Then comes "balance eight" and the other two men go through the same movements with all the girls. Sometimes all four men cross the hall at once and this makes it a fast set. The boys have a chance to show off while crossing the room, "cutting a Dido," as they call it, though they never heard of *The Iliad*.

Dancing contests are sometimes held between sets and prizes are given for the best jiggers. It is said that the men sometimes danced barefoot in the old days but I have never talked with an old-timer who would admit it. Vance Randolph in his *Ozark Mountain Folks* reports a story, told to him by natives of the Missouri Ozarks, about an Arkansas politician who was run out of his native settlement for fraud in a backwoods dancing contest.

"They was all a-dancin' t' see who could stomp th' loudest," the story goes, "an' this feller he win easy, but some o' th' boys suspicioned somethin', an' purty soon they ketched him a-cheatin'. He had went an' stuck some o' these hyar chinkapins betwixt his toes—'t warn't no wonder he raised sich a clatter!"

Some of the popular Ozark dance calls are: "Old Joe Clark," "Cheat or Swing," "Grapevine Twist," "Indian Style," "Bird in a Cage," "Arkansas," "Rattlesnake Shake," "Chinese Puzzle," "Old Jim Lane," "Two Little Sisters," "Ocean Wave," and "The Girl I Left Behind Me." There are fiddle tunes to fit each call but they are sometimes used promiscuously. "Indian Style" goes well with "Big-Eared Mule" and "The Grapevine Twist" seems to fit with "Sally Goodin."

Mountain girls usually wear neat print dresses of percale or gingham at dances, but the boys frequently attend wearing denim shirts, overalls, and stout brogan shoes. It is not considered out of place to work all day in the field or woods and then go to the dance without changing clothes. Recent years have brought changes in dress, however. Most mountain men now follow the fashions set by their city cousins and the girls, with rouge and lipstick and permanent waves, keep pace. One must go deep into the backhills to get away from modern trends of fashion.

The barn dance, now a favorite radio feature, was once a popular pastime in the hills. Let us look in on one of these old-time frolics in its natural setting.

The main floor of the barn has been swept clean and given a thorough scrubbing. Kegs and boxes are provided as seats for the musicians, but the spectators perch in hay-filled mangers or lounge in spring seats carried in from their wagons. Lanterns are hung on the walls for lighting and the doors flung open for ventilation.

I got a gal at th' head o' th' holler,
She won't lead an' I won't foller.

These words seem to spring from the fiddle as the orchestra tears loose on "Sourwood Mountain." The dancers rule on the floor and the caller is shouting directions. The cares of the day are locked out.

A group of young folks, waiting their turn, climb to the loft and sit on the hay with their feet dangling over the edge. Loud laughter rises spontaneously and almost stops the dance when a young swain sits down on a nest of eggs while trying to maneuver closer to his sweetheart.

The hour of midnight arrives. The older folks yawn and wiggle their tired toes methodically. Some of them doze in resignation. But the younger members of the crowd continue to balance and swing with tireless ecstasy. The dance may continue until the morning star peeps over the horizon and shoots its rays into the open doorway.

Farewells are said as wagons and buggies are loaded by the light of swinging lanterns. Young men on horseback yodel and sing as they ride through the night. A cock, roosting in a persimmon tree, flaps his wings and crows as jolt-wagons rattle homeward bound over the rocky roads.

Social Pastimes

The social life of the Ozarks a quarter of a century ago had many of the primitive trappings of pioneer days. Recreational activities harmonized with the ways of life conditioned by the stern backwoods existence. The social scheme had traditional patterns which were followed almost exclusively. But the tempo of fun and frolic has been greatly accelerated in recent years by the use of the automobile, and by the invasion of modern entertainment in the form of movies and roadhouses. A new order of social life is being established in the backhills.

When youth reaches the age of indiscretion, romance sets the stage for the social drama. Nature maneuvers in strange ways to accomplish her purpose. It is good usage to encourage Cupid in his quest. Tame social pastimes, firmly anchored by convention, may have subtle motives.

One of the rural customs that takes the starch out of sophistication is the husking bee. Its double purpose cannot be denied. First, it gets the work done in a satisfactory manner with a minimum of expense. Second, it offers romantic incentives and rewards, and ultimately leads to court-ship and marriage. Without doubt, it is the search for the red ears in the pile of corn that puts zest in the husking. To a bashful country lad, who could never muster the courage to kiss a girl in secret, it is opportunity given social approval.

The husking bee is strictly an American institution and used to be popular throughout the Midwest. It was only one of the many neighbor-hood "bees" such as logrolling, house-raising, quilting, hog killing, and soapmaking, but its romantic slant gave it special appeal and unending popularity. It was "folklure" at its best.

Sometimes the husking bees were conducted on a stag basis with the womenfolks gathered at the house for the frolic to follow the husking. To stimulate and add relish to labor, the farmer who owned the corn would measure the crib and stash a jug of corn whiskey in the very center of the pile of ears. Captains were appointed to choose up so that the crowd would be evenly divided. With wooden pegs or bare hands, the men worked fast and furiously, tearing the shucks from the ears. The winners had the privilege of emptying the jug in the presence of their opponents; such an opportunity was worth working for.

Kissing games were popular at Ozark parties a generation ago. Some of the popular games of this type were: "Post Office," "Log Chain," "Build the Bridge," "Spike in the Wagon Wheel," "Wade the Swamp," "Lost My Glove Yesterday," and "Possum Pie." The note of sentiment is outstanding in these games and there was no attempt at disguise. Even children encouraged love's conquest in their play by "Marching 'Round the Levee." Perhaps many a mountain courtship began in the acting out of this old song.

> We're marching 'round the levee,
> We're marching 'round the levee,
> We're marching 'round the levee,
> For we have gained the day.
>
> Go in and out the window,
> Go in and out the window,

Go in and out the window,
For we have gained the day.

Go forth and face your lover,
Go forth and face your lover,
Go forth and face your lover,
For we have gained the day.

I kneel because I love you,
I kneel because I love you,
I kneel because I love you,
For we have gained the day.

I measure my love to show you,
I measure my love to show you,
I measure my love to show you,
For we have gained the day.

One kiss before I leave you,
One kiss before I leave you,
One kiss before I leave you,
For we have gained the day.

"Build the Bridge" is a party pastime played without the formality of blueprints. Vance Randolph found it popular with young folks in south-western Missouri. "In this game," he says,

> a boy and a girl stand facing each other holding hands with arms extended to form an arch. Then the girl chooses a second boy who walks under the arch or span and kisses the girl as he passes. Then he takes his position by the side of the girl, locking his arm with hers, and calls the name of another girl. The girl kisses boy number one as she passes through the arch, then locks her arm into his and clasps hands with her partner, so as to form the second span of the "bridge." The boy whose name she calls kisses both girls and locks arms with girl number two, after which he

calls a third girl to be his partner, and so on. The completed
bridge has as many spans as there are couples in the game, and
the last few couples to line up certainly do a lot of kissing.

But not all the party games in the backhills were so richly flavored
with sentiment. In some communities, kissing games were restricted by
straitlaced folks or entirely prohibited by social ethics. Tamer diversions
were known at parties in these neighborhoods. Snap was a popular game
at such parties.

In playing Snap a boy and a girl take a position in the center of the
room holding hands. A boy is usually the first "it." He walks around the
room, finally snapping his fingers in a girl's face. The girl chases the boy
around the couple in the center until she catches him. He then takes the
place of the boy who was standing and the girl who caught him "snaps"
another boy. The chase continues until the girl is caught. She takes the
place of the girl standing and the game goes on. This game is a good
warmer-upper at parties and continues to be a favorite with Ozark young
people.

Other conventional party pastimes, sometimes called "parlor games,"
in the backhill country are: "Spin the Plate," "Cross Questions and
Crooked Answers," "Going to California," "Philadelphia," "Clap-in and
Clap-out," "The Duke of York Has Lost His Hat," "My Ship Comes
Sailing In," and "Going Walking." Some of the games are so arranged
that forfeits are given as penalties. These pawns consist of knives, rings,
watches, pins—anything of value. After the peddler makes the rounds
collecting these things, a judge is appointed to decree the acts that must
be performed to redeem the article. "Heavy, heavy hangs over your head,"
says the peddler. The judge inquires whether it is "fine or superfine." Fine
means that the article belongs to a boy, superfine to a girl. The penalty
for redemption is left to the judge. He may have Jack Elzey doing a
barefoot dance while Millie Stout tries to kiss her elbow. Ted Richmond
is sentenced to eat three crackers and then whistle "Dixie." Opal Garton
must walk around the house with Claude Johnson to redeem her engage-
ment ring. Tom Anthony sings a solo, Payne Mitchell calls hogs, Anna

Bolinger proposes to Fred Berry, and so the game goes on until each person in the room has performed a stunt to redeem his property.

In nutting time the young folks play "Hull-gull." This is a guessing game played with chinkapins. With one or more nuts secreted in the closed hand, the antagonist challenges a companion with "hull-gull" which, being interpreted, means "How many chinkapins have I?" The person challenged makes a guess and, if correct, wins the handful of nuts. If incorrect, which is usually the case, the guesser must pay his companion the difference between his estimate and the actual number of nuts.

"Candy-breakin'" is a popular party pastime throughout the Ozarks. In the old days sorghum molasses was boiled down and pulled into strands to be used at the breaking. In recent years store-bought stick candy is used. It is broken into pieces an inch or two long and placed in a box or utensil and covered. A boy selects a girl as his partner and they draw one of the short pieces from the container. With the candy between his teeth, the boy challenges his partner to bite off the free end. If she accepts the challenge, she clamps the offered sweet between her teeth and the contest begins. The rules of the game compel the couple to stand without touching each other, hands clasped behind their backs. The one who is first to bite through the candy wins the contest and may choose a new partner for the next "chawin'."

Other pastimes that have become institutions in the hills are: marble playing, horseshoe pitching, the shooting match, the medicine show, horse racing, card playing, and the annual picnic or old settlers' reunion. Marble shooting is considered to be a sport for boys in most sections of the country, but I found many men enjoying this pastime when I entered the Ozarks a quarter of a century ago. Contests were sometimes held between communities with the best players taking part. Gambling usually accompanied such tournaments.

The more modern card games such as auction and contract bridge are unknown in the backhills, but both draw and stud poker are relished by many hillsmen. The law against gambling requires strict secrecy and such games are usually carried on in the woods with stumps for tables, or behind closed doors. Pitch is played everywhere "jist fer th' fun of it," in hotel lobbies and country stores, and checkers helps the hillsman pass many pleasant hours. At Caddo Gap, Arkansas, checker squares are painted on the concrete in front of two business buildings for the convenience of the players.

The medicine show is a transient institution that makes the rounds of the villages and it seldom fails to get a crowd. Entertainment is provided by a blackface comedian or two who crack jokes and sing catchy songs and dance with guitar or banjo accompaniment. Health lectures by the "Doc" are interspersed, and herb bitters, snake oil, or goldenseal salve are recommended for about all the ills imaginable. If you have jitters, stomach trouble, rheumatism, kidney trouble, freckles, boils, or bunions, the Doc's remedies, "compounded from an old Indian prescription," will do the work. The proposition is baited with special offers and a money-back guarantee, and it pulls "foldin' money" from the hillsman's pocket. "Honey Boy" and "Lasses" carry the products to customers with cries of "Sold out, Doctor" when a sale is made. Within an hour or two, the show ends and the Doc and his helpers head their car toward the next village.

Annual picnics or reunions are held in the late summer after the crops are laid by and there is a rest period before harvest. A convenient grove, where plenty of drinking water is available, is selected for the occasion. Concessions include hot dog and cold drink stands, a dance platform, and sometimes a homemade swing pulled by a mule. Speeches are made by local politicians during the afternoon, but the night is for fun and frolic. These picnics may be one-day affairs or may be reunions that continue for a week or more. "Folks shore have good times at them thar picnics."

CHAPTER VI

Customs and Traditions

. . . .

Hillbilly Barter

"I'd like t' have that thar yaller dog o' yourn, Tobe," said Ed Bullock as he took a seat on the counter near the stove at Tuttle's store, "but I jist can't give ye whut yer askin' fer him. Tell ye whut I'll do. If'n you'll put in th' grubbin' hoe with th' dog, I'll swap ye this here crosscut saw an' five pounds uv th' best homegrown tobacker ye ever chawed on. You'ens 'ill need th' saw fer makin' ties an' bar'l staves this winter an' this is th' best one ever brought into th' county, I reckon. Don't need a thing done t' hit but a leetle sharpenin' and settin'. That's a good offer, Tobe, fer that dog o' yourn ain't much account no way."

But Tobe Mullins was not inclined to trade that way. In fact, no hillsman ever accepts a first offer unless it is a bargain beyond the shadow of a doubt. Such procedure would spoil all the fun of barter and ultimately bring ruin to an honorable profession. The custom of barter is as old as the hills themselves. Mountaineers, with little cash on hand, always have been inveterate swappers. It isn't necessary to designate the first Monday or the third Saturday of the month as trade's day at Woodville. Every weekday is an open day for swapping in this Ozark community and the men sometimes deal in worldly goods on Sunday in spite of all the parson does to prevent it. Everyone remembers the time Deacon Jed Taylor was caught trading horses with a band of gypsies on Sunday morning when he should have been saying his prayers at the church house.

Tobe chewed his tobacco hard and fast as he whittled long shavings from a pine slab that he had picked up outside the store. It was a tense moment in the commercial life at Woodville. Half a dozen village loafers awaited the outcome with interest. Hite Lindsey was already figuring that if the trade went through he would borrow the dog from Ed for squirrel hunting.

P-futt went a stream of tobacco juice at the stove's door. Tobe wiped his mouth on his shirtsleeve and continued whittling. The pine slab began to take the shape of a butter paddle. At last the old trader spoke.

"I can't swap that way, Ed. This here dog is th' best cur in these parts fer night huntin'. Refused ten dollars in cash money fer 'im last fall a year ago when I took that big hunt with Dan Freeman on White River. Treed four coons an' seven 'possums in one night. Ye ort t' put in a bushel o' them taters ye growed in th' bottom 'long with th' tobacker. Best I could do would be t' swap th' dog an' th' horse collar fer th' saw an' tobacker, an' a tow sack full of them taters."

After three or four hours of parley, the deal was made and the property changed hands. Ed seemed well satisfied with the trade as he went whistling down the trail, leading a yellow cur with a frayed rope, and carrying the horse collar on his shoulder. The trade had cost him a cross-cut saw, a worn file, six pounds of tobacco, and two gallons of sorghum molasses.

Jed Taylor holds the record as the best trader in the Woodville community. Last year he started a string of trades with a coonhound and when he finished swapping he had the dog back and a pony and a pig for profit. He began by swapping the dog to Ed Bullock for a broken-down plow horse. Ed took the dog to the Posey neighborhood and traded it for a couple of calves. Jed then contacted the dog's new owner and swapped him the horse he got from Ed for the dog and a good-sized shoat. So far he was a pig ahead. Then he traded the dog again, this time for a cow. This farmer swapped the dog to another party on a hog deal. Taylor then bartered with the dog's new owner and got the dog and a pony in exchange for the cow he had recently acquired. He had retrieved his coonhound and had a pig and a pony as profits on his trading.

Under the hill by the river stands Tom Peden's barbershop. It might be called a variety shop for although Tom began as a barber forty years ago, he has gradually enlarged his business to include many of the arts and sciences. At Tom's place you can get a modern haircut, a late-model whisker trim, or a slick shave. In the old days he had to use the sap from wild grapevines as a hair restorer, but now he has the latest commercial tonics with which to scent the young bloods for their social encounters. At Tom's shop you can have your shoes half-soled, get your watch fixed, or leave a rifle to be rebored. At one time he pulled teeth, but the coming of a "tooth dentist" to the county seat has relieved him of this work.

Tom never was much of a dentist, but he served his neighbors in this capacity as best he could. His regular price for extracting a tooth was two bits for home folks and fifty cents for "furriners." But a native did not need cash in hand. He would do the work with the same promptness for a 'possum hide or a bucket of huckleberries. Of course, the procedure wasn't painless and sometimes the homemade pliers slipped off the tooth and fractured a jawbone, but Tom was persistent in this work and would continue the torture all day if necessary. The patient sat in the barber chair and laid his head against a board padded with flour sacks. Tom is cross-eyed and it is rumored that he sometimes pulled the wrong tooth. Of course, many of the old-timers did not patronize him. When they had teeth to be removed they cut around them with a pocketknife, or a pair of scissors, worked them loose and jerked them out without dental assistance.

On Saturdays, Tom gives most of his attention to barbering. He looks all dressed up in clean blue denim overalls. Fifteen cents pays for a shave; a quarter of a dollar buys a haircut. Tom owns only one razor but it is a good one, given to him by his father years ago. He knows the exact amount of snake oil to put on the strop for conditioning the blade.

Tart Tuttle, the merchant, has more trade sales than cash ones. A good mink hide or coonskin will pay for a pair of brogans and a few ounces of "sang" root will get the best hat in the house. Overalls that sell in towns at a dollar fifty are swapped for two bushels of corn or five gallons of molasses. It takes a generous slab of hickory-smoked bacon or a pail of wild honey to pay for a couple of cotton work shirts. Tart owns the best string of foxhounds in the country and if a fellow comes along with a dog that suits him, he will trade almost anything in the store for it. Old Lead cost him a ten-gallon hat, a box of cigars, and five dollars in money. Two other hounds in his pack cost a suit of clothes and an assortment of snuff, stick candy, and fishing tackle. Tart considers them good trades, for the dogs furnish the best of entertainment when the moon is up and the foxes are out.

Farmers in Woodville community have the happy practice of swapping work of all kinds. During the haying season, neighbor swaps with neighbor in getting the crop into barn or stack. Sometimes a man gets behind with his spring plowing or planting and the neighbors help him out. He pays this work back at some time during the working season. Suppose Tobe Mullins decides to dig a pond to hold water for his stock during the dry months of the summer season. He has no money available to hire laborers and teams to help him with the work and he can hardly do it all by himself. But Ed Bullock and Hite Lindsey are available and they help with the project. A few weeks later Tobe pays Ed by helping him make molasses. Hite calls on him to help shingle a barn. These farmers keep no books but they do not lose track of the work due.

Swapping picks up "right smart" during the sessions of circuit court at the county seat. Many Woodville folks go to court to listen in on important cases, to meet old friends and neighbors, and to do a little trading. Jockey row is on the vacant lots back of the old livery stable. Here the men from Woodville meet traders from other parts of the county and spend many happy hours in barter.

Going to Mill

History hangs like an aura over the old water mills of the Ozarks; tradition clings to them like moss to an oak tree. In the annals of folklore, few things compare with the waterwheel of an old burr mill, monotonous perhaps in its slow revolutions but providing, ever providing, food for the rural table and toll for the thrifty miller. The folklore of Missouri and Arkansas is enriched in flavor by the seasoning of romantic milling days.

One of the first water mills west of the Mississippi was established by John Carter near Eleven Point River in Randolph County, Arkansas. It was built in 1805 and operated by Carter and his son for eighty-three years. For a long time it was the only gristmill within a radius of one hundred miles. It continued operation through the Civil War period and was one of the mills of the Ozark war zone that escaped destruction. A man named Hufstedler bought the mill in the eighties and christened it Birdell in honor of his two daughters, Birdie and Ella. Birdell Mill is still in operation after 138 years of continuous service.

In pre-motor days water mills dotted the streams throughout the Ozark area. The burr mill was an institution necessary to the life of the mountain people. Farmers and frontiersmen of that day went to mill weekly, monthly, or yearly, depending upon the supply of meal or flour needed and the distance to be traveled.

Among the early settlers of the Ozark region were many men who knew the milling trade. Some of them brought milling machinery with them, up the rivers in keelboats or by torturous overland hauls to choice sites near flowing springs or streams. To utilize a hillside spring, a wooden flume was built to carry the water to the top of a large overshot wheel which assisted in developing the power by its immense weight. If a stream was to be harnessed for power, and an undershot wheel used, a crude dam was built to provide a millpond which supplied water through a sluice gate as needed. One method of constructing a dam was to build pens of logs and fill them with stones. Some of these early dams were lashed with strips of bark when wire was not available. The structure was weighted down with large rocks which held it in place except in times of immense floods. The dam was usually twelve or fifteen feet high and twenty feet in depth. The logs were laid in pigpen style and fitted closely together. Gates or crude openings were provided to release the surplus water in flood time. The size of the millrace itself depended upon the type and size of the wheel to be used in developing power.

Much of the machinery of the early mills in the Ozarks was manufactured by the millers themselves. The waterwheel was built of wood capable of long wear in the water. Shafts and pulley wheels were hewn from seasoned hickory. The burrs were of native stone cut to a thickness of twelve or fifteen inches and with a circumference of three or more feet. Belts were sometimes cut from home-tanned cowhide with the hair left on.

Three types of waterwheels are known in the Ozarks. The earliest and, for many years, the most popular type was the large overshot wheel. It is twenty or more feet in diameter and the rims of the circumference are four or five feet apart. Wooden paddles are inserted at the proper slant to use the water to good advantage. The stream pours upon the wheel from the flume or race, turning it forward. The old Woodlock Mill in Crawford County, Missouri, had a wheel of this type. The main shaft of this large circular contraption extended into the mill proper and operated the machinery by means of pulleys.

The undershot wheel is smaller in diameter than the overshot type but it has greater width. The water from the millpond enters the race through a sluice or gate and strikes the lower part of the wheel, turning it backwards. The axle shaft runs into the mill and operates a bar fitted with pulleys for the attachment of belts.

The third type of wheel is more modern than the other models and is called a turbine. It has a vertical shaft, lies flat in the millrace, and is seldom more than three or four feet in diameter. It is driven by the impact of the flowing stream upon the blades of the wheel, utilizing a high percentage of the potential energy of the flowing water. Pioneer millers made turbines from the butts of large logs and carved the buckets in the solid wood. Modern turbines are made of iron. The vertical shaft from the center of the wheel is attached to a horizontal bearing on a level with the mill machinery.

In the early days the water mill was a vigorous community center, a popular meeting place for all classes of hillfolks. It was no uncommon thing to ride fifty miles to mill and camp for two or three days while waiting a turn. The burrs ground slowly and quite often the output did not exceed two or three bushels an hour. This gave opportunity for sports and amusements and valuable social contacts. Frequently the whole family rode to mill in a jolt-wagon to enjoy the recreation the occasion afforded. The men carried their rifles with them in order to provide meat for the camp, to compete in tests of marksmanship, and for protection. Women knitted and gossiped around the campfire. The boys played marbles, gathered wild fruits, hunted with "bonarrows," and went swimming in the clear pools. Sometimes they fished from the windows of the mill.

The mill was a good place to exchange ideas about farming, tell tall tales, sing old ballads, and catch up on news from the outside world. Tom Keener from over on Bull Creek had foolishly planted his turnips in the light of the moon, much to his regret. John Johnson from the head of Bee Fork had seen the brush rabbits lying in shallow pits along the way, which meant fair weather for at least two or three days. A fellow from the knob country of north Arkansas told how he had "whetted a banter" on his cradle Thursday a week ago and had outdone every other man in the neighborhood.[1] Susie Black, arriving muleback from Finley River, told about a neighbor's baby being born with a veil over its face. Nate Sellers, who had carried his sack of white corn from the foot of Breadtray Mountain, was always ready with a hunting story in which he invariably played the heroic part. Of course, the old "yarb" doctor was there giving free advice on the use of catnip tea, hoarhound, sassafras, and slippery elm. The circuit rider shook hands all around and invited everybody to attend the fourth Sunday meeting and foot washing at the log church on Sow Coon Mountain. Sometimes marriage vows were said in the shade of the mill and the parson needed to be on hand to tie the knot and collect his fee.

In the picture of pioneer milling days, honesty and integrity stand out like a harvest moon. The toll of the miller was seldom questioned. The customers waited their turns with salutary patience. Good sportsmanship was an accepted fact that seldom met contradiction. Of course, occasional fights occurred but the records say that trouble was the exception rather than the rule. Such an exception happened one time when a certain hillsman grew tired of waiting his turn. He had been at the mill three days and had not yet been served. Jokingly he remarked that he would just dust the miller and go home. A fight followed but it was the hillsman himself who got dusted.

Sometimes the little brown jug went to mill along with the sack of corn. One miller in Christian County, Missouri, combined distilling with milling. Corn was ground or liquefied as one might desire. A sack of burr meal and a jug of good corn liquor made a happy combination to the isolated hillsman.

At midnight on Saturday the water gates of the mills were usually closed and not opened until Monday morning. It was the custom at a mill in Madison County, Arkansas, to auction the fish that might be caught in the race during the Sabbath. The closed gate provided an excellent trap and sometimes the catch was good. The auction was held on Saturday afternoon before the gates were closed and if no fish happened to get in the successful bidder paid just the same.

Sometimes a section of the mill was used for a dance when the day's work was done. If no fiddler were present, the young folks stepped to the tune of "Buffalo Girls" or other old party songs, singing as they danced. Many an old mill was the scene of this beautiful custom which today has lost out in competition with the modern dance. One of the favorite party games in the backhills comes from the milling tradition.

> Happy is the miller boy who lives by the mill;
> The mill turns 'round with a free goodwill.
> One hand in the hopper and the other in a sack;
> Ladies step forward and the gents fall back.

The old water mills are passing rapidly due to modern methods of milling, but the taste of burr-mill bread made from water-ground meal lingers in the memory of every old-time Ozarker. Old-timers claim that such meal escapes being heated during the slow grinding process and is more palatable when made into bread. Add to it a few cracklings and bake in a Dutch oven, and no other corn bread on earth can compare with it in flavor and goodness.

The water-mill epoch of the Ozarks is marked by the principles of individualism, with liberty and justice for all. It is a period that should adorn history's pages as a golden age of democracy.

Special Days

Folk life is embellished with practices connected with red-letter days on the calendar. The observance of long-established customs dispels the rigid monotony of everyday life. Hillfolks like to give play to the imagination on special days: to visualize George Washington cutting the cherry tree, Abraham Lincoln splitting rails, men in powdered wigs and knee breeches signing the Declaration of Independence, rabbits miraculously laying eggs at Easter time, oxen kneeling at midnight on the eve of Old Christmas, St. Patrick driving the snakes out of Ireland. There are love charms for St. Valentine's Day, devilish pranks on Hallowe'en, the groundhog running from his shadow on February 2, signs and omens on May Day, and the usual Yuletide fancies on Christmas. The majority of these practices are old Anglo-Saxon traditions transplanted in the Ozarks by the early settlers.

May Day has an ominous setting in the backhills. Activities begin on the last night of April when lovelorn maidens hang handkerchiefs on bushes or clotheslines with romantic purpose. Every girl knows the superstition, whether she believes it or not, that when the handkerchief is dried of dew by morning sun on May 1, it will have on it the initials of the man she is to marry.

Another romantic experiment may be tried on the first morning of May. Without a word to anyone, the girl goes to the well or spring before the sun is up. She takes a glass or bottle, fills it with water, and lets the sun's first rays shine through it. In the water, she expects to see the image of her husband-to-be. But according to the old wives' tales, she may see a coffin instead. In the old days that meant an early death.

Or perhaps the young woman goes to the spring at sunrise, breaks an egg into a glass, and pours water over it. In it she may behold not only her future mate, but the number of children to be born to the union.

If these charms do not work, the romantically inclined maiden may bake a salt cake on May Day and eat a generous portion of it just before retiring. The man who gives her a drink of water in her dreams is to be her Romeo. Or she may look into a deep well at high noon and view the image of her intended through the reflection of a mirror.

"There isn't a blame thing to those old signs," the older folks say, but the younger generation continues to look for them just the same. Perhaps there is a subconscious feeling that they might after all prove true.

Early in May is the proper time to set a "dumb supper." At least it was considered so in grandmother's day. On the day set for this romantic event a group of girls would get together and follow the old, old tradition taught to them by their mothers. The table was set with dishes but no food was placed in them. An apparition was not supposed to partake of food. It was his business to come out of the night and occupy the place laid for him by his prospective bride. Each girl fixed the place for her lover and then stood behind the chair to await his coming. Of course, he never showed up in ghostly form but the event caused much merriment for the girls.

It is recorded that on one occasion a prospective groom did appear in flesh and blood to astonish the girls. It happened in this way. Two boys overheard the planning of the dumb supper and decided to have a little fun at the girls' expense. No sooner had the girls taken their places behind the chairs than a noise was heard outside the house. They were frightened but made no outcry. The door opened slowly and into the dimly lighted room walked a man. With hat pulled over his eyes, he walked straight to the chair at the head of the table and calmly seated himself. The girl gave her prospect careful scrutiny and then screamed, for the young swain was none other than a boy she had recently spurned. He made no move to leave, but sat there undisturbed by the girl's wails. But when she fainted and fell to the floor, her lover came to life. From that time on the despised admirer met with more favor. In fact, they were soon married and settled in a home of their own. The dumb supper wasn't such a dumb affair after all.

The Fourth of July is a day for fun and festivity in the Ozarks and hillsmen know how to make the eagle scream in the good old-fashioned way. Suppose we select the village of Buffalo, in Baxter County, Arkansas, as the site of our patriotic funfest. It is well to arrive early on this holiday for parking space is limited in the little White River town and everyone for miles around will be there. Cars, wagons, buggies, "horse-backers," and folks on foot will line every road leading to the picnic grounds.

We crowd into the community schoolhouse to hear the reading of the Declaration of Independence by a local boy who attends college at Batesville, and to listen to the patriotic oratory of the county judge and other regional celebrities. Buffalo takes pride in this annual celebration and it has a right to do so. The community is steeped in history and tradition of long standing. This scenic spot was a pioneer trading post and the head of navigation on White River in territorial days. It is a fitting place to celebrate the birth of the nation in the good old American way.

Contests follow the speaking and we shake with laughter as a squad of hillbillies give the greased pig a run for the money. Perspiring boys take turns at the greased pole with covetous eyes on the top where a silver dollar is anchored. We cheer heartily when a freckle-faced urchin reaches the goal and pockets the dollar. Grizzled hillsmen call hogs in true hillbilly fashion and housewives give exhibitions of husband calling and rolling-pin maneuvers that lift the hair on one's head. Chips as large as cowcumber leaves fly in all directions as husky men swing axes in the log-cutting contest. There is keen rivalry in horseshoe pitching and a lanky hillsman from Big Flat takes the honors. Contests in shooting, swimming, boating, foot-racing, and pie eating give young and old a chance to prove their skills and carry away prizes. The grand climax is the tug-of-war between the fats and the leans. The heavyweights puff their way to victory much to the chagrin of their lanky opponents.

There is barely time to slip over to a stand for a hot dog and a bottle of pop before the afternoon program begins. Everything runs as scheduled. Fiddlers vie with one another in scraping mountain melodies from vibrant strings. There is competition in singing old ballads and shape-note ditties. Sacred Harp singers from downstate give an exhibition of their singing technique. Square dancing occupies much of the afternoon with two sets going at the same time. Prizes are awarded to the women for proficiency in canning, baking, and sewing and the men get awards for woodcarving and leather work. The largest family present receives a sack of flour, the tallest man gets a brand-new ax, and the most recently wedded couple takes home a pair of bedsheets.

The big night attraction, of course, is the traditional free fireworks display, sponsored by the chamber of commerce. Then fiddles croon and guitars strum and the dance is on till the wee small hours of the morning. Nothing modern or streamlined in Buffalo's Independence Day celebration.

Christmas is a day of expectancy to young and old in the mountains. The Yuletide season in the backhills may lack the colorful, artificial pageantry of the town, but it is Christmas just the same and sentiment tugs at the heart even in the midst of poverty and isolation. Let us, for the moment, turn back the clock of time one hundred years, setting the hands on December 25, 1841.

The Ozark region in 1841 was a wilderness mecca for the hunter, trapper, and trader, but its agricultural epoch had not yet begun. Although the land had belonged to the United States thirty-eight years, settlers had trekked in rather slowly. The first ones came, so the records show, during the first decade of the century, pushing their way over rough mountain trails or moving in keelboats up the White, Black, North Fork, and Current Rivers. Most of the Indians had been moved westward before 1830, but a large portion of the country remained an untrodden wilderness with no roads and few social opportunities. Subscription schools of three months' duration provided the formal education for the youth. Law courts were few and far between. The religious needs of the people were cared for by circuit riders who traveled the mountain trails on horseback to shepherd their flocks. Trading posts were sometimes fifty miles apart and the roads, especially in winter, were practically impassable. One would naturally conclude that Christmas in such an isolated region would be a dismal affair. Of course, there was no exchange of fancy gifts, no packages coming by parcel post from mail-order houses, no radios to wish you a merry Christmas and to follow it up with the suggestion that you could make it merrier with a carton of a certain brand of cigarettes or by installing an oil heater in the old fireplace, but regardless of the handicaps of isolation, the Christmas spirit pervaded the hills and the children worshipped Santa Claus even as they do today.

In 1841 the backhill Ozark region was made up of settlements of a few families, usually kith and kin. The weather was never too cold nor the roads too bad for them to get together on Christmas Day. If the parson happened to be present they would have religious worship for they were pious people and chips off the old block of Puritanism. The dinner was not a series of elaborate courses, but it was a substantial meal such as hillsmen relish. It consisted of wild meat such as deer and wild turkey, or perhaps a fat hen boiled in a big pot and surrounded by tasty, tender dumplings. Corn bread was the staff of pioneer life, but on this occasion there was sweet bread with wild honey or sorghum used as sweetening. Toys were few, and candy, when obtainable, was invariably of the striped-stick variety, but the children, knowing no better, were easily satisfied. A backhill Christmas one hundred years ago was, without doubt, a comparatively simple affair, but it fitted well into the prosaic of human life at that period.

Parade of Folklore

Folklore has been defined as the beliefs and practices of barbarians and illiterates, but this definition is incomplete and only partially true. In its broadest sense, folklore includes all customs, beliefs, mannerisms, legends, and lore of the folk, regardless of the cultural status of the class in which they are found. Its sources may be divided into three classes:

1. The traditions and practices of uncivilized peoples.
2. The beliefs and ways of the uneducated portion of civilized society.
3. Survivals of primitive lore which linger in the customs of cultured peoples and influence their activities.

Each of these groups is a fertile field for the folklorist. There is an abundance of material to be found even among the elite. Take, for example, the subject of superstition which is one of the strongest survivors of the fear element to be found in human nature. One of the most progressive merchants in Arkansas will not permit his janitor to sweep dirt out through the door after dark because of the mythical bad luck penalty connected with this practice. A keeper of a big city hotel refuses to number a room "13" and never starts a journey on Friday. Many cultured people continue to believe in superstitions and regulate their conduct accordingly. In fact, it is an almost universal trait of mankind.

The parade of folklore is colorful pageantry, pristine in its simplicity but pregnant with meaning. Traditions thrive best in a land which refuses to succumb to the plow. Ozarkians, who recognize cultural values, take pride in their folkways and consider them a noble heritage from a glorious past. Let us lift the curtain for a look at the shadowy land of yesteryears with old-timers who recognize the historical value of backhill lore and logic. The items that follow are contributions of old-line Ozarkers who have helped shape the destiny of the Ozark Country:

> The good old days in the Ozarks. Our best doctor had his saddlebags stuffed with quinine, castor oil, turpentine, and calomel. His admission to the profession may have been obtained by a grade of sixty-seven percent in these four medicines, but we had faith in his practice. Ozarkers in those days didn't have modern ailments, and a hot onion poultice usually cured the inflammation of the bowels now called appendicitis. The doctor gave us blue mass pills for constipation—that is, if our home supply of mayapple roots had run low.
>
> We used a "mad stone" to draw the poison from a wound made by a dog having hydrophobia. We secured the stone from the stomach of a buck deer. It was laid upon the wound and allowed to draw. It was then removed and placed in a bowl of hot milk. If it had been effective, the poison would turn the milk green. The treatment was continued until the stone could be dipped into a bowl of milk without coloring the liquid.

Our neighbor across the creek would stand at the corner of his five-acre patch of wheat and "whet a banter" on his cradle. This was done by stroking the blade with a whetrock, producing a code or tune recognized by all hillsmen. This challenge would bring other cradlers helter-skelter to the spot to compete with him in cutting around the field. Sometimes the winner was entertained with an oyster supper or a squirrel stew at the expense of the losers.

Almost every settler had a small field of wheat to be ground into flour for home consumption. If his land was not suited to wheat, he would take a "passel o' corn" to the mill and trade it for flour. The grain was first cut with reap hooks, which was a very slow process. The cradle was thought to be a great improvement over the old way of harvesting. A good cradler could cut four acres of grain a day. Threshing was accomplished by tramping or with a flail. One method was to build a rail pen four or five rails high and place a sheet on the ground within the pen. Rails were laid across the top and the bundles of grain laid upon them and beaten with a flail.

Before the days of the fan mill the wheat was winnowed on outstretched sheets, agitated in a natural or artificial draft. Sometimes a hollow log was used as a winnowing machine. A handle was attached to one end and the log rolled from side to side, separating the grain from the chaff.

Some of the first settlers beat their wheat in mortars to make it into flour. Then came the small horsepower gristmills and after that the larger water-power mills.

The first breaking plows used in the Ozarks were of the "barshears" type. The bar and shears of the implement were made of metal by the local blacksmith or the pioneer farmer himself. These were attached to homemade wooden moldboards and stocks. These plows were not strong enough to break up the sod of blue stem grass on the prairies and this fact caused many settlers to pass the lucrative level lands and locate on the ridges. After the timber was cleared, they broke the land with

a bull-tongue plow which had a jumping coulter in front of it.
This plow could take lots of punishment among stumps and
roots. By the second year the barshears plow could be used for
the breaking. Corn and other "rowed" crops were cultivated with
a "double shovel," drawn by a single mule or horse. Many hill
farmers still use this implement in preference to modern two-
horse cultivators.

Fences in the backhill country were restricted to crop lands
in the old days. Horses, cattle, sheep, and hogs were marked or
branded and turned loose on the range. Horses were branded as
in the West, on hip or shoulder, usually with the initials of the
owner. Hogs were marked by cutting holes or making slits in
the ears. Sheep had labels placed in their ears to identify them.
Cattle were branded or labeled as the owner preferred. These
brands and marks were sometimes recorded at the county seat
to avoid infringement of rights. There was always a bell horse, a
bell cow, and a bell sheep among the stock turned on the range.
Most of the stock would stay near the one that carried the bell.
Roundup time was in the fall. Neighbors joined together in collecting and identifying their herds.

We used linchpin wagons, so named because the wheels
were fastened on with linchpins stuck through the ends of the
wooden axles. The old Anglo-Saxon term for axletree is *lynis*.
"Lynispin" was shortened to "linchpin" by the early settlers. The
outer end of the hub was slotted to admit the pin which was
dropped through the slot and hole in the axle and the wheel end
keyed on. The reverse operation, and the wheel was off.

One hundred years ago there was a scant population in the
Missouri Ozarks. Travel between the sparsely settled communities was over rough trails, or along watercourses in various types
of boats. A few roads linked some of the more important towns
with St. Louis.

A stagecoach line was operated between St. Louis and
Springfield, but the speed of which people boasted in 1841
would try the patience of Job today. It was a matter of pride that

the traveler could leave St. Louis by stage and be in Springfield at the end of three days. High water and muddy roads often held up travel for days or weeks at a time.

There was no highway department in Jefferson City—first called The City of Jefferson—to petition when a community needed a new road. There was but one thing to be done; people did it. They organized "road bees" and went to work with axes, picks, and shovels to build roads along the best route between two points. The shortest distance was not considered. The roads were routed along the ridges where they were least affected by flooded streams.

There were no bridges, so men applied for permits to operate ferries across the larger streams. Rates of ferriage across streams varied, but it is interesting to note the rates of an Osage River ferry, operated by Thomas O. Witten in 1841. Witten had to file a $500 bond and pay the county collector the sum of two dollars for a license to operate his ferry one year, and was permitted to charge the following rates:

Man and horse . . . 25¢
Footman . . . 12½¢
Wagon and team . . . $1.00
Two-horse carriage . . . 75¢
Hogs and sheep, neat head . . . 3¢
Horses and cattle, neat head . . . 6¢

There was a special half rate for citizens of Osage Township crossing the ferry to attend elections, which put the cost at 12½¢ for man and horse and 6¼¢ for a footman. I have never learned just how the ferryman made change involving the fractions of a cent. Jurors were given free passage on the ferry if they were on the way to duties at court.

Today huge transport trucks go shuttling back and forth through the Ozark Country, carrying all sorts of cargoes. In the days before the highways, boats on the rivers carried raw materials from the Ozarks to St. Louis, and brought manufactured goods from the city to supply trade throughout a large section of the hill country. At one time Linn Creek, in Camden County, was an important distributing point for river traffic.

One firm, J. W. McClurg and Company, sold more than half a million dollars' worth of goods annually for a good many years. Dodson, Roberts, and Company was doing a thriving business at the same time. For about six months of the year, boats could run from St. Louis to Linn Creek, and from this point freighters with ox or mule teams formed the transportation system of the Southwest. Goods went into Arkansas and the Indian Territory, and raw materials came from those distant points to be marketed and shipped to St. Louis.

Sometimes there would be enough water in the Osage River to carry boats as far as Warsaw in Benton County. But when the river was low, the supplies were transferred to flatboats and these boats were propelled by manpower. Ten or twelve men were employed to pole a loaded flatboat up the river. Warsaw shipped a surprising amount of produce to the city, such as wild honey and beeswax, hides, and deer meat.

It is on record that during the height of prosperity, an average of twenty wagon loads of wheat per day came into Linn Creek the year round. However, the building of railroads changed the status quo of this little Ozark town, and the people could only look forward to the time when a railroad would be built to their village. It was a dream that never came true, and now there is no Linn Creek, only the deep water of the Lake of the Ozarks where the old town once stood. There is a new Linn Creek a few miles away, but it lacks the halo of romance that surrounded the old town.

The first settlers built their homes on the ridges at the heads of the creeks. The fear of malaria kept them from the fertile river valleys. The land was cleared and heavily cropped with little rotation. Within a few years, erosion set in and farmers found it necessary to change locations. Some of them occupied the valley lands and built permanent homes there. Villages sprang up at strategic points. Others moved out of the Ozarks, seeking greener pastures in Oklahoma, Kansas, and Texas. A few drifted to the mining centers around Joplin; many engaged in the timber industry. The deserted ridges were soon covered with second growth and became open range for hogs and cattle.

The first tourists in the backhill country were sportsmen who came from St. Louis and Kansas City. They came in large parties to hunt deer, bear, and wild turkey. These hunters were good spenders and the natives gave them a warm welcome. The modern tourist invasion began with motor transportation and the building of highways early in the twentieth century. Many of these furriners were not considerate of property rights and the practice of posting land against trespassers came into vogue. One farmer in the backhills put up the following sign.

> NOTIS! tresspassers will B persecuted to the full extent of 2 mungrel dogs which never was over-sochible to strangers & 1 dubble brl shot gun which aint loaded with sofa pillors. Dam if I aint gittin tired of this hell raisin on my place.

Saturday evening was an exciting time at our house. The big boys curried the horses and filled the wagon with straw. Mother sent out one of her best quilts for us to "set" on. A basket of cookies and baked ham was placed near the spring seat where father and mother sat. We were going visiting and would stay all night, all day Sunday, and Sunday night at Aunt Mary's or Cousin Jim's. Either we visited friends and relatives on Sunday or they came to see us.

On Sunday we went to church. But after a deacon in one of the churches accused father of stealing his silver spoons and they had a church trial, and the deacon gave father a libel written on paper cambric, my parents decided that we could get to heaven without mixing up with such hypocrites. But I can see our family at church now. Father on the end of the backless seat, mother next, and then the eldest child and so on down to me. I can hear the preacher denouncing sin with a vengeance and outlining the miseries of hell. After the energetic parson had expostulated and pounded the stand for an hour and a half, I usually fell asleep and missed the rest of the service.

Beauty parlors were unknown in that day but women made use of simple devices to enhance their loveliness. Buttermilk was used to keep the skin soft and white. For a quick bleach, tomato juice was applied to the arms and face before retiring. Tallow was melted, perfumed with petals of flowers, and used in massaging the face. A curling fluid was made by pouring hot water over flax seed. When young ladies wanted to put a pink glow on their cheeks, they took soft young mullein leaves and pressed them gently but firmly against the face. For "whitening" they used rice flour in little flannel bags "starched" or dusted on. Shoes were shined by rubbing black from the bottom of a kettle.

We carefully guarded the chunk of fire on the hearth, wrapping it in ashes between usings. If perchance it did die out, we could borrow coals from a neighbor, use flint and steel, or start a fire with gunpowder. We would place a little powder on the hearth, place a gun cap in it, cover with lint cotton and spread with fine pine splinters, then strike the cap with a hammer and a blaze would start. Sometimes we would "spin fire" with a yarn string which had been soaked in copperas solution and dried. One end of the string would be wrapped around the "whirl" of a spinning wheel and turned so fast that the string would catch on fire. We would blow the spark and catch the blaze with a piece of cotton sprinkled with powder. This was transferred to pine splinters on the hearth.

One day a peddler came along selling matches, twelve in a little wooden box for a dime. We purchased some of them but they were used only on special occasions or when we "lost fire." Even after the regulation-size five-cent boxes came in, matches were used sparingly. One neighboring family used the same box for more than twenty years.

Candles were our only means of lighting in the days of my

youth. They were made from beef tallow and beeswax. We had learned to steep the wicks in limewater and saltpeter and dry them. This made a brighter flame and prevented the tallow from running. The parlor candle was made with a double wick to give it a brighter light. We had discovered that putting a little salt on the candle would make it last longer.

We didn't have to live on corn bread and spring water or eat sowbelly with the buttons on.[2] We always had a few hams in the smokehouse, some of them two years old, and plenty of pork sausage, properly seasoned with sage. A woodsman could eat a pound of this sausage at a meal without discomfort. All through the morning hours, hog jowl and cabbage were cooked soft and tender in a big black pot, and these potlicker memories linger with me still.

If we broke a looking glass, it meant seven years of bad luck, for it was usually that long before we got another mirror. If one of the boys thoughtlessly carried a hoe into the house, it brought a storm of protest and he was ordered out immediately. If anybody twirled a chair on one of its legs, we knew father would come home mad as a wet hen about something.

One day my oldest sister dropped the dishrag and neglected to throw a little salt over her left shoulder. She did not report the incident to the rest of the family. Of course, mother could not take the usual precautions against calamity when she did not know it was coming. Sure enough, that very evening one of my little brothers stuck a thorn clear through his foot and probably would have had lockjaw had my sister not realized her neglect and reported the dishrag affair to mother. A vinegar application was applied to the boy's foot and in almost no time he was outside trying to get a doodlebug to stick up his horn "so that he could give it a barrel of corn." These superstitions seem ridiculous now but many of them were taken seriously in the old days.

We broke green gourds above our old dog's head to make him bark up a tree. If a cow swallowed her cud, we wound a ball of wool thread, fried it in lard, and made her swallow it. If a white moth lingered around us, we thought it was the spirit of one of our deceased grandparents hovering over us. A poultice of droppings from black hens, mixed with lard and applied to the chest, was a sure cure for pneumonia. For itch (we called it "each") we used a paste made from gunpowder and cream. It didn't matter to us whether a hen set or sat on a nest of eggs, but it did make a difference how the eggs were carried and how the "set" was started. We thought that eggs carried in a woman's bonnet invariably hatched pullets while a hen set on Sunday brought a hatch of roosters. Eggs set in the dark of the moon would not hatch; chickens hatched in the month of May would not live. We never burned sassafras wood in the fireplace for we didn't like the idea of the devil sitting astraddle the comb of our house roof. Yes, we *were* superstitious, but many of these odd beliefs provided a veil of protection that was needed. Logic is sometimes bedded in a strange way.

A "water witch" was an important man in the community. My father could locate a vein of water with a forked stick. He would take the stick firmly in both hands, fork upward, and start walking across a plot of ground in search of a location for a well. When the stick turned down it meant water below. To determine the distance to the vein, the "witch" walked away from the spot, counting the steps, until the stick regained its upright position. Six steps meant eighteen feet to water. To make sure of the location, he would approach the spot with his witching stick from all directions. We never dug a well without first witching for water. It is my opinion that what scientists call "corpuscular philosophy" is just plain old water witching gone to college.

A few men in our neighborhood claimed they could locate metals with the witching stick. To locate silver, the witch would cut a slit in the forked stick and insert a silver coin in it. Gold was supposed to locate gold. To find mixed ores he used two coins of different metals, usually a dime and a one-cent piece. A stick reinforced with metal would not react to water. My father didn't take much stock in this treasure lore. He stuck to plain water witching. He believed that only one member of a family could possess this witching power.

Marriage was regarded as a serious matter in the old days and divorces were rare. The sexual code was strictly masculine. No matter how much tomcatting a young man might do, he was determined to select a virgin for his wife. It was thought that virginity could be detected by a tiny depression in the end of a woman's nose.

When getting married, we stood on the floor the way the boards ran. We thought an unhappy marriage would result if we set our feet at right angles with the planks.

Many trivial happenings were accepted as signs of death. A bird flying in the house, a ringing in the ears, a cock crowing from the housetop, a dog howling at night, the falling of a window sash, or the breaking of an object without anyone touching it—these were definite signs of the approach of the Grim Reaper.

We were awed by the appearance of "angel wreaths" or "heavenly crowns" in the pillow on which the head of a dying person had lain. These perfect wreaths are of artistic design and appear in sharp contrast to the mass of feathers surrounding them. They are not made with human hands.

"Telling the bees" at the time of a death in the family was a common practice in the old days. Some member of the family would knock on the beehives, call the name of the departed one, and report his death. Sometimes the hives were draped with black cloth. Failure to do this meant that the bees would either die or depart.

We left our home in White County, Arkansas, in the nineties and moved to Texas. My grandfather (mother's father) remained behind at the old home in Arkansas. We owned a large grandfather clock which sat on a shelf against the wall in the dining room of our new home. One summer evening, a few months after our arrival in Texas, all the family was sitting on the front porch talking. Suddenly the clock began rumbling and ringing in a strange manner. It had no alarm on it and had never done that way before. We all rushed into the house, but the ringing ceased as we entered. The clock struck nine and stopped. My stepfather remarked that someone we knew had died and that the sound we heard was a "death bell." News traveled slowly in those days, but three or four days later came a letter from Arkansas, edged in black. The missive informed us that grandfather had died. The time of his passing coincided with the death-bell warning.

We saw many will-o'-the-wisps or "Jack-o'-lanterns" along the river and thought they would lure men and animals astray. Sometimes it was a ball of fire shooting through space horizontal with the earth. Or it might be a flame-like appearance hovering in a swamp. My father saw one that had little bluish flames as long as a man's finger, moving in a group like a flock of blackbirds.

During an electric storm, all the dogs were driven out of the house as we thought a dog's tail drew lightning. We were taught to stand still and hold our breath when meeting a mad dog. By doing this we avoided all danger of being bitten. If birds made their nests from the combings of our hair, we thought we would have headaches. If we could succeed in spitting between the eyes of a red worm, we would live to a ripe old age and never wear glasses. It was considered bad luck to kill a bat. We had a superstitious fear of these creatures for it was believed that if one entered the house after nightfall, someone in the family would be missing before morning. If we "took bread and had bread," someone was coming to our house hungry.[3] We always tried to kill the first snake we saw in springtime as that meant we would be able to conquer our enemies. To cure asthma, we would back the patient up against a tree and peg a lock of his hair into a hole bored into the trunk, and snip it off with a pair of scissors. When the bark grew over the hair, the asthma was supposed to be gone.

A child born out of wedlock was called a wood's colt. If it grew to school age, the neighboring children would refuse to play with it, or loan it slate and pencil. If, as was sometimes the case, this child could diagram a sentence better than the rest of us, our home folks would conclude that Lum Skinner was surely not its father as the gossipers supposed.

A loose woman was considered a disgrace to the neighborhood. She was a bitch, and hillsmen did not mince words in voicing their contempt of her. Of course, there were immoral women in the hills, plenty of them. But they kept themselves in the background and did not court respect, even from their men associates. They were not "commercial daughters of joy" like their city cousins.

The better class of people refused to countenance immorality in the community and they frequently used force to subdue it. If a person disregarded the conventions of decency, he was warned by placing a bunch of switches on his doorstep. The number of switches indicated the number of days allowed for the man and woman to wind up their local affairs and get out of the country. Failure to comply meant that they might be "drummed out" of the neighborhood.

"To plow with one's heifer" was an expression that meant to deal with the wife to get something from the husband. "Saltin' the calf to catch the cow" was a phrase frequently used to explain a man's unusual attentions to a widow's child. We never used the word "bull" in mixed company, but said "cow brute" instead. Prudery put reticence into our speech but there were exceptions to the rule. Many women used salty expressions when referring to members of their sex whose conduct was under suspicion. Profanity was used freely by both men and women but even it had its acknowledged propriety. A man who would "gawddam" at almost every breath would carefully avoid obscenity in the presence of women.

Acts of sexual perversion between men were practically unknown in the hill country, but the practice of sodomy, that is copulation with animals, was more prevalent. A belief existed that such unions are sometimes fruitful and monstrosities were frequently rumored.

Every peculiarity in appearance or oddity of action had a definite cause. The pop-eyed idiot of the neighborhood owed his tragic condition to the fact that his mother stepped on a toad two or three months before the child was born. The seventh son of a seventh son was endowed with strange powers and could remove warts, take out fire, stop blood, and provoke cures of all kinds. A baby born with a veil over its face was likewise empowered with supernatural gifts.

Birthmarks were thought to be caused by shocks or fright during pregnancy. A neighbor woman watched the butchering of a calf and her child's feet were formed like hoofs. Our hired man could show a mark on his leg caused, he said, by his mother being frightened by a betsy bug. One woman had the mark of a snake coiled around her ankle. She explained that her mother had been frightened by a snake at about the time it was shedding its skin and that the scales on the birthmark peeled off at that season each year. One of the strangest markings was reported to us by a maiden aunt. The woman had been frightened by a cow brute during pregnancy and the mark resembled a cow with two small growths protruding from the head like horns. But the marking did not stop there. It was psychological as well as physical. The woman emitted low, mumbling sounds like the bellowing of a bull.

. . . . . .

Midwifery is an old, old custom, carried to America from England by early migrants. It was a Victorian institution firmly established in English life. Charles Dickens is credited with having ridiculed this practice to its eventual ruin. But it made a new start in backwoods America and again became an institution of importance. The midwife knew obstetric lore by experience and, like the boy on the burning deck, she remained at her post "when all the rest had fled." Her methods were crude, but she was a godsend to the hillswoman in the throes of childbirth.

Midwives had plenty of abnormal grist for the mill of gossip. They told of babies born with two faces, with heads like serpents, with gold teeth and pop eyes and numerous other peculiarities. Discussions of cause and effect produced many strange theories.

Many of the older folks believed in witchcraft and it was no uncommon thing to hear stories of people and animals that had been bewitched. One woman related a weird experience in this realm of the supernatural. A neighbor hillsman came into the house one morning, picked up her baby girl, and looked at her. When he departed the child began to cry and scream and nothing could quiet her. A neighbor woman came in and told her that the baby was bewitched. She said that to break the spell the other should take the child to the door before sunrise, lick her from nose to hairline, and repeat the three highest names in the Bible. She was to do this for nine mornings, and on the ninth day the one who cast the spell would come to borrow something. They were not to let him have *anything*.

The mother did as she was told and on the ninth morning the neighbor hillsman came to borrow as was foretold. He was refused everything he requested. Finally he asked for a tow string to tie a hog. Even this was refused him. This made him angry and he went home. The baby was all right from that time on, but the woman who told how to break the spell had a nice heifer die the following day.

A man was out hunting one morning when something like a shot seemed to hit him in the back. He realized he had been shot by a witch. Such shooting by supernatural means was called "elk shooting." He believed a certain neighbor was responsible, so he drew an outline of the man on a board, chalked his name on it, and set it against a tree. A silver dollar was melted, a bullet made from it, and shot into the picture. A few days later he heard that the suspected neighbor had been injured in an accident.

Another story current in the backhills appears to be a survival of the old werewolf legend except that, in this case, the man was transformed into a horse instead of a wolf. A farmer was riding through the woods on horseback late one night when a witch cast its spell and overpowered him. He was changed into a horse and tied to a tree, where he spent the remainder of the night gnawing bark and kicking up dirt. The spell

broke at daylight and he made his way home. It is said that to convince
his family and neighbors of the reality of the incident, he took them to
the spot, showed them the tree with its torn bark and the ground he
had trampled into dust. He had the added proof of a sore mouth "frum
chompin' th' dang bit."

Formerly, the word "witch" was applied to persons of either sex who
were given to sorcery or enchantment. Later, the term was restricted to
a woman who was thought to have made a compact with evil spirits and
through their means operated supernaturally. In the Ozarks, the name
was applied to both male and female.

Men who had power to overcome witches were called witch masters.
If a witch was stripping the cows, making the hogs act hoodoo, or causing
other devilment or injury, an expert witch master was called to put the
demon out of business. He would draw a picture of the witch and plug
it with a silver bullet from his rifle gun. A bullet had to be made of silver
to subdue a witch.

A Missouri woman told me a story of witchcraft that had been
handed down by her ancestors. Here is the tale as her grandmother
reported it.

> There was a certain woman in our neighborhood who was
> thought to be a witch. There had been several strange occur-
> rences she was thought to be responsible for, some of which
> would identify her in my community if I repeated them, even yet.
> One morning, after she had been dead for some time, I
> was driving past her old home, which I knew was deserted and
> had been for some time. As I came in sight of the house I was
> amazed to see smoke coming out of the chimney. It was thick,
> blue smoke, appearing just as it does in the early morning when
> one is starting a fire. I stopped to investigate, thinking that per-
> haps someone had moved in, but there was no one there and no
> fire in the fireplace.
> The hair rose up on the back of my head, but I was deter-
> mined to find the reason for the smoke, and forced myself to go
> up to the fireplace and stir the dead ashes with a stick. There was

no sign of fire, no hint of warmth. I thought there might be a swallow's nest in the chimney and that the birds had stirred up a dust which deceived me. I looked carefully but found absolutely nothing. Yet all the time the curls of thick blue smoke were coming out of the fireplace chimney. I have thought of this many times and have never found any natural explanation.

Little Log Schoolhouse

The little log schoolhouse still sits by the side of the road, "a ragged beggar sunning," in a few isolated communities of the Ozarks, but it is a dilapidated structure succumbing to the ravages of decay. The old oaken door sags on its hinges and the spectral windows are curtained with cobwebs. The homemade desks, scarred with initials, have been removed and only a remnant of blackboard remains as a relic of other days. The district is now consolidated with other schools in the county and the scholars ride to the central school at the county seat in comfortable motor buses. Almost every school from Bee-gum Holler to Pokeberry Ridge has adopted the consolidation plan. Perhaps Dirt Dauber and Bug Tussle have held out against this modern trend but they cannot do so indefinitely. The die has been cast by legislative action and there is no turning back.

Educational traditions in the backhills are interwoven with the romantic lore of the one-room schoolhouse and it will be many years before this pestilent influence is wiped out. Terms were short in the old days and the teachers were poorly paid. The children sometimes walked three or four miles in all kinds of weather to "get a little schooling." The curriculum was limited to a few essential subjects. Hot lunches were not provided for undernourished youngsters and directed play was unknown. But the rural school, like the church, was an institution of vast importance to the pioneer settlers. It was both a house of learning and a community center. Its departure has cast a shadow over the community that cannot be lifted by modern ingenuity.

The teachers who carried the torch of learning in the dark day of isolation deserve much credit for the work they did. They were usually men of talent and integrity and they knew the fundamentals they taught. They endured many privations in order to promote the educational traditions of that day.

Thomas Smith Evans, who began his teaching career in Searcy County, Arkansas, is the type of pioneer teacher to whom we point with pride. He taught one of the first free schools in Arkansas, provided by an act of the state legislature in 1854. Before then schools were conducted on a subscription basis and continued in session for only three months of the year. Evans taught a number of these schools before accepting his first free school at $22.50 per month, payable in gold. His prodigious industry made him an outstanding teacher. He manufactured all the pens for his pupils from the quills of goose feathers. He made ink for his penmanship classes from the "ink balls" that grow on oaks, boiling them in a little water and setting the fluid with copperas. He was an expert shoe cobbler and would frequently make a pair of shoes after school hours, using wooden pegs and leather from his own tanyard. In Carroll County, Arkansas, he had fourteen young women in his school and "all but thirteen of them wore shoes." He was in the first teachers' examination in the state, held the first free-school contract, and was the first speaker in the first Teachers' Institute.

This backhill pedagogue with his bag of ink balls and homemade pens was made a county examiner in the seventies. He is said to have licensed the first woman teacher in his county. The teachers' examinations were mostly oral, the examiner asking questions until he was convinced of the applicant's fitness for the position. The examiner's salary was $200 per year, in scrip at forty percent value.

Thomas Evans began preaching the gospel in 1855 and carried this work along with his teaching. Church debates were a fad in those days and he took an active part in them. But his strong doctrinal arguments in the debates caused him to be "deeded out" of one church. The deed to the church property gave preachers of all denominations the right to preach in the building "except Uncle Tom Evans." He never asked for pay for preaching, but he did receive donations totaling thirty dollars during his long period of service. Evans ran the gamut of life as teacher, preacher, singing-school teacher, shoe cobbler, rail splitter, farmer, traveling salesman, hunter, and Confederate soldier during the Civil War. He died at Newburg, Arkansas, in 1920 at the age of ninety-eight.

The course of study in the little log schoolhouse included the McGuffey's Readers, Ray's Arithmetic, the Blue Back Speller, and *Webster's Dictionary*. Schools were seldom graded, but when a pupil could read the Fifth Reader intelligibly, work the problems in Ray's "Third Part," and spell all the miscellaneous words given on pages 169 to 174 in the old Blue Back, he was ready for a diploma. Spelling was oral and the pupil pronounced each syllable of the word as he came to it, and then the word as a whole. After a few years the course of study was enlarged to include grammar, history, and geography. Scientific subjects such as physiology and general science were added later.

Friday afternoons were always set aside for spelling and ciphering matches and literary programs. The recitations were usually taken from the readers that were being used as textbooks and most of the selections were literary masterpieces. The technique followed in "speaking a piece" was to face the audience, make a bow, repeat the lines of the recitation, make a bow, and retire. Courtesy was an important part of elocution. Debates were frequently held on such vital subjects as, "Which is the more important: the broom or the dishrag?" or "Which is the mightier: the pen or the sword?" These debates were a vocal free-for-all for the older pupils and each side tried hard to outwit its opponents.

Spelling matches were frequently held on Friday nights and all the community took part. When the crowd had gathered and leaders had been selected, the teacher would take the spelling book, insert his finger between pages, and have the two leaders guess the number of the page. The one coming nearest to the number got the first choice of spellers. They chose back and forth until the entire crowd was divided and lined up on opposite sides of the room. The teacher then began pronouncing, alternating from one side to another. When a word was missed, the speller took a seat and the word was passed on to the opposite side. This was continued until it was spelled correctly. The person turning all the others down was declared winner. Sometimes the last two spellers would hold the floor a long time and the teacher would turn to page 174 of the Blue Back Speller and test them out on such words as ren'dez-vous, nau'seous, da-guerre'o-type, phlegm, and caout'chouc.

Numerous affiliated institutions have been established in recent years in the hill country to enlarge the scope of educational opportunity for both young and old. Adult schools have been conducted in practically every county throughout the area and the percentage of illiteracy has been greatly reduced. Educational agencies through the 4-H clubs and NYA and CCC camps have pushed back the horizon for thousands of young people in the Ozarks. Now and then we find an educational missionary like James T. Richmond who operates his Wilderness Library in the backhills of Newton County, Arkansas. But even now educational conditions are deplorable in some sections of the hill country.

Charles Morrow Wilson, in his recent book *Corn Bread and Creek Water*, reveals the inadequacy of our schools in the backhills through the startling information that there are schools in Arkansas where teachers "turn back" their pupils when they arrive at decimal fractions and the sixth reader because the teachers are not prepared to go further. He points out, however, that inadequacy of rural schools is common to many areas of the United States and that the Ozark Country is not necessarily the horrible example of deplorable insufficiency in rural education.

Attempts are being made to eradicate these inequalities by legislative action; short terms, low standards, and poorly paid teachers will probably have to go. But the stupidity and corruption of past years cannot be blotted out in an instant. It will take time to establish equality throughout a region that is a part of three states, each differing from the other in educational standards.

A ray of light in the political darkness is the Ozarkian folk school. An outstanding example of such a school is the one held each autumn at Shannondale Community Center in Shannon County, Missouri. Qualified leaders are secured to teach classes in vocational agriculture, forestry, and stock raising. Agricultural extension agents, forest rangers, county agents, and local teachers aid in the program. The students learn how to test soils for mineral content and general fertility. They learn how to diversify crops so as to build up ground which is deficient in certain elements. They learn how to raise better and more profitable crops. They make a thorough study of animal husbandry, breeding, feeding problems, dairying, and inoculation against diseases.

There are classes in home economics for the rural women at Shannondale. Basketry, rug weaving, and woodcarving are given special attention. These art crafts hold a cherished spot on the folk school curriculum.

The social program of the school is planned with special care. There are recreational periods which include such activities as ballad singing, group singing, guitar playing, folk dancing, and the playing of folk games.

The Shannondale Folk School is not a philanthropic venture. It is not one group of people trying to help another, but, in the words of the headmaster of the project, "a group of people trying to help themselves."

CHAPTER VII

Sports Afield

. . . .

The Shooting Match

The squirrel lay on a sycamore limb fifty feet from the ground. I took deliberate aim with my rifle, sighting at the bark of the tree a quarter of an inch below the gray patch of fur over the rodent's heart. Bang! Scraps of bark jumped into action and fell to the ground. The squirrel slid from the limb and took refuge in a den tree nearby. I had shot too low to accomplish my purpose. I concluded that "barking" was all right for the native, but a furriner should stick to the old way if he wants to pocket the game.

White River folks judge a hunter's skill by his ability to bark his game. The Nimrods aim at a point to hit the bark of the tree near the animal's head or heart. The concussion of the bullet knocks the game from the tree, sometimes killing it. Disgrace shadows the Ozarker who brings in a squirrel showing an ugly bullet wound. Anything less than a shot between the eyes is counted a miss.

I had just reached the top of Smackover Ridge and was planning to move over into the Clabber Creek bottoms when a shot rang out in the river valley to my right. This was followed by others at somewhat irregular intervals. I hurried to the edge of the cliff to see what might be the cause of such an extravagant use of powder. Rounding a boulder, I looked down into the pocket-like valley. A colorful sight presented itself. It was the day of the community shooting match at Woodville, an annual event of great importance, and I had forgotten all about it. I descended into the valley to take part in the fun.

A shooting match in the Ozarks is an affair to be remembered. It is an old custom in the backhills that men get together occasionally and try their skill at shooting. In the old days muskets or muzzle-loading "rifle guns" were used, but on this occasion, it being a "turkey shoot," most of the men carried modern, breech-loading shotguns.

I arrived just in time for the "splatter match." Tobe Mullins was tacking the large cardboard on a tree just as I joined the group. It cost only ten cents to enter and as the prize was a fine turkey hen, I paid my dime and took a chance. Each man who entered had made an X on the board and put his initials near it. When thirty chances were sold, the stage was set for the splatter match.

Ike Foster, a disinterested man from the Posey neighborhood, was selected to do the shooting. He used a long-barreled, single-shot, twelve-gauge gun, loaded with number six shot. At twenty steps he aimed point-blank at the center of the board and fired. We all rushed up to see whose X had a hole nearest the intersection. I saw at once that I had a chance to win, but it was up to the judges to decide. It lay between Hite Lindsey and me, but after much measuring and arguing, Tobe Mullins announced that I had won the turkey. It was the first, and last, prize I ever won at a shooting match.

The big event of the afternoon was the rifle shoot. Several turkeys were placed in a coop on the hillside some thirty yards from the log on which the men rested their guns. When a turkey pushed its head between the slats on the coop, it was an ideal target for the hillsmen lying behind the log. To win, the bullet must pierce the head, killing the bird instantly. Bill or neck shots did not count. One by one the turkeys were picked off by the expert riflemen.

Before my arrival, the men had tried out their guns in the big gobbler match. In this contest each man had his own card on which was drawn a circle the size of a silver dollar. The man who succeeded in placing the most number six shot in his circle at twenty paces was declared winner. This was a test of guns rather than marksmanship for, other things being equal, the gun with the smallest "choke" placed the most shot in the circle.

When the turkeys were disposed of, the men retired to the flat ground near Tart Tuttle's store to pitch horseshoes and play marbles. A few men sauntered into the ravine back of Lem Logan's blacksmith shop to play poker. Corn liquor flowed freely but it was not drunk openly. The sentiment produced by the recent local-option movement held the men in check. Most of the men went inside the blacksmith shop or into the bushes to do their drinking. There had been but little showing of liquor during the match. The hillsman knows that corn liquor produces unsteady nerves. I did see one man go behind a tree, take a flask from his pocket, pour some liquor into the palm of his hand, and rub it into or around his eyes. He did it just before it came his time to shoot. I assume that he considered the fiery stuff to be a good eye-opener.

The day following the match, the store-porch jury assembled at Tuttle's store to talk things over. Shooting matches, ancient and modern, were discussed. Tobe Mullins was there to remind us that a twentieth-century shooting match wasn't to be compared with the ones held fifty years ago. It was an easy matter to get a story out of Tobe.

"I wus jist a kid of a boy, 'bout ten, I reckon," began Tobe, "when th' match I'm tellin' ye about happened. Th' Mullins clan lived over in the Bug Tussle neighborhood then an' me an' pap rode over hyar t' try out his rifle gun, Ole Buck, agin th' Woodville fellers. They had shootin' matches regular them days, most ever' Saturday evenin'.

"Ole Buck wus a monster gun with a fifty-six-inch bar'l. Hit wus made by an ole gunsmith named Hankins in Kentucky. Hit had a double set o' triggers an' a lock that took a cap. Pap could pick out a squirrel's eye at thirty steps 'thout no trouble.

"In them days we shot fer beef. A feller would drive a steer t' th' match, butcher hit an' sell chances on th' beef. Get maybe ten er twelve dollars out'n it. Th' first- an' second-best shots got th' hindquarters, th' third an' fourth got th' front quarters, th' fifth got th' taller an' th' hide, an' the sixth got t' pick th' lead out'n th' tree.

"A feller got six shots fer a silver dollar. In this here shoot twelve men taken chances, but Bim Steele frum Bee Crick, havin' only fifty cents in cash money, had only took three shots. That left three shots over but Bum Tuttle, who had butchered th' steer, said t' go 'head, an' if nobody didn' want th' three extras, he'd take 'em hisself.

"Pap had cleaned Ole Buck t' suit him an' had greased his patchin's with taller frum th' taller box that set in th' right side o' th' stock o' th' gun. He laid his cleanin' rag an' stick on a stump right handy-like. He then cut out a paper fer th' mark an' tacked hit on a piece o' board that had a black spot burned on it. All th' men fixed their marks that thar way, cuttin' a V out'n th' paper, four by five inches, an' layin' it agin th' burnt part o' th' board so that it would show up well.

"Th' front sight o' pap's rifle gun wus made out'n a silver coin an' wus jist a little off, but pap had shot Ole Buck so many times that he knowed jist how t' hold it t' center th' mark. I wus t' set pap's board up fer him an' I sure wus a-honin' fer som o' that thar beef.[1] Crops had been scanty over at Bug Tussle that year an' we didn't have much t' eat. Some beef along with our beans an' taters would taste mighty good, I thought.

"When hit come pap's turn t' shoot, I set th' board an' ducked behind a big tree. Pap laid Ole Buck cross th' log an' fired. I run t' th' board expectin' a center shot. You can guess how I felt when I seed that pap, th' best shot in th' Bug Tussle neighborhood, had jist nicked th' edge o' th' paper. Fer some reason Ole Buck had gone wild.

"Pap took th' other five shots he'd paid fer but they all went th' same way, splatterin' here an' thar all over th' danged board. I jist couldn't understand hit fer Ole Buck wus a good gun an' hadn't never done that way before. An' Zeke Mullins wus given up t' be th' best shot in th' country.

"After firin' th' sixth shot, pap called me over t' whar he wus an' give me a half a dollar.

"'Tobe,' he says, 'see Bum Tuttle an' buy them other three shots quick. Cy Watkins put rosin on my wipin' rag an' throwed me off.'

"I hurried an' bought th' three extra chances an' then went with pap t' the blacksmith shop whar he give th' gun a good cleanin' with wood ashes an' coal ile. Then we went back fer him t' take th' three shots.

"I set up th' board an' waited. Pap rested Ole Buck on th' log an' took a steady aim. I thought he never wus goin' t' pull that thar front trigger. At last th' ole gun spoke an' I didn't lose no time gettin' t' th' tree. He had centered th' fork o' th' V as purty as ye'd ever seen.

"I stuffed th' hole with leaves an' he shot ag'in. 'Nother center, cleanin' out th' leaves jist as nice as ye please. I stuffed th' hole th' second time an' th' third shot jist lapped th' hole 'bout half an' half. This give us three quarters o' beef an' I wus th' happiest kid in them parts.

"Pap didn't say nary word 'bout th' rosin on his wipin' rag. He fig-gered he'd git even with Cy th' next time they swapped horses enyway."

Hunter's Paradise

Game authorities estimate that there are less than fifty black bears now living in the wild state in the forests and canebrakes of Arkansas. Deer are more plentiful, being found in sixteen of the seventy-five counties of the state. Wild turkeys thrive in the wilder sections of the hills under the protection of watchful game wardens. All three of the Ozark states (Missouri, Arkansas, and Oklahoma) are succeeding in propagating deer and turkey but things are not going so well with bruin. This noble animal is having a struggle to survive with civilization pushing him on every front.

Time was when black and brown or cinnamon bears roamed the Ozark region in great numbers. They lived upon small mammals, frogs, fish, bees and their honey, ants, fruits, berries, and roots. By early fall the animals were sleek and fat and considered a prize kill by hunters. The young are born in midwinter while the mother is hibernating. These babies are smaller than kittens and do not open their eyes for several days after birth.

Folklore gives the bear a high intelligence rating. It is said that during the rutting season the male bear will mark every object he passes with his claws as he trails the female. If another comes along on the courting quest and cannot make a mark higher than his predecessor, he gives up the chase. I have seen scratches on the walls of caves and cliffs, said to be the markings of bears, but I have no proof of their authenticity.

Bear hunting was a favorite sport in the early days and many are the stories told of encounters with these animals. Two hunters in the Ouachita hills tried hitching a yoke of oxen to a live bear and, in the words of the participants, "hell really broke loose." It happened in the Greasy Cove country where the mountains are high and the hollows deep. The men had crippled a black bear and lost it in the rough terrain of the mountainside. After searching for some time, they discovered the leg of a bear protruding from a shelf of rock far up on the side of the cliff. It was impossible to reach the spot so the men decided to lasso the leg and pull the carcass from the crevice. Everything was made ready with the oxen hitched to one end of the rope and the other ready for the throw. One of the hunters was an expert roper and easily tossed a loop over the protruding leg. But when the rope tightened, it was discovered, much to the hunters' surprise, that the bear was alive and not even wounded. It was a ferocious female sunning herself in front of her lair and guarding her cubs. It was too late to make amends. As the rope tightened, the bear went into action and pandemonium resulted. The frightened oxen plunged into the woods, dragging bruin from the cliff. The men grabbed their guns but circumstances alter cases and gunpowder was wasted. The steers broke their yoke and parted company. The bear got loose from the rope and disappeared in the underbrush. It all happened so quickly that neither of the hunters had opportunity to fire a shot.

Fox, both red and gray, inhabit all parts of the Ozark region and timber wolves continue to trouble the farmer by taking toll of his lambs, pigs, and poultry. Wildcats of the bobtailed variety are quite plentiful in many sections, but the panther or "painter" is now a legendary shadow stalking the aisles of the past with stealthy tread. The smaller game consists of squirrels, rabbits, quail, and migratory fowl. Raccoon, opossum, mink, muskrat, and skunk are the chief fur-bearers of the region. Beaver and otter were plentiful along the streams in the old days but they have gone the way of the elk and the buffalo. The ferocious wild hog with its powerful "tushes" is a thing of the past

Fifty years ago the Ozark region was a hunter's paradise. Tall tales are told, and retold, by old-timers who hunted in this era preceding the machine age. At that time, hunting wild game was both a sport and a business.

Sam Hudson of Newton County, Arkansas, is an example of the rugged type of woodsman who leaned upon ax and rifle for a living. It is said by his descendants that he killed hundreds of buffalo, and rode nine packs of hounds to death during his lifetime. Hudson and some of his relatives were chasing a bear when they discovered the great cavern now known as Diamond Cave.

Hudson came from Tennessee more than one hundred years ago and settled on Panther Creek, a branch of Buffalo River. The log house which he built for his home is still standing and in good condition. It stands near the mouth of Diamond Cave and is viewed by thousands yearly. This vigorous pioneer cleared up three farms and was married three times. His three wives bore him forty children. He was an expert gunsmith and repaired more than a thousand guns during his residence in the Ozarks. The region he selected for his home was an untamed stretch of wilderness, for he was a Davy Crockett type of man—liked elbow room and plenty of it. But other settlers followed him and he courted their daughters, repaired their guns, and led them on many hunting excursions.

One of Hudson's best-known adventures, told in Fred Allsopp's *Folklore of Romantic Arkansas*, was a death struggle with a huge panther. The hillsman was cutting a bee tree and had stopped to rest when he noticed the big cat a few steps away, "sitting down with its forelegs elevated." Sam wasn't afraid of the devil himself, so he sailed a chip at the beast to see what would happen. He didn't have long to wait. The animal advanced a few feet and sprang in his direction. Hudson had no gun with him so he used his ax as a defense weapon. But he swung so hard that the handle flew from his hands, leaving him at the mercy of the ferocious beast. But the pioneer was not easily daunted, though he had no hunting knife and had to fight with his bare hands. When the animal sprang at him with open mouth, he rammed his fist and forearm into its throat almost to the elbow, at the same time pounding the beast over the heart with his left fist. The heavy blows caused the panther to relax its grip, and a few more blows killed it. Hudson's right arm was badly torn by the beast's fangs and he carried ugly scars the rest of his life.

A symbol of extravagant folklore in the Ozarks is the legendary tales concerning the wild razorback hog. Popular legend states that this ferocious animal descended from a herd of swine brought into this country by Hernando de Soto in 1539. Some historians say that the hogs escaped from the Spaniards while they were battling the Chickasaw Indians in what is now Alabama. They ran wild, multiplied, crossed the Mississippi, and took up residence in the forests and canebrakes of Arkansas.

J. Frank Dobie, in his *Vaquero of the Brush Country*, confirms this legend by quoting the statement that de Soto and his six hundred men had thirteen sows with them when they landed in Florida in 1539. A year later this brood stock had increased to three hundred swine and the adventurers subsisted largely on pork for the time being. The daily allowance was half a pound to the man and it was eaten with boiled herbs. Not all the animals were killed for food, however, and the herd continued to increase in size. But the theory that these hogs were the seed that produced the wild boar of the Ozarks is based upon pure legend.

Regardless of its origin, the wild boar has a reputation for ferocity seldom equalled in frontier lore. To have three hundred pounds of enraged hog charging at express-train speed might lead one to believe that the brute was sired by a cyclone and mothered by a witch. To shoot into the mass of wild ham would establish the theory that the monster had been suckled by a gowrow of the pachyderm family.[2] A more plausible solution, however, is that it descended from ordinary barnyard hogs which escaped from early settlers and went wild. But the animal was once the terror of the backhill country. To meet it in the woods was to flirt with the graveyard. The species is now almost extinct, but not forgotten. In November 1927, *Ozark Life* magazine carried a news item of a wild boar episode in southern Missouri. Here it is:

> Armed with a twelve-gauge shotgun, and twenty feet from the
> hog when he discovered it, the farmer fired a load of number

four shot into the animal's left eye. The enraged boar immediately charged him and he fired a second volley from not more
than ten feet, striking the beast between the eyes. The third load,
fired into the neck at the base of the skull when the animal was
within two feet of the gun, stunned it long enough for the farmer
to kill it with a knife thrust into its heart.

In general appearance it resembled our domesticated Poland China
hog. Though in only moderate good flesh, its weight was estimated at
five hundred pounds. The tusks, or tushes, were three-fourths of an inch
thick and an inch wide where they emerged from the jaw. In form, they
described a complete semicircle, measuring nearly a foot in circumference. About two inches from the tip, the tushes had been worn to a razor
edge on two sides, and had points as keen as any knife blade.

There are two theories regarding the name "razorback." One is that
the term was applied because of the animal's lean, skinny back. The man
who wrote *Three Years in Arkansas* probably held to this theory, as the
cover of his book has a picture showing two men sawing a log with a
razorback hog for a saw. Others say the name comes from the razor-
like edge on the back of the tusks. But regardless of its origin, the word
"razorback" has popular appeal and is the adopted emblem of athletic
teams at the University of Arkansas.[3]

Perhaps the leading outdoor sport in the Ozarks is foxhunting.
There are many strings of hounds in the backhills, veterans of the chase,
"honin' t' scent." They will stick to Reynard's trail throughout the night,
radiating music that is sweet to the hillsman's ears. The fox may outsmart
the dogs but that doesn't matter. Love for the chase is bred in the bone
of both man and dog. It is a passion whose fires never die.

"One of the best chases I ever had was on a moonlight night
about a month ago," said an old-timer whose avocation is foxhunting. "I took the dogs over on the glade where we can usually
find a trail. The dogs had not been out for quite a while and they
were covering every bit of the ground back and forth in front
of my horse as we went along. It wasn't long before Old Trump

found the trail, stuck his head up, and bawled as loud and long as he could. In an instant all the pack fell in behind him and the chase was on.

The varmint led the dogs over the roughest country it could find, trying to escape them, but you can't lose these dogs of mine once they get on a warm trail. Their noses are as sensitive as the needle to the pole. The varmint took them across the creek and over the ridge until they were almost out of hearing.

But after a little while I could tell they were coming back. Their voices grew plainer as they came near, and they were really making music. I never heard them so much in earnest as they were that night. They passed to the west of me, almost in sight, and then they circled to the east and passed a dense thicket of brush. Suddenly they barked as if they were about to take hold of the animal.

It was a wolf they had started and these animals are about the smartest that roam the woods. When the pups are young both the male and female help in protecting them. When one of the parents is out foraging the other stays close by the young to see that nothing molests them.

It was the mother wolf the dogs had jumped, and she had tried hard to lose them, but failing to do so, had circled back to the den where the sire stood guard. When they neared the brush patch the male wolf ran out and took a position behind his mate, playing along until he had pulled the dogs off her track. The mother then circled back to her pups and the old dog wolf led the hounds as straight away from those pups as he could. I sat on my horse and listened to them as their voices gradually faded from my hearing. The wolf took them into the distant hills so far away that it was way up in the morning of the next day before they all came back.

The passenger pigeon, or "wild pigeon" as the pioneers called it, migrated to the Ozarks each fall in the early days. These birds came in such flocks that they "blotted out the sun." Millions of these pigeons came to the hill country to feed on the abundant mast of the forest.

Hunting was engaged in both for profit and for pleasure. Nets were used to capture the birds and a thousand or more were frequently taken at one haul. These were packed in barrels and freighted to the nearest railroad points where they were shipped to eastern cities. Harold Wales says that the New York market alone would take one hundred barrels a day for weeks, without a break in price. Prices ranged from seventy-five cents to $1.50 a dozen.

The last big hunt by Indians in the northern section of the Ozarks occurred in Camden County, Missouri, in 1846. These Indians were Delawares and had been moved to the Indian territory several years earlier but they were permitted to return on hunting trips. They camped a few miles above Linn Creek at a spot now covered by the Niangua Arm of the Lake of the Ozarks, two miles above the mouth of the Niangua. This was no warring band but the palefaces took note of their presence. The Indians held religious services at their camp and several white people went to hear the sermon by the Indian preacher. "He preached Christianity as it is taught in the Bible," was the report of one of the listeners. Strange ammunition for the Indian to use on the paleface so soon after the tumultuous years of removal, but such is the record of history. Gospel is a great relief after tomahawks and poisoned arrows.

But religion did not weaken the ardor of the hunt. The Ozarks woods must have been teeming with game for this band of Indian hunters killed two hundred deer, seven bears, a vast number of wild turkey, raccoon, and other small game. The meat was cured on scaffolds suspended above slow fires and taken away with them at the end of the hunt, which lasted three weeks. It was the last organized Indian hunt in the northern section of the Ozarks.

Fisherman's Luck

Bill Biles, a White River habitant, once told me that, when he was a boy, the fish were so plentiful in Ozark streams that they "pushed one 'nother out of th' water, clean up on th' bank." Perhaps he was referring to redhorse suckers at shoaling time. I have seen great schools of these fish swarming in the water, thick as ants in a bed. But game fish travel in smaller schools and are more cautious in their antics. They test the angler's skill with almost incredible ingenuity.

The bass is the most popular game fish in Ozark waters. There are white bass, locally called "stripers," largemouth, smallmouth, and the rock bass or goggle-eye. According to Robert Page Lincoln, the last three are not bass at all but belong to the sunfish family. The white bass, however, is a true bass and a member of the sea bass family, *Serranidae*. Natives frequently apply the name "trout" to all members of the bass family.

. Other game fish found in Ozark lakes and streams are: perch, channel cat, jack salmon,[4] and the rainbow trout that live in the cold-spring branches. Buffalo, redhorse, and yellow and blue cat are called rough fish and do not get the legal protection given the game varieties. Natives gig them in winter and "noodle" for them in summer.

Ozarkland, with its thousands of springs supplying more than five hundred fishing streams with crystal-clear water, is a popular region with sportsmen. Floating may be combined with fishing in any one of forty of the larger streams. Outfitters, located along shore at convenient points, supply boats, guides, food, and camping equipment. Let us focus our fancy upon a recent James–White River float from Galena to Branson, Missouri, with Walt Guilliams as guide.

Guilliams knows Ozark streams and the fish that inhabit them. For twenty years he was a market fisherman and has learned all the tricks of the trade.

"I have handled every species of fish that live in Ozark waters," said Walt as he pushed the boat from the pier and, with swift strokes of the paddle, shot it into the current. "But my favorite is the smallmouth black bass. This fish differs from the largemouth in several ways. Both of these fish have oblong-shaped bodies, shaded with dark green over black and with broad tails slightly forked. The largemouth species shows dark stripes along the sides and we sometimes call them 'lineside bass.' The smallmouth has vertical bands over its sides, and the mouth does not extend beyond the eye. Bass average two or three pounds in weight but occasionally run to five or six pounds. They are good fighters and show plenty of action in fast water."

"What are some of the questions fishermen ask you on these float trips?" I inquired.

The guide rested his paddle, as we idled along in an eddy, took a chew of tobacco, and gave answer.

"Usually the first thing they want to know is what the fish are hitting. By that they mean what kind of artificial bait. I tell them which baits have been successful on recent trips. Tackle has lots to do with fishing but it isn't everything."

I had seated myself on a campstool near the front end of the boat and was casting, right and left, into the swift water. Walt knew how to handle the boat to put me in range of the best spots for fishing. He shot around huge boulders and skirted beds of water lilies, guiding the boat with expert stroke. I had been casting for an hour without a strike and was beginning to get discouraged. Walt offered advice but it was of no avail.

"Couple of years ago," said the guide, "I guided a man and his wife from Kansas down this same stream. They were dead game sports and the bass soon realized that fact. I was on an eight-day trip with this couple. Neither of them had ever tried to cast before. Imagine two people in one boat learning to cast at the same time and you will sympathize with me. But they had good tackle and learned rapidly. By the third day they were catching bass right along and I never had to tell them where or when. All that I did was to loosen up the bearings on their reels so they could cast farther with ease. With the beginner, I always fix the reel so it won't run too fast as he naturally casts too hard at the start."

This was said to encourage me, no doubt, but my luck didn't change. I tried almost everything in my tackle box without success. I began to think I was about the sorriest fisherman that ever wet a line. But Guilliams liked to talk and I enjoyed his patter.

"Some fishing parties are hard to please. I have guided men who thought because they could throw a bait forty feet they were good fishermen. They are the ones a guide finds hard to please. One such man I remember quite well. He was just as apt to throw his plug into a treetop as anywhere else. Once we were passing through a stretch of fine water with big rocks sticking up, and plenty of submerged ones, and a nice current twisting through them. He made two or three wild throws and then wound up his line, looking sarcastic at me, as if to say, 'No bass here. Your river is a fake.' Just at that time I let the boat bump a rock and a bass weighing around three pounds jumped into the boat. I picked it up and threw it back into the river. The man asked me what I did that for. I said, 'Figure it out. That bass is a particular friend of mine.' In fact, all fish are my friends and I will not allow them to be abused by heartless fishermen.

"Bass frequently jump in muddy water and some fishermen are poor enough sports to take them in this manner. Two men usually pole a boat upstream close to the bank. The bass seem blind in muddy water and as they jump for deep water they sometimes land in the boat. Both Missouri and Arkansas have laws prohibiting the taking of fish in this manner.

"I was a guide in a three-boat party a few years ago that carried a Negro servant. He was permitted to paddle one of the boats. On the first day out the Negro sank the boat that carried his boss. On the next day the Negro was placed in a boat with two boys who wore bathing suits. One of the boys carried a shotgun. I told them that since the river was muddy a bass might jump into their boat. Sure enough, it happened. The Negro let the boat get near a weedy bank and a big fellow jumped in. The boy with the gun took a shot at the bass, and the colored man took to the water. Of course, the kid shot a hole in the bottom of the boat and I had to patch it before we could go on. Next day I carried the gun with me."

I learned many things about fish and the ways of catching them while on this float trip. The bass in southern Missouri streams begin nesting around April 20 if the weather is normal. They move to water about two and a half feet deep, and in a sheltered place away from the current. They do not all nest at the same time but most of them are through by the first of June. The Ozark states have a closed season on bass during the nesting season.

Bass will not always take the lure even when they are breaking water on both sides of the boat. Guilliams made a statement in this connection that puzzled me but I did not doubt the truth of it. "Not more than two percent of the bass in a stream are in a mood to strike at the same time," said Walt. "In other words, out of every one hundred bass that see the lure, one will strike and possibly one will follow for a short distance. But at this ratio, the expert angler will make a good catch in any of the bass streams of the Ozarks."

By this time we had reached the landing near the yawning mouth of Gentry Cave and stopped for lunch. We filled our canteens at the spring which gushed from the rocks near the entrance of the cavern and then lounged in the deep shade with a basket of eatables between us. Walt continued his harangue as we ate.

"The smallmouth bass is an active fellow and good at playing pranks. One of his favorite tricks is to keep minnows away from a trap. Last summer, I fished for yellow cat for the market, using three or four trotlines. It took a lot of minnows to supply these lines and I kept two minnow traps set and baited all the time. Bass bothered my traps so much that I had to wade from one to the other continually to drive them away. Finally, I tired of doing this, so I caught a few soft-shelled crawfish for bait and, taking my rod and reel, changed the tune of these playful bass. I caught five within a few minutes. After I had secured my supply of minnows, I turned them loose.

"Another way in which bass have given me much trouble is by killing the minnows on my trotline. Sometimes if the water is clear they will bite at night. I have caught a number of smallmouth on trotlines at night. They seem to bite best just at the time the moon is rising. Last spring we caught a bass on our line that weighed four and one-half pounds. We had our scales with us and after weighing it, threw it back. We were fishing for cat for the market at that time."

The mention of soft-shelled crawfish gave me an idea and I suggested that we catch a few of them to use for bait. We turned over a few rocks at the water's edge and soon had a sufficient supply of them. I tied a hook on my line and baited it with one of the soft-tails. About one hundred yards below the cave I tossed the bait near a partially submerged log. *Whang!* The battle was on! The reel sang a siren's song as the fish headed for deeper water. I let out plenty of line but it looked like all of it would be taken from my reel. Walt kept the boat in position to give me the best possible advantage. I fought that fish for several minutes, up and down the stream, and at last landed it in the boat. It was a channel cat and weighed six pounds.

CHAPTER VIII

Boy Meets Girl

. . . .

Pride of Posey

I do not ordinarily believe in signs, but when a pretty red-haired girl riding a white horse crossed my path on the Woodville–Posey road, I instinctively interpreted it as an omen of good luck, even though she was whistling as she rode by. Everyone knows that "a whistling woman and a crowing hen always come to the same bad end," but I could not conceive of such an attractive girl ending her career ingloriously.

My search for beauty and adventure had led me to the Posey settlement in the shadow of Breadtray Mountain. I wanted to fish, and to exercise my soul. I sought an isolated haven where one might drink from the bowl of the gods unmolested. It was June, the month of wild roses, and I felt a thrill of vagabondish ecstasy as I followed the old trail down James River. I had resolved to capture every bit of inspiration I could. Lem Logan of Woodville had told me there was good fishing in Posey Creek, and that I would enjoy the hospitality of the people who cropped the ridges for a livelihood. But he warned me of Breadtray Mountain. Tradition had put a mark on this flat-topped peak and it was whispered that ghosts made it a favorite rendezvous. But that is another story.

I had crossed White River and was approaching the general store at Posey when Joyce Delmar crossed my path on her white charger. She lifted the veil of conventionality to smile a pleasant greeting and then, like a dream girl of the sunshine, disappeared down the trail. Ten minutes later I inquired at the store for a boarding place in the neighborhood. The merchant directed me to Nate Delmar's farm at the foot of Saddleback Mountain.

Joyce Delmar was the will-o'-the-wisp of the community in which she lived. No one understood her; everybody liked her. She was sixteen and so winsome in appearance that men invariably turned to take a second look at her. She was the loveliest hill girl I had seen, a child of the forest as Venus was a child of the sea. She had that tricky beauty of Andromeda which lures men on but leads them to be respectful and protective. Naturally, she had many admirers. Nate tolerated them with customary White River hospitality when they called on Sundays. But his eyes were ever open in thoughtfulness of Joyce. Her mother was dead and she was all that he had in the world.

I secured board and lodging at Nate Delmar's home and settled down for a week of angling in Posey Creek. I like to fish little streams that have quiet pools frequented by perch, goggle-eye, and bass. I like to rummage in the liquid pockets of these crystal spring branches that go tumbling and singing toward the river. Posey Creek is such a mountain stream and my excuse for loitering along its winding course was to wet my fishing lines and air my sentiments.

One Sunday morning, shortly after my arrival in the settlement, I arose at dawn to test my skill with some white bass that were chasing minnows in a neighboring pool. Morning announced a day full of promise and a few minutes after sunup, I had six beauties on my string. I was about ready to pull my line and call it a day when I heard hoofbeats on the trail below. From my place of concealment I saw a young man riding a bay horse. It was Charlie Griggs from Bull Creek going courting.

Charlie was a gay young Lochinvar of the White River hills. He had just turned nineteen, was brown as a nut and stalwart as an oak. A thrill of expectancy lighted his face as he guided his mare into the churning water at the ford. As the animal drank from the clear stream, the young man's voice rose in song. Young Griggs had the voice of a bird—a mockingbird. It was an experience to hear him yodel the weird White River yell while choring in early morning or riding from a dance late at night.

Who-ah, who-ee, who-ee, who-ee!
Who-ah, who-ee, who-ah, whoo!

Only such veterans as Tobe Mullins and Dan Freeman could do this yodel with a greater turn of artistry.

On this occasion it was an old English ballad he sang—an Elizabethan romance taught to him by his mother. Tragedy lurked in the shadows of Charlie's mind, it seemed to me, as he shaped his baritone voice to the words of "Gypsy Davy."

Oh, would you leave your house and home,
Oh, would you leave your honey?
Oh, would you leave your babies three
To go with Gypsy Davy?

Raddle-um-a-ding, a-ding, ding, ding,
Raddle-um-a-ding-a-dary,
Raddle-um-a-ding, a-ding, ding, ding,
She's gone with Gypsy Davy.

Oh, yes, I'd leave my house and home,
Oh, yes, I'd leave my honey,
Oh, yes, I'd leave my babies three,
To go with Gypsy Davy.

The old man came home that night
Inquiring for his honey.
The maid came tripping along the hall;
"She's gone with Gypsy Davy."

Go saddle for me my milk-white steed,
Go saddle for me my brownie;

I'll ride all night and I'll ride all day
Till I overtake my honey.

Oh, come go back with me, my love,
Go back with me, my honey;
I'll lock you up in a chamber so high
Where the Gypsy can't get to you.

I won't go back with you, my love,
I won't go back, my honey.
I'd rather have one kiss from Davy's lips
Than all your land and money.

The song ended, the boy paused thoughtfully for a moment as if deciding his next move. He looked in the direction of the Delmar house, half hidden by a hill. Squinting one eye at the sun to get the time of day, he climbed from the saddle and tethered his mare to a sapling. It was a bit early in the day to start courting. Sitting down on a rock near the water's edge, he removed his shoes and bathed his tortured feet in the soothing water. Sunday shoes did not fit his plebeian feet.

Without making my presence known, I slipped through a crevice of rock and up the path to the house. I found Nate sitting in his favorite hickory-bottom chair in the living room of the cabin smoking his clay pipe and enjoying the Sabbath quiet. Joyce flitted about the house, setting things in order. Her expression told me that she intuitively knew of Charlie's coming. Perhaps he had said nothing about it. Social custom in the Ozarks does not require advance dating. But in the heart of youth, dreams border closely upon realism. The Fates had whispered into the girl's ear that this day would not pass uneventful. Nate smoked his pipe thoughtfully, and apparently without suspicion. I wondered how he would accept the young swain's visit.

An hour passed and Charlie had not made his appearance. Joyce began preparing dinner. She took antique silver that her mother and grandmother had used before her and set three places at the table. She sang as she worked. It is the way of youth in love. Surging emotions are

quieted or aroused by song. Joyce sang an old, old song, one that the
hillfolks use at play parties for their swinging games in the absence of the
fiddle. Perhaps it was only a coincidence that her song was "Handsome
Charlie." Perhaps it wasn't. No one will ever know. The words of the song
were centuries old, written to ridicule a foppish English monarch. The
girl half hummed them as she worked.

> Charlie's neat and Charlie's sweet,
>   And Charlie he's a dandy;
> Every time he goes to town,
>   He brings the girls some candy.

> The higher up the cherry tree,
>   The riper grows the berry;
> The more you hug and kiss the girls,
>   The sooner they will marry.

> Over the hill to feed my sheep,
>   And over the river to Charlie;
> Over the hill to feed my sheep
>   On . . .

She stopped the song suddenly and listened. The flock of sheep
never got "the buckwheat cakes and barley" that were intended for them.
Something of greater importance was about to happen. Charlie Griggs
was approaching.

Nate's bulky frame almost filled the doorway. Joyce peeped shyly
over his shoulder.

"Light an' look at yer saddle," greeted the host. Charlie needed no
second invitation. He dismounted and tied his horse to a young hickory.
Awkwardly he ambled up to the cabin.

"Joyce, bring them cheers out in front. Hit's gettin' hot inside." The
girl did as her father commanded and I was invited to join them. We
occupied ourselves with talk about the weather and crops and local happenings. The race for county sheriff and the hog-stealing case on Blair

Creek were prime topics. Nate reported that some fishermen had heard a "hant" while camping near Breadtray Mountain a few days before. The girl seldom joined in the conversation but listened attentively to what was said. She appeared to be undisturbed, carrying herself with dignity, but I thought I could detect a sudden pouring of pink into her cheeks when she brushed Charlie's arm in passing. The strange thing about it was that Joyce gave no special attention to her guest. From all appearances, he might have been visiting her father. I had much to learn on the subject of backhill courtship. Charlie conducted himself as all well-bred hillsmen do on such occasions. He knew it would never do to portray eagerness.

Joyce soon had dinner on the table and politely invited us inside to eat. She stood aside, according to the custom of the hills, to wait on the table. Later, she would eat a few bites in the kitchen. She kept an eye on our plates and what Charlie might have missed through bashfulness, she supplied generously. Silently but joyously he ate the fluffy biscuits baked by fairy hands and dipped his knife deep into preserves sweet as the lips of the one who had prepared them. The sage-flavored sausage, baked potatoes, greens wilted in grease, and fried pie made it a feast fit for an epicure. Romance danced in the coffee as we poured the hot liquid into saucers for cooling.

Dinner over, we walked leisurely to the barn and fields to look at Nate's livestock and growing crops. We examined the corn almost knee-high in the creek-bottom field. Charlie apparently took a deep interest in everything. Only once did I see him look over his shoulder toward the house as if he preferred being there helping Joyce with the dishes. There would be little chance to talk this Sunday with Nate present. But he had no need to worry. Hadn't he gone into the clearing a month ago and bent a mullein stalk in the direction of her cabin? It had lived and all was well.

We returned to the house, moved the chairs to a shady spot, and continued our discussion of community affairs. Mention was made of the recent marriage of Jesse Lindsey and Millie Owens. They were mere children, seventeen and fifteen, and I had inquired about the custom of child marriage in the hills. Nate explained that such marriages were quite

common in the White River country but added as an afterthought that
a girl ought to be eighteen and a boy twenty-one.

Charlie's eyes fell and I could see disappointment in them. Some
folks throw their emotions on the facial screen that acts as a curtain
for the soul. I could read the young man's thoughts: "Must I wait two
years for Joyce and take a chance of some other fellow getting her?" The
thought had its effect. It took all the vim out of sparking. Half an hour
later he swung into the saddle and rode away. There was no song on his
lips as he splashed through the ford homeward bound.

But paternal objections cannot easily extinguish the candle of true
love. Three years later I revisited the Posey community and called at the
Delmar home. Charlie met me at the door and the first thing he did was
to lead me to the cradle where Charles Junior lay sleeping.

Courtship and Marriage

Courting customs in the backhills have a technique that harmonizes with
the traditional code of the mountains, and the invasion of modern social
practices has done little to change them. The process is comparatively
slow as the young folks have a bashful reserve which acts as a protective
halo. Marriage is the high point of life and it is taken seriously. Girls
grow up to become wives and mothers and there is no attempt to break
the tradition. The majority of young men take wives by the time they
reach voting age and begin cropping parcels of land without paternal
supervision. Child marriages have been checked somewhat by the estab-
lishment of high schools throughout the hill country. Many rural boys
and girls now graduate from these institutions and spend from one to
four years in college before settling down. They may remain single for a
few years after that to teach school or do office work in nearby towns. But
the ultimate aim is matrimony and, in most cases, it is not long delayed.
For a hill girl to reach mature womanhood without a beau or a proposal
is not in line with the customs of the hills.

Time was when love charms were thought to be potent in affairs of the heart. One of these charms was a carved peach seed filled with a highly perfumed powder. The maiden wore it on a string tied around her neck. Whiskey in which a girl's fingernail trimmings had been soaked was thought to be especially potent in swaying a young man's affection. Mountain girls did not know all the answers to the questionnaire of love but instinct prompted them. To test her lover's devotion, a girl would take a hair from her head and pull it between her fingers. If it curled, he loved her; if it remained straight, he did not. She frequently relied upon nature in solving her romantic problems. A mullein stalk would be bent in such a way as to point toward the home of her Romeo and the results were observed carefully. If the plant withered and died, his love had done the same and she should waste no more time on him. But if it straightened and lived, all was well. The hill girl knew that she must sweep down the cobwebs in the parlor, for if they were left hanging her lover would not visit her again. When corn bread burned in the oven, the boy was angry. If the fire she kindled burned brightly, her man, for whom it was named, was faithful, but if it smoldered the opposite was likely to prove true. The mountain lass could force her lover to visit her on Sunday by trimming her fingernails the preceding day. And if a red bird flew in front of her, she would be kissed twice before nightfall.

Superstition played an important hand in the game of hearts.

The young man tested the devotion of his sweetheart in divers ways. He was determined to marry a virgin at all costs and could not pardon unfaithfulness in the woman he loved. This caused a double standard of morality and it is still firmly entrenched in backhill provincialism. The code of the hills is dyed in the wool of tradition.

Ozark girls are home girls and they are carefully guarded during the age of indiscretion. There is very little nightlife in the hills and the automobile is not yet widely used as Cupid's chariot. Young women attend church and go to neighborhood frolics, but usually they are chaperoned by their parents or other kinfolks. The young men have more freedom and ride long distances on horseback to spark the girls of their choice. They are not immune to the lure of passion and frequently seek amorous adventures. But the conventions of time, place, and conduct are

discreetly followed in courting respectable girls. Every youth knows that
social custom is firmly fixed and that a misstep may bring tragic results.
Of course, there is petting or "spooning" wherever boy meets girl, but
affection between the sexes is checkmated by traditions that are bred in
the bone and carefully guarded.

When a young man in the hills gets interested in a particular girl,
he calls at her home on Saturday evening or on Sunday, visits with her
and her folks but does very little sparking. He may walk with his girl
to church or singing, but usually there is a crowd along and privacy is
denied. Sometimes the girl's parents invite him to spend the night and
this is considered a sign of paternal approval.

G. W. Clark relates a story of courting in the old days which gives
us enlightenment on the social decorum of that age. He has given me
permission to repeat it.

> Our grandfathers and great-grandfathers not only walked long
> distances to visit their girlfriends, but they frequently went bare-
> foot, which was in perfectly good taste at that time.
>
> I have heard my maternal grandmother tell how her father
> took his first lesson in real courtship, as he afterward related the
> adventure to his family.
>
> It was on one of those warm, romantic Sunday afternoons
> when great-grandfather, all togged up according to the styles of
> that time, but minus any kind of footwear, made a call at a neigh-
> boring home that boasted a pretty, though bashful, young lady.
> Not being so sure of his ground, he addressed most of his remarks
> to the old folks or the family in general. Finally as the shadows
> of the trees began to lengthen, he could endure the suspense no
> longer; so picking up the hickory-bottom chair in which he had
> been sitting, he carried it across the room, set it beside the girl,
> and awkwardly tumbled into it. The girl blushed but said noth-
> ing. As to the youth, his every word stuck in his mouth, his lips
> became dry, his tongue clove to one side of his mouth.
>
> The shadows of the trees were now fading into dusk. The
> young man had made the visit with the expectation of spending

the night with his neighbors, having a good time in general, and incidentally gaining some information as to his standing with the girl beside whom he was now sitting. But there he sat like an animal in a trap. How to get out was the question. He thought about as fast as one in such a predicament could think, and finally something practical dawned in his mind. Suddenly he arose and started for the back porch, saying as he went, "Well, I must go and wash my feet."

Ike Foster once had a widow "jist about sparked" when a stranger came along and married her. This old hillsman testifies that "lovemakin' and settin' up t' a girl is mighty rattlin'." He backed up his testimony with this information: "When th' widder let me walk home with her frum th' spellin' at th' schoolhouse one night, I got so blame rattled that I plumb fergot my fine saddle mare left tied t' th' schoolyard fence. Th' mare had a brand-new saddle on, too. Left her thar till nearly midnight."

In the old days it was customary for a girl to "sack" a suitor whom she wanted to get rid of. Sometimes it was called "giving him the mitten." The girl would knit a little sack or a mitten and send it to the boy, or give it to him at some social gathering. It meant for him not to come back, and the verdict was final. May Kennedy McCord says that this is an old, old custom and originated in England. One old-timer tells me that he collected enough sacks and mittens in his courting days to make a saddle blanket.

Marriage is the trailblazer for happiness in folk life. Dream lore is full of images that relate to marriage.

To dream of bad weather means a wealthy marriage with a person living outside the hills; bereavement experienced in dreams means matrimony, and the nearer the relative the happier the marriage. An altar foretells marriage and domestic happiness. Dream of a tomb and you will attend a wedding. Orange blossoms, pigeons, garden rakes, and a legion of other things mean a happy marriage. The majority of dream superstitions relating to matrimony are happy ones.

In the old days wedding dates were sometimes determined by the

changes of the moon or signs of the zodiac but these things are seldom
thought of now. Any month except May is a good time to marry in the
Ozarks. Just why May is considered unlucky for the start of the marital
adventure I do not know, for it is next to impossible to trace a popular
superstition to its beginning. Perhaps a Scotsman would say that May
is an unlucky month for brides because of the unfortunate marriage of
Mary, Queen of Scots, to Bothwell during that month in 1567. But the
superstition goes farther back than that. Ovid, the Roman, wrote that
the common people of his day considered it unlucky to marry in May.

June is the most auspicious month of the year for weddings, and the
time of the full moon is especially propitious. But superstitions creep in
even during this favorable month. It is a disturbing element for a cat to
cross the path of the bride and groom as they approach the church or
other place where the rites are to be solemnized. But let a toad hop down
the path in front of them and good luck is assured.

Time, tide, and shotgun weddings wait for no man. The irate sire
names the hour for this ceremony of honor and there is no appeal. No
wedding bells ring out the glad hour when a marrying takes place at the
point of a gun.

There are so many things to be taken into consideration in getting
married that it is remarkable that the mind can retain all of them. It is
always considered an unlucky match if a girl marries a man whose sur-
name has the same initial as her own.

> Change the name and not the letter,
> Marry for worse and not for better.

Color in the wedding dress is a serious consideration. Every mountain girl knows the rules.

> Marry in red,
> You'll wish yourself dead.

> Marry in black,
> You'll wish yourself back.

Marry in brown,
You'll live in town.

Marry in yellow,
You'll be ashamed of your fellow.

Marry in green,
You'll be ashamed to be seen.

Marry in blue,
You'll always be true.

Marry in white,
You'll always do right.

Weather is a vital factor on the wedding day. "Happy is the bride that the sun shines on," but the outlook is dark if the day happens to be a cloudy one.

A marriage in the backhills may be a "meetinghouse tie-up," but in recent years most of the young people don't stand on ceremony when approaching the altar. Vows are said before a justice of the peace or in the minister's home. The nervous groom and the blushing bride are anxious to get the ordeal over as quickly as possible.

A few years back elaborate home weddings were held in the better homes of the Ozarks and followed by feasting and celebration that usually lasted two days. It was a formal affair with the bride properly gowned and the bridesmaids wearing brideknots made of leaves and flowers. The time of the ceremony was high noon. The groom with other young men as companions would leave the groom's home on horseback to reach the bride's domicile in the nick of time for the wedding. They rode at breakneck speed, whooping and yelling, hurdling fences and defying all caution. Arriving at the girl's home, they rode around the house three times and then dismounted and walked in for the ceremony.

The rites were comparatively simple, but the wedding feast that followed was an elaborate affair. In the afternoon they sang songs and played games, and perhaps took down the dummy of a rejected suitor which had been hung on the limb of a tree nearby. The whole affair was punctuated by the hilarious conduct of the menfolks. The women might weep at the solemnity of the occasion, but nips from an overflowing jug kept the men in boisterous humor. The wedding night was the time for a big dance if religious scruples did not interfere. The lid was off the barrel of hospitality and everybody enjoyed themselves. A wedding meant more than just going to the preacher in those days.

When it came time to retire, the women put the bride to bed. Then the men came in and put the groom to bed with her. The hour that followed was an embarrassing one for the newly married couple. The crowd walked around the bed looking at them and making witty remarks. Sometimes they tormented them all night by playing music and dancing in the room. They would not let the young couple get out of bed and dress, neither would they leave the room. Sometimes the watchers would sleep in relays with alert guards to keep the bride and groom awake.

In many communities it was the custom to have an "infare" dinner at the home of the groom on the day following the wedding. Sometimes a dance was held that night to complete the celebration. Noisy charivaris were customary and the groom was forced to treat his guests with candy and cigars, or take a dunking in the river.

Parenthood usually followed the wedding at the accredited time, and life began to have serious obligations for the young married couple. When a wedding was reported in the hills, the doctor and midwife knew that they would soon be on the trail of the honeymoon.

CHAPTER IX

Mountain Music

. . . .

"Arkansaw Traveler"

The Ozark region is a geographical center of artful fiddling and expert guitar and banjo picking. These instruments belong to the folk and nowhere in the world are they used to greater advantage. Ozarkers fiddle by the feel of the tune, and notes hung on a staff have little meaning. "Banjer" and "git-tar" pickers likewise play by ear and are the last representatives of that ancient race of gleemen and jongleurs who once brought gaiety to a darkened world.

The James–White River country grows fiddlers as a principal crop and many of them have won state and regional championships with their playing. Joe Spears, who lives on Big Clabber, can neither read nor write, but he knows the muse and mood of his listeners and could sway a jury or break up a revival meeting with his fiddle. Perhaps it is the rattles from the tail of a mountain rattlesnake that give Uncle Joe's fiddle such enchantment for, as every hillsman knows, a few rattles in the box are absolutely necessary to make a fiddle talk "like it ought to." Sometimes it may be a single rattle but more often there are several. Some fiddlers have their instruments half full of them. Old-timers claim that these rattles give a rustling sound which adds a pleasing tone to the strings of the instrument.

Visit with me the home of Joe Spears on Clabber Creek. A soft autumn twilight is creeping over the hills. Neighbors have gathered in, pipes are lit, and Uncle Joe is tuning his fiddle. A bullfrog in the nearby swamp emits measured croaks as regular as the pulse of time. Katydids click in the surrounding trees and a whip-poor-will joins the congruous chorus. Other creatures of the wild lend their voices to welcome the approach of night.

Darkness envelops the rural scene and a lantern is hung in the gallery where the crowd has gathered. Chairs are tipped back and all is expectancy as Uncle Joe tunes the fiddle, touching an ivory key now and then and testing the strings with his thumb. New resin is on the bow and the old instrument responds with a tone as soft as the voice of an angel. At last everything is in readiness. The instrument breaks loose in rampant glory as the fiddler heads the bow in the direction of "Arkansaw Traveler."

In imagination, the listener sees the traveler ride up to the old squatter's cabin in the forest, and the words of the racy dialogue come to mind as the fiddle loosens the melody. Uncle Joe dramatizes the conversation and makes intermittent runs on his instrument. He touches the notes of emotion and holds to the key of human sentiment in his vivid portrayal.

> Hello, stranger!
>
> Hello, yourself!
>
> Can I get to stay all night?
>
> You can git t' go t' hell.
>
> Have you any spirits here?
>
> Lots of 'em. Sal saw one last night by that thar ole holler gum, an' hit nearly skeered her t' death.
>
> You mistake my meaning, have you any liquor?
>
> Had some yestiddy, but Ole Bose he got in an' lapped all of it out'n th' pot.
>
> You don't understand me. I don't mean pot liquor. I'm wet and cold and want some whiskey. Have you got any?
>
> Oh, yes—I drunk th' last this mornin'.
>
> I'm hungry, haven't had a thing since morning. Can't you give me something to eat?

Hain't a damn thing in th' house, not a mouthful of meat nor a dust o' meal hyar.

Well, can't you give my horse something?

Got nothin' t' feed him on.

How far is it to the next house?

Stranger, I don't know. I've never been thar.

Well, do you know who lives here?

I do.

As I am so bold, then, what might your name be?

Hit might be Dick an' it might be Tom, but lacks a damn sight of it.

Sir, will you tell me where this road goes to?

Hit's never been anywhar since I've lived hyar; hit's always thar when I git up in th' mornin'.

Well, how far is it to where it forks?

Hit don't fork atall, but it splits up like th' devil.

As I'm not likely to get to any other house tonight, can't you let me sleep in yours? I'll tie my horse to a tree and do without anything to eat and drink.

My house leaks. Thar's only one dry spot in hit, an' me an' Sal sleeps on hit. An' that thar tree is th' ole worman's pet persimmon. You can't tie to hit, 'cause she 'low t' make beer out'n 'um.

Why don't you finish covering your house and stop the leaks?

Hit's been rainin' all day.

Well, why don't you do it in dry weather?

Hit don't leak then.

As there seems to be nothing alive about your place but children, how do you do here anyhow?

Putty well, I thank you, how do you do yourself?

I mean what do you do for a living here?

Keep tavern and sell whiskey.

Well, I told you I wanted some whiskey.

Stranger, I bought a bar'l more'n a week ago. You see, me an' Sal went shares. After we got it hyar, we only had a bit betweenst us an' Sal she didn't want t' use hern fust, nor me mine. You see, I

had a spiggin' in one end an' she in t'other. So, she takes a drink
out'n my end an' pays me a bit fer it, an' then I takes un out'n
hern, an' give her th' bit. Well, we's gittin' 'long fust rate till Dick,
damn sulkin' skunk, he bourn a hole in th' bottom t' suck at an'
th' next time I went t' buy a drink, they wurn't none thar.

I'm sorry your whiskey's all gone, but, my friend, why don't
you play the rest of that tune?

Got no rest t' hit.

I mean you don't play the whole of it.

Stranger, can you play th' fiddle?

Yes, a little.

You don't look like a fiddlur, but if ye think ye can play any
more onto that thar tune, ye can git down and try.

In fancy, we see the traveler dismount from his horse, sit down on the
stump, and, taking the fiddle, complete the tune the old squatter has been
trying to play. Old Joe knows just how to impress this part of the story on
his listeners. He puts the bow into vigorous action and the strings emit
tones that loosen the shackles of conventional behaviorism. It is easy to
picture the squatter's change of heart as Joe Spears fiddles the rollicking
tune. Then again comes the dramatization.

Stranger, take a half dozen cheers an' sot down. Sal, stir yer-
self 'round like a six-horse team in a mudhole. Go 'round in th'
holler whar I killed that buck this mornin', cut off some of th'
best pieces and fotch em an' cook 'em fer me an' this gentleman,
directly. Raise up th' board under th' head of th' bed an' git th'
old black jug, I hid frum Dick, an' give us some whiskey. I know
thar's some left yit. Till, drive Ole Bose out'n th' bread tray, then
climb up in th' loft an' git th' rag that's got th' sugar tied in it.
Dick, carry th' gentleman's hoss 'round under th' shed, give 'im
some fodder an' corn, as much as he kin eat.

The fiddle moans the melody and we visualize the confusion of the
household as each member goes into action. We see Till rushing up to
her father with the complaint that "thar hain't enuff knives to set th'
table." Then Old Joe resumes his impersonation.

Whar's big butch, little butch, ole case, cob-handle, granny's knife, and th' one I handled yistiddy? That's 'nuff to sot any gentleman's table with, without you've lost 'em. Damn me, stranger, if'n ye can't stay as long as ye please, an' I'll give ye plenty t' eat an' drink. Will ye have coffee fer supper?

Yes, sir.

I'll be hanged if ye do, tho! We don't have nothin' that way here but Grub Hyson, an' I reckon hit's mighty good with sweet'nin'. Play away, stranger, ye kin sleep on th' dry spot tonight.

Colonel Sanford C. Faulkner is usually credited with the authorship of "The Arkansaw Traveler," but he never claimed parentage of either the dialogue or the ditty. The scene of the story is thought to be in Pope County, not far from the present site of Russellville—the time, 1840. Perhaps the incident is pure fiction, originated by some versatile funmaker. If so, it has a record of which few legends of recent origin can boast. Both the tune and the dialogue have circled the globe and brought laughs from the masses everywhere. It is the best example of comic legend the state has produced.

The question of which came first, the dialogue or the music, is like considering the age-old riddle of the chicken and the egg. Folklore appears in strange ways and it is not easy to put a finger on origins. The tune may have preceded the dialogue many years but no one knows. Blodgett and Bradford of Buffalo, New York, published the music and a version of the dialogue in 1850. Fred W. Allsopp of the *Arkansas Gazette* gives us the following information which we quote with his permission:

> To trace the history of the Arkansas brand of humor is interesting to the analyst and the antiquarian. The story of the *Arkansaw Traveler*, which the people of the state are sometimes squeamish about referring to, is supposed to have originated about 1840. It is the best known piece of Arkansas folklore, and its vogue is attested by the fact that innumerable articles have been branded with its name. It has been brought into being by pictures in lithograph and oils, at least two plays, a fiddle tune, and numerous versions of the ridiculously amusing dialogue. Evidencing

the wide circulation of the story, Opie Read, in 1882, in his first issue of his *Arkansaw Traveler*, quotes Archibald Forbes, a war correspondent, as saying that "in England people who live in retired districts know Arkansas only through Colonel Faulkner's *Arkansaw Traveler*; in France, everyone has heard of the famous fiddler, as they term Colonel Faulkner, and some of the most ignorant suppose that he was a great violinist, rivaling Ole Bull; along the Rhine, and even among the people who live on the Danube, the *Arkansaw Traveler* is a familiar name."

One writer has said that no other region as young as Arkansas has produced as great a mass of comical legend and genuine native genius. Much of the humorous literature connected with the state, however, has been written by outsiders and cannot be considered authentic Arkansas folklore. The author of *Three Years in Arkansas* trekked in from Oklahoma and squatted in Polk County for a while, but he got out before the reaction to his absurd "classic" set in. Neither did native genius produce that rollicking piece of wit and humor, *On a Slow Train Through Arkansaw*. Thomas W. Jackson was the furriner who pictured the train, on which he said he rode, as the slowest contraption on wheels. The railroad companies have never appreciated this book, and not long ago its sale was banned on the trains of one of the important lines operating in the state. But I cannot understand why folks should be squeamish about this type of humor. Here is an example of Jackson's "slow train" pleasantry.

> "Conductor, what have we stopped for now?"
> "There are some cattle on the track."
> We ran along a little farther, stopped again, and I said, "What's the matter now?"
> He said, "We have caught up with those cattle again."
> We made good time for about two miles. Then one cow got her tail caught in the cowcatcher, and she ran off down the track with the train. The cattle bothered us so much that we had to take the cowcatcher off the engine and put it on the hind end of the train to keep the cattle from jumping into the sleeper.

Opie Read ranks as one of the best writers of Arkansas wit and humor, but he was not a native, and resided outside the state much of the time. He wrote somewhat in the vein of Mark Twain and he is not noted for scurrilous remarks about Arkansas.

Ballad Hunting

Ballad hunting is a favorite hobby of mine. Wherever I go along the shady, flower-spiced trails of the backhills, or in the sunny valleys that rim the tortuous streams, I find adventure in capturing folk songs. It may be around the fireplace in the dead of winter, or in a stony field where a singing lad guides a lanky mule to a bull-tongue plow, that the simple music of a people finds its spontaneity most readily. Or perhaps it is in the voice of a tie-hacker in the forest or the chorus of floaters on a tie-raft going to market. Folk music is inspired by emotion and does not have the technique of formal music. It is the product of centuries of isolation and is earmarked with certain stock phrases that distinguish it from modern imitations. It has a naturalness that gives it subtle charm.[1]

Someone has said that the tests of a folk song are its simplicity of theme, its sincerity, its childishness, its crude sentiment, its distinguishing melody and, most of all, the traditional trappings it has carried with it through the years. Unlike formal music it is seldom touched with literary tradition but it does carry a tone of antiquity in its lines. The real folk songs of the Ozarks have a distinctive Anglo-Saxon tone that harks back to Elizabethan England—to the days of William Shakespeare and Ben Jonson.

Folk songs may be called the rhythmic idiom of the people. The old ballads match the moods and manners and emotions of the folk. In the Ozarks, there are merry, skipping songs that delight young people at their parties and frolics, pathetic tunes for those who have experienced sorrow, and folly ballads for amusement. Cradle songs have been handed down from generation to generation. Household songs are sung by women doing housework or mending clothes. Men, young and old, whistle ancient tunes as they do the farm chores or follow the plow. There are somber tunes for burials, and swinging melodies, done in shape notes, for community singings. In the category of song we find the hopes and longings, sorrows and disappointments, loves and hates of people who have lived so close to the earth that it has fully seasoned their personalities.

The songs of the Ozarks belong to four distinct classes. First come the old English ballads, or "ballets" as the natives call them. These songs, for the most part, are laden with tragedy and have many different versions or variants due to the fact that they were handed down by word of mouth. Some of the stock phrases of the old ballads are "lily-white hands," "milk-white steed," "snow-white bosom," "red, red rose," and commands or entreaties—usually at the end of the song—such as, "Go dig my grave both wide and deep" and "Put a turtledove on my breast." It is interesting to note the frequent reference to the British homeland in these ballads. Kings and king's daughters and royal scenes and incidents were ever on the lips of the Ozark pioneers, who were the regal vagabonds of the Elizabethan age, spinning a thread of Anglo-Saxon continuity in the deep pockets of the Ozark Mountains.

A second class of songs which permeates Ozarkian life is the more recent ballads which deal with fires, floods, railroad accidents, explosions, tornadoes, shipwrecks, outlawry—calamities of all kinds. Examples of these songs are "Jesse James," "The Death of Floyd Collins," "Casey Jones," and "The Brooklyn Fire." If the ballad is composed in the Ozarks, it frequently gets a start through local newspapers, or the author may have a leaflet printed to promote distribution. If it is a foreign product, it is introduced through the medium of phonograph records, or over the radio. Jean Thomas, in her *Ballad Making in the Mountains of Kentucky*, explains how these songs are put before the public in the Blue Ridge Mountains:

> Tragic events always bring forth a number of ballads. Some ballad makers, alert to commercial value, hasten to the printer and have their composition struck off forthwith.
>
> A printer in an isolated county seat in the Kentucky moun-

tains, who had only a poor assortment of battered type and a picture frame with which to work, once told me he did "moughty well with the song-ballet of Floyd Collins," selling them to wandering fiddlers who, in turn, sold their wares to eager listeners who gathered at the court house on Court day.

The improvised ballads follow the plan of the old English songs both in type and tune, but they lack the pedigree of age—and that is a big item with collectors.

Another type of song popular throughout the Ozark region is the gospel tune, set with shape notes and modernized with a touch of swing. These songs have religious sentiment, but they show little kinship to the solemn hymns of camp-meeting days. They are distinguished by the range and tempo of the composition, which give the singers opportunity for elaborate vocalization. Nearly everyone in the rural Ozarks attends singings and it is estimated that at least sixty percent of the people sing, or try to sing, these gospel tunes.

Singing schools of two or three weeks' duration are held from time to time in almost every community. An enterprising singing teacher visits the neighborhood and "gets up" a class. Young and old attend, spending an hour or two each evening in learning the rudiments of music and practicing singing.

At the first session of the school the instructor explains how to identify the notes. *Do* looks like the roof of a house wherever it appears on the staff; *re* has the appearance of a coffee cup with the handle broken off; *mi* is a diamond; *fa* looks like a flag; *sol* resembles a grain of buckwheat; *la* is rectangular in shape; and *ti* looks like an ice cream cone.

The teacher spends a few minutes each evening giving instruction in fundamentals, but most of the time is given to singing. On the last night of the school, a special program of solos, duets, quartets, and group singing is presented to the public. It is remarkable how much a person can learn in ten or twelve lessons at a singing school. Some teachers offer to refund the tuition money if a student fails to learn to sing by note during the first five or six lessons. The fee for attending the school is usually a dollar per person, but sometimes the group have a pie supper or cakewalk and pay in a lump sum.[2]

The itinerant teacher is agent for songbooks and makes a small profit on his sales. Shrewd publishers put out new editions every two or three months, knowing that the singers will want to try the new songs. It keeps two or three publishing houses busy supplying the demand. That the new books receive a hearty welcome is evidenced by the following news item from a country correspondent in the *Log Cabin Democrat* of Conway, Arkansas: "Remember that next Sunday is our regular singing date and everybody is invited. We have our new books now, so everybody come and let's mingle our voices together in glad song and sweet praise to Almighty God for having made these wonderful books possible."

The fourth group of songs includes both the popular and classical types of music that are taking the place of the old ballads and fiddle tunes. But this is art music and has little kinship with the folk songs grandfather sang.

A special technique is required in collecting ballads in the backhills. I have learned by experience that the best way to capture a folk song is to appear unconcerned about it and talk about the weather or foxhunting. As the conversation proceeds, I casually express my dislike for modern jazz and mention a few old favorites of which I am especially fond. This usually gets the song, but sometimes one must go "all the way 'round Robin Hood's barn" to get it. Vance Randolph, Ozark folklorist, gives a plausible reason for this reticent attitude of hillsmen. He says:

> In order to fully appreciate just how seriously the old songs are taken by hillfolks, one must note the reaction of the native audience as well as the behavior of the singer. I have seen tears coursing down many bronzed old cheeks, and have more than once heard sobs and something near to bellowings as the minstrel sang of some more or less pathetic incident, which may have occurred in England three or four hundred years ago. The old song of "Barbara Allen" which Samuel Pepys enjoyed in 1666 is still a moving tragedy in the Ozark hills, and women in Missouri

and Arkansas weep today for young Hugh of Lincoln, murdered across the sea in 1255, whose story lives in the ballad of "The Jew's Garden."

One of the tarnished echoes of yesteryears which, if given proper rendition by a native singer, never fails to bring emotional reactions from the audience, is that symbol of tragedy, "The Jealous Lover." This ballad was popular years ago throughout the Appalachian region as well as in the highlands of Missouri and Arkansas, but it is rarely sung any more. The style and the story are typical of the old English ballad but its pedigree has never been established. Some students of folk song contend that it is founded upon the murder of a girl named Pearl Bryan, who was decapitated by two medical students near Fort Thomas, Kentucky, in 1896, but this is contradicted by old ballad singers who say they heard the song as early as 1870. Some think the song was derived from another old ballad called "The Murder of Betsey Smith," which was published in England early in the nineteenth century. But whatever may be the facts of its origin, "The Jealous Lover" was certainly known to many Ozark ballad singers at one time and no collection of Ozark folk songs would be complete without it. The version given here was heard in the Big Springs country of the Missouri Ozarks.

Down by yon weeping willow,
Where the violets gently bloom,
There sleeps our young Florilla
So silent in the tomb.

She died not broken-hearted,
Nor from sickness nor from woe,
But in one moment parted
From the one that she loved so.

'Twas on a Sunday evening
When early fell the dew,

Up to her cottage window
Her jealous lover drew.

"Come, Love, and let us ramble
O'er meadows green and gay;
Come, Love, and let us wander
And name our wedding day."

Deep, deep into the valley,
He led his love so dear.
She said, "'Tis for you only,
That I should ramble here.

"Oh, Edward, I'm so tired,
I care no more to roam,
For roaming makes me weary,
Please, Edward, take me home."

"Down in these woods I'll show you,
You cannot from me fly.
No mortal hand can save you;
This moment you must die."

"What have I done, dear Edward,
That you should take my life?
You know I've always loved you
And would have been your wife."

He saw not when he pressed her
Against his cruel heart;
He saw not when he kissed her
For he knew that they must part.

Down on her knees before him
She pleaded for her life,

But in her snow-white bosom
He plunged the fatal knife.

"Oh, Edward, I'll forgive you,
This being my last breath,
I never have deceived you."
And she closed her eyes in death.

The best-known folk song of ancient lineage in the Ozarks is
"Barbara Ellen" or "Allen." It was carried to America from England by
the earliest colonists and transplanted in the highlands of Missouri and
Arkansas by the pioneer settlers, and it has been a favorite ever since.
This old ballad was popular in England at the time of Goldsmith. It
probably originated in the thirteenth or fourteenth century but was not
printed until 1740. Few songs have been preserved so well and carried so
far as this one. Sometimes the version is fragmentary as the one I heard
in the Boston Mountains recently.

'Twas in the early month of May
    When all the buds were swellin',
Young William on his deathbed lay
    For the love of Barbara Allen.

He sent his servant to the place
    Where his true love was a-dwellin',
"Arise you up and quickly go
    If your name be Barbara Allen."

Slowly, slowly she got up
    And came to where he's lying,
And when she reached him thus she spoke,
    "Young man, I think you're dying."

She started to go down in town,
    She heard the death bells ringin'.

She looked due east, she looked due west,
   And saw the corpse a-comin'.

"Oh, mother, mother, make my bed,
   And make it long and narrow!
Since William died for me today,
   I'll die for him tomorrow."

The folly ballads were popular in the backhill country a generation or two ago and some of them are still heard in the out-of-way places. These songs are distinguished by their nonsensical last lines or choruses. A favorite in the Ozarks is "Rolly Trudum."

When I was out walking
To breathe the pleasant air,
I saw a lady talking
To her daughter fair.
Rolly trudum, trudum, trudum, rolly day.

Now hush up, dear daughter,
And stop your rapid tongue,
You're talking about marrying,
And you know you are too young—
Rolly trudum, trudum, trudum, rolly day.

Now hush up, dear mother,
You know I'm a lady grown,
I've lived seventeen years
And I've lived it all alone—
Rolly trudum, trudum, trudum, rolly day.

Oh, if you was to marry,
Oh, who would be your man?
I know a jolly farmer

And his name is handsome Sam.
Rolly trudum, trudum, trudum, rolly day.

There's doctors and lawyers
And men that follow the plow,
But I'm going to marry
For the fidget's on me now—
Rolly trudum, trudum, trudum, rolly day.

They've gone for the parson,
The license for to fetch,
And I'm going to marry
Before the sun sets.
Rolly trudum, trudum, trudum, rolly day.

Oh, now my daughter's married,
And well for to do.
So hop along my jolly boys,
I think I'll marry, too.
Rolly trudum, trudum, trudum, rolly day.

Many of the old folly ballads, with their whack-fol-loddy and bob-a-lob-a-loosy refrains, have no meaning whatever and they are said to be among the oldest ditties on record. Their original purpose seems to have been lost in the shuffle of history. Sometimes the refrain monopolizes practically all of the composition. The tail wagging the dog. Here is an example.

When I get on yonder hill,
There I'll sit and cry my fill,
All my tears will turn a mill,
Sing bob-a-lob-a-loosy larry!
Surely, surely, surely mat-a-rue,
Surely mat-a-rac-back, surely barbecue,

When I sought my Sally bob-a-linktum,
Bob-a-lob-a-loosy larry!

The revolution in Germany in 1848 brought a large number of
German immigrants to the United States. Many of these settlers wandered westward and settled at St. Louis. Some of them drifted on to the
Ozark hills. When the Civil War broke out, many of these foreigners
lined up with the North under General Franz Sigel. They were good
soldiers, due to their previous military training, but they were taught a
lesson, long to be remembered, at the Battle of Wilson's Creek. Their
"Dutch" war song, sung to the tune of "The Girl I Left Behind Me," is
a relic of these strenuous days. The words of this song were supplied by
the late A. M. Haswell, Ozark novelist.

I FIGHTS MIT SIGEL

Ven I come from dot Dutch country,
I vorks sometimes at bakin'.
Und den I keeps a beer saloon,
Und den I tries shoe makin'.
But now I was a soldier been,
To safe dot Yankee eagle;
Und so I gits mine soldier clothes,
Und go and fight mit Sigel.

Yah, dot been true,
I speak mit you,
To go and fight mit Sigel.

Dose Dutchermans of Siegel's band,
At fighting haf no rival,
Und effer time der meets der foe,
Dey shosh 'eem like der devil.
Und so I vas er soldier been,
To safe dot Yankee eagle,

Und gits me ein big rifle gun
Und go and fight mit Sigel.

Chorus (repeated)

Old Ben and Price at Vilson Creek,
Fights mit us like creation,
Und ve falls back to get recruits,
To safe dot Yankee nation.
Und if de vorst comes to de vorst,
To safe dot Yankee eagle,
I puts britch-loons upon mine frau
To go und fight mit Sigel.

Chorus (repeated)

The most popular fiddle tunes of the Ozarks are folk music without made-to-order markings. Some of them have historical or legendary
origins, like "The Eighth of January" which, it is said, was composed
to celebrate the victory of Andrew Jackson at New Orleans, January 8,
1815. But the majority of rollicking melodies one hears at the country
dance or musical have been handed down from generation to generation
and are real folklore. Most of the tunes played by ear in the Ozarks are
in the following list:

"Arkansaw Traveler," "Buffalo Girls," "Black-Eyed Susie," "Cacklin'
Hen," "Devil's Dream," "Eighth of January," "Fisher's Hornpipe," "Gal
I Left Behind Me," "Gray Eagle," "Hell Among the Yearlin's," "Irish
Washerwoman," "Limpin' Sally Waters," "Leather Britches," "Midnight
Breakdown," "Money Musk," "Ocean Wave," "Old Jim Lane," "Pick
the Devil's Eye Out," "Pop Goes the Weasel," "Rattlesnake Shake,"
"Sally Goodin," "Soldier's Joy," "Sixteen Days in Georgia," "Sourwood
Mountain," "Sugar in the Coffee," "Turkey in the Straw," "Wagoner,"
and "Woolsey Creek."

One of the strangest musical instruments in the Ozark hills is the "jawbone of an ass." Kermit Shelby of Reeds Spring, Missouri, explained to me how his neighbor, Albert Smith, plays this unusual instrument. He holds the jawbone on his left knee with his left hand, small end up, the teeth turned outward. In his right hand he holds a plain old barlow knife, blades closed so that either end knocks against the jawbone from underneath. He beats a rhythmic double-time tattoo. Shelby says that it sounds something like the Cuban rumba players shaking their dried-seed gourds. It also resembles the music of the bone knockers, only more violent. To add variety the player gives the smooth side of the jawbone a vigorous slap-slap in the manner of the swing boys who slap bull fiddles. This makes the loose teeth vibrate in an unearthly fashion like skeletons jumping up and down. Albert Smith certainly has got rhythm.

CHAPTER X

Things Eternal

. . . .

Death and Burial

Nate Delmar loped his gray mare around the bend toward Woodville, carrying a six-foot coffin stick in his hand. He stopped long enough at my camp on the Devil's Eyebrow to say howdy, and to tell me a neighbor had died the night before and that he was riding to Mart Hull's place to have a coffin made. The light hickory stick, cut a few inches longer than the dead man's body, would give Mart the correct measurement. This veteran woodcarver would build a durable pine coffin, lined in white and covered with black sateen cloth. If all went well, Nate's neighbor would be buried in the Antioch graveyard in true traditional form before sundown that day.

The conversation with Nate, and the sight of the ominous stick he carried, started my investigation of Ozark death and burial customs. An old schoolteacher by the name of John Higgins lived near my camp and I questioned him. He had lived his life in the James–White River country and knew the lore of his people.

"Here in the backhills," began the teacher, speaking slowly between puffs from his clay pipe, "we are superstitious enough to highly respect our dead. We may go unwashed while living, but we can't escape a good scrubbing when they lay us out. A grave never remains open overnight and a body is always laid with its feet to the east that it may rise facing the sun on Resurrection morning. A rain on the day of a burying is a good omen and we respect our dead by remaining on the ground until the last clod of dirt is in the grave. We give funeral processions the right of way on the road and toll bridges and ferries don't charge any fees. As a youth I was taught never to count the wagons in a funeral procession nor to meet one on the road if there was any possible way to avoid it. A coffin is always made about six inches longer than the remains to allow for stretching. Many people in the hills believe a corpse will stretch and become too long for the coffin if burial is delayed."

I interrupted with a question. "Do all the natives stick to the old traditions concerning death and burial?"

"Yes and no. There is a set way of doing things at the time of death and no respectable citizen would think of doing differently. Only now and then do you find a man who has no regard for tradition. Old Zeke Walters was such a man. Zeke was thought to be possessed of a devil, and it surely did shock the neighbors when he buried his wife, Sally, the way he did. The old man didn't believe in funeralizing and when Sally died he didn't even call a preacher. It wasn't that they were scarce in the country either. You could shake a bush on almost any ridge and two or three preachers would drop out. But Zeke didn't have anything to do with any of them. He was so wicked he wouldn't ask one of them to ride if he passed him in the road.

"Of course, Zeke followed certain rules for his own protection. Just as soon as Sally breathed her last, he stopped the clock and covered up the looking glass with a white cloth. He knew right well that if the clock should stop of itself while the corpse was in the house, one of the family would die within a year. Zeke seldom used the glass at any time, but he might forget himself and look in, you know, and that meant death. Zeke Walters was as mossbacked a hillbilly as ever swung a broadax, but too smart to take chances on a thing like that. Neighbors went in, of course, to lay out and set up with the corpse, but the old man seemed unconcerned about the whole affair. Of course, he had Mart Hull make a coffin, but whether or not he ever paid for the work, I don't know.

"Sally died early one morning and the next afternoon we loaded the corpse into Zeke's wagon and, with a neighbor and myself sitting in the back end, drove to the old Antioch burying ground. Three or four men had gone ahead to dig the grave in a patch of weeds in the corner of the cemetery.

"When we pulled up alongside, Zeke didn't even get out of the wagon. He left it up to me and the other neighbors who were there to lower the coffin into the grave. We did it as best we could with an old pair of lines I had thrown into the wagon. It surely didn't seem right to do a burying like that with no parson and no mourners. Even the children had been left at home.

"The coffin lowered, we began to shovel dirt. It didn't quite fill the grave and Zeke suggested that we throw in a few old rails to fill it up. When we had done this, he drawled in his unconcerned way, 'Wal, boys, that's good enough,' and drove on to town.

"Zeke had boasted that when Sally died he would be married again 'fore th' wagon tracks war out'n th' yard.' He was a man of his word in this instance for, before the next full moon winked over Eagle Rock bluff, he had married a woman of the Posey neighborhood and brought her home to stepmother his eight or nine tousle-headed youngsters."

When I first came to the Ozark Country, undertakers were almost unknown in the backhill sections. When a person died, neighbors gathered in and did the work now taken care of by the professional funeral directors. Two chairs were set facing each other and rough boards, long enough to accommodate the body of the deceased, placed upon them. A sheet was placed over the boards and a pillow laid at one end. Then the corpse was laid on the boards with the head carefully placed on the pillow. A cloth was tied around over the top of the head so that the mouth would be closed when rigor mortis set in. The eyes were closed with coins, usually twenty-five-cent pieces for adults, placed on them to hold down the lids until they were set.

Sometimes a cloth was saturated with soda and placed over the face to bleach the skin and keep it from turning. The body was washed thoroughly and dressed for burial. There was no embalming, and burial followed as soon as possible.

The majority of hillsmen now hold membership in burial associations and are served by professional undertakers. The funeral service may be held at the home or in the church, but the general custom is to have the last rites at the cemetery. When the procession arrives at the cemetery, the casket is opened and friends and relatives are invited to view the remains. A song is sung and the casket is lowered into the grave. Bible verses are read, a short talk is made, and then the officiating minister, taking some rose petals or dirt in his hand, says: "We therefore commend his soul to God and commit his body to the ground: earth to earth [here the rose petals or dirt is dropped into the grave], dust to dust, looking for the general resurrection in the last day, and life in the world to come." That concludes the ceremony, but it is customary for the friends and relatives of the deceased to remain until the grave is filled with dirt and banked with flowers by sympathetic neighbors.

John Higgins was emphatic in defense of the customs and traditions of his people. He was "to the manor born" and might have been a famous educator, but he preferred the simple life in the hills.

"My heart goes out to the common man," he said. "Call him the dung of the social strata, if you wish, harpoon him with criticism, rob him of his solitude, but leave him free to worship his God and bury his dead as his own conscience and traditions dictate."[1]

The Church at Hog Scald

If you like an old dirt road that winds through the hills like a misty dream in a world of make-believe, turn off Arkansas State Highway 23 a few miles south of Eureka Springs and head toward Hog Scald. No signs mark the way and traffic is noted for its absence. The erosion of time has stamped out the ruts and hoofprints of other years, but the spirit of the old trail remains. It is a byway to an undiscovered country, as far as tourists are concerned, but for riches of tradition and excellence of scenic beauty, it cannot be surpassed in the Ozark highlands. It is a land of clear gushing springs, laughing brooks, and tumbling waterfalls—water everywhere, spilling over rocky ledges and twisting through granite-lined canyons. It is a land of massive oak, stately pine, and verdant cedar, of purple grapes that cling to broad-leafed vines and red berries that tinge the cheeks of the hills with crimson blushes. It seems a land of divine favor and it is indeed fitting that the early pioneers of the thirties and forties found here, in a temple not made with hands, an ideal place to worship their God. Under a giant ledge overlooking Hog Scald Creek they held religious services for more than three-quarters of a century.

The sturdy pioneers who trekked to these hills from Kentucky and Tennessee were the salt of the earth in character. Religion was the bulwark of their natures. The person who loiters for a season in their Promised Land will realize, a little, the influence of such an environment upon a people whose feet were deeply set in the soil of mediocrity, so far as learning was concerned, but who saw divine imprints in every work of nature.

The spacious rock shelter below Auger Falls on Hog Scald Creek attracted these settlers as a suitable place for a church. A natural auditorium stood on one side of the stream with a rock pulpit for the preacher. In a convenient shelter opposite were choir stalls for the singers. Between audience and preacher was an immersion pool where the rites of baptism could be administered without leaving the sanctuary. The drone of falling water from Auger Falls was just loud enough to be the pipe organ divine, never out of tune, always doing its part to make the service effective. When the preacher prayed, these musical waters seemed to echo: "Ho, everyone that thirsteth, come ye to the waters, and he that hath no money, come buy and eat—without money and without price."

Hog Scald soon became an active community center. It was the meeting place of settlers for such activities as butchering hogs, canning wild fruits, and making sorghum molasses. The idea originated during the Civil War when the entire valley was a Confederate camp. The inviting springs and cozy shelters made it an ideal campsite. The shut-ins at the elbow of the falls offered opportunity to hem in herds of wild hogs and kill them in a cove convenient to the butchering grounds.

The creek secured its name from the practice of the soldiers in scalding the wild hogs in the kettle-like holes of the rocky creek bed. The water was diverted from its regular course into these holes which are four or five feet deep and average six feet in width. The method of heating the water to the scalding point was to drop hot stones into the pits. The hogs were then immersed in the hot water until their hides were soaked sufficiently for the removal of the hair with knives.

When the war ended, the hillsmen of the community continued this practice and enlarged upon it. Families would drive many miles through the hills to camp at Hog Scald, butchering and canning, and enjoying a few days of social contact. On Sunday they held religious services. The young folks might play party games on the rocks Saturday night, but the fun ceased at midnight. Sunday was for the good things of the soul.

Every student of human behavior knows the truth of the adage— "the mills of the gods grind slowly, but they grind exceeding small." The customs of the folks of this particular community have borne fruit in a sober, righteous, contented people. I have been told that almost every home in the community has its altar of prayer.

CHAPTER XI

Primitive Panaceas

. . . .

The "Yarb" Doctor

Mart Hull's professional life was spiked with paradox. This Woodville
citizen was not only the best coffin maker in the neighborhood, but a
yarb doctor of great repute. He was sincere with his panaceas and made
every possible effort to relieve suffering and save life, but he recognized
the inevitable and prepared for it. He was equally skilled in making bitters from the herbs of the field and in building coffins from the pine
or walnut of the forest. Live or die, it was profit for Mart Hull. All the
community paid tribute.

Doc Hull had an indiscriminate clientele within a radius of five miles
of his backwoods home. It was a widely recognized fact that he possessed
an unusual knowledge of herbs and knew the secret alchemy for compounding them into healing remedies. I spent much time with him while
at Woodville, observing him at work both in field and laboratory, and
making calls with him to witness the effects of his herbal compounds on
sick folks. These observations increased both my knowledge and appre-
ciation of Ozarkian plant lore. He showed me how to season meat with
the seed of the wild peppergrass, and explained the use of this herb as
an ingredient of the medicines he recommended for stomach complaints
and blood disorders.

One day the old doctor showed me the wizardry of a persimmon seed. Taking a seed from the fruit, he cut the end of it off squarely and split it carefully. In the heart of the seed was the perfect image of a spoon. This formation in the persimmon seed, according to Hull, is a sign that the following crop year will be a good one. When the image of a knife and fork appear in the seed, a crop failure is ahead.

The persimmon is not only a fattening food for the opossum but a delicacy for humans, if it is permitted to dry on the tree. I discovered that the flavor improves with freezing.

The folklore of the Ozarks has been greatly enriched by the herb specialists who, before the dawning of modern science, did the best they could to relieve physical suffering through the use of plant products found in nature's great laboratory. A knowledge of many of these early panaceas has been lost in the shuffle of readjustment in recent years. We may class the yarb doctor as a survival of primitive society or a relic of our own racial childhood, but his work is not to be discredited even in the light of scientific contrast.

As a rule, hillsmen are reliable authorities on plant lore. They know the habits of plants and how to identify them. They are schooled in their medicinal properties and know the legendary connections that have been handed down for generations. To the superstitious individual, herbs possess the power to ward off evil as well as heal disease. Naturally it is assumed that the practice of using certain plants to guard against demoniac influences originated in the folk-mind at a time when magic and science were badly mixed. It is the "old science," as one hillsman told me.

The old-time doctors did not rely entirely upon roots and herbs for their remedies. Most of them had attended medical school and knew how to use quinine, turpentine, calomel, and castor oil. A few just "took up doctoring" because they had talent in that direction and possessed a fair knowledge of herbs and their healing properties. These men and women did not practice medicine as it is practiced today by legalized physicians, and surgery was practically unknown. Bleeding was about the only surgical operation performed by the old-timer in the backhills.

Doc Hull was an institution at Woodville and his practice reached beyond the boundaries of his neighborhood. He did not magically remove warts as the witch doctors do by spitting on a stone and throwing it over the left shoulder, or by placing the blood of the wart in a white bean and burying it. He did not use buzzard oil as an application for cancer. But he did make certain recommendations when folks visited him, and he had a few herbal compounds ready for emergencies. He had discovered that a tea made from parsley roots was excellent for dropsy and that the seeds could be used to kill head lice. He knew that wintergreen tea was a heart stimulant if taken in small doses but that larger doses had the opposite effect and caused vomiting. Wild plum bark was used to relieve the distress of asthma and bull nettle root for skin diseases. Slippery elm was found valuable in stomach complaints and was used externally as a poultice for inflammations and boils. Tonsillitis was relieved by gargling a tea brewed from white oak bark, and common colds were treated with hoarhound. Hull's favorite liver remedies were mayapple and dandelion root. He believed horsemint good for rheumatism and neuralgia. Various other mints were used in compounding his extracts. In some cases he recommended the rubbing of the inflamed or sore parts of the body with crushed mint leaves. In others he advised that a tea be made and taken internally. The mint was also a popular ingredient in his "smelling" medicines.

Mart liked to tell of his experiences in relieving the physical ills of mankind. One of his favorite stories was that of the Till Berry family who lived at the forks of Big and Little Clabber Creeks. Till's family consisted of himself, his wife, and two children. At the time of the incident that made the story, one of the children was a boy four years old, the other a nursing baby girl of three or four months. The baby was ill and Doc Hull was consulted. He gave the mother some of his pills to take as indirect treatment for the babe. The cure was rapid and it made a deep impression on the parents. A few months later the four-year-old boy became ill. The supply of pills had not been exhausted, and it was decided to try them again. On this occasion, however, the father took the pills for the boy. Strange as it may seem, a prompt cure was effected.

Household remedies are still quite common in the Ozarks. A boy's stone bruise is treated with a generous slab of fat meat, applied to the bruised portion. Boils or "risin's" are thought to be caused by bad blood and such foods as raisins and onions are recommended. Itch is a backhill scourge which is no respecter of persons. The remedy is sulphur and molasses taken internally with external applications of a salve made from sulphur and hog lard. Devil's shoestring may be used to restore women to health after childbirth. This plant is rare in the Ozarks and is not often used.

Doc Hull believed in his herbs but he discounted magic and the traditional beliefs that health is influenced by changes of the moon and signs of the zodiac. Neither did he advise such practices as the wearing of a bag of asafetida on a string around the neck to keep germs away, or the use of stump water for skin diseases. So far as possible, he relied upon herbs and tried to find a scientific basis for his remedies. He had just one discrepancy in his behavior. Regardless of his wisdom and experience, he carried a buckeye in his pocket to prevent rheumatism.

Home Remedies

A Golden Fleece! A Holy Grail! Utopia! A Pot of Gold at the Foot of a Rainbow! These dreams are the lure of mankind and the quest is eternal. Men endure desert heat, Arctic cold, cloistered privations, and sometimes they turn worlds upside down to titillate their egos or satisfy their desires. Likewise, the search for health is conducted by rich man, poor man, beggar man, thief. The path may be broad or narrow but all are on the go and the direction is the same. Even a devil needs steady nerves and a good liver to get satisfaction from his deviltry.

The road of good health, traveled by pioneer peoples, was a long, dark lane with many pitfalls. Nature was the great laboratory but there was no scientific key to unlock her abundant stores. Because of this, folkways are sometimes dark ways, and the school of experience is a dear school in which to learn the secrets of successful living. Curious panaceas, many of them with supernatural attributes, were accepted by the people as necessary to their welfare. If tradition said squirt sow's milk in the eyes to see the wind, they did so even though common sense told them better. In matters of health they proved that expediency sometimes outweighs prudence.

Advocates of the old remedies still exist in the Ozarks, but most of them have folded their tents and stacked their guns and accepted the new order which science has imposed upon them. But enough of the old is left to trouble the waters of the new. A neighboring woman has a large goiter which causes her much discomfort, but she wears a small sack of salt tied by a string around her neck in preference to having an operation. Another woman relates that she once had that strange disease called shingles and that all remedies failed to give her relief until she used the warm blood of a black hen. She explained the treatment in this way:

> They laid me on a bunch of newspapers spread out to catch the surplus blood. Then they chopped off the hen's head and let the blood run on the eruption. It was from the small of my back and down one leg to a little below the knee—very painful, swollen, and a solid eruption all around my leg. They spread the warm blood to cover it all.
>
> That was one night at bedtime. I slept restfully and awoke the next morning to find the soreness, swelling, and inflammation all gone. My leg peeled off and came clean. There were faint spots for a while, but I never suffered any after the hot blood was applied.

Modern science has outflanked the old folk cures to such an extent that the younger people know little about them. But the older folks cling to them with leech-like tenacity. Profuse bleeding is stopped by charm, warts are removed by forms of magic, thrash is cured by a person who was a posthumous child breathing into the mouth of the afflicted child.[1] There are men expert in "taking out fire" from burns and scalds and women who know how to make "skillet bark tea" for "blue babies." But many of the cruder remedies have disappeared along with the belief in witchcraft and the practice of the midwife.

In grandmother's day a mouse's head tied around the baby's neck prevented certain ills. A mole's skin was placed against a woman's breast to prevent swelling. A remedy for sore mouth was to drink water out of a shoe. A sure cure for frostbite was to kill a young rabbit, cut it open, and while it was still warm thrust the frostbitten member into the body of the rabbit, letting it become thoroughly bathed in the warm blood. A bad cut was doctored with soot from a chimney mixed with a little sugar.

One of the strangest Ozark remedies I have found is a treatment for asthma. I first learned of it through May Kennedy McCord's "Hillbilly Heartbeats." Here it is:

"Kill a steer and set the patient's feet in the hot guts, and let them remain there until the entrails cool. Be sure to remove the pouch or maw as the acid from it will pull out the toenails."

Another curious panacea is the "silk cure" for the chills in children. First, find out the age of the child and the number of chills it has had. Go away by yourself and tie a knot in the string for every chill. Tie them one inch apart. Then bury the string under the eaves of the barn or stable. This works only on children over one year and the person handling the string must not be a relative of the child. A somewhat similar remedy is the "yarn cure." Knots are tied in a yarn string, a knot for each chill. This cure is used for people of all ages.

One of the most interesting faith cures I have observed is that of stopping blood. There are a few people in almost every community who claim to have this power. It is not necessary to see the person who is losing the blood, but the full name and the place of wound must be known. With this information, the individual who possesses the power to stop the bleeding calls the person's name and the name of the wound and then repeats a certain verse from the sixteenth chapter of Ezekiel. He walks toward the east while repeating the lines. Thousands of people in the hill country have faith in this charm and it is used repeatedly for both man and animal. A man who has the power may tell the secret to three women; a woman may tell three men. Some think they will lose the power if they tell the secret to the third person.

The charm formula is used in taking out fire from a burn. Hazel

Dagley Heavin of Rolla, Missouri, tells me of her experience with this charm.

> My father possessed the power to take out fire. When I was a child, I always ran to him with my burned fingers and he made the pain leave. He told me the mystic words just before he died and said an old lady had taught them to him. She told him that it could be passed to but one person and that one must be of the opposite sex.
>
> The other day I was dyeing some material and in removing it from the kettle, some of the boiling dye splashed into my hair, burning the scalp. I repeated the words my father had taught me and the burning stopped. Whether I was too busy even to feel the burn, I don't know; anyway the pain stopped immediately when I spoke the words. But I had a sore spot on my head for several days as a result of the accident.

There is an age-old belief that toads cause warts. Science has discovered that the toad secretes a substance through its skin that irritates the mucous linings of the human body but does not affect the outer skin. If this secretion causes warts, the fact remains unknown to science. Probably the fact that the toad has a warty appearance gave rise to the belief that to touch it would cause warts on the hands. It is true that the appearance and disappearance of warts on the human body remain a mystery even to science. Some authorities believe that this tendency is hereditary, others hold to the theory that warts are caused by irritation and that the growth is nature's attempt to heal the wound.

The removal of warts by charms is even more mysterious than their sudden appearance. I have collected more than a score of methods used in the Ozarks to remove these growths. Here are a few of the outstanding ones:

Spit on a stone, stir the saliva with the finger and repeat these words: "What I see decreases." The stone is tossed aside and the wart disappears.

Split an Irish potato and rub the wart with it. Bury the potato at the time of the moon's decrease and when the potato rots the wart will go.

Pick the warts with a needle until they bleed, then rub a thin piece of wood over them, wiping them free of the blood. Close the eyes and throw the wood away. To watch it fall spoils the effect of the charm.

Pierce each wart enough to make it bleed. Rub a grain of corn in the blood and feed it to a goose. The growth will disappear.

Go to a home where there is an orchard and borrow or steal a knife of any kind from the house. Go to a fruit tree and cut as many notches as you have warts. Go away and forget the incident and the warts will soon leave.

Take three grains of corn and go to a place where the road forks into three branches. Put a grain of corn in each road and cover with rocks. The warts will leave you and go to the persons knocking the rocks off the grains.

Other charm methods of wart removal included such stunts as pricking the wart with a thorn and then throwing the thorn over the left shoulder; catching a katydid and letting it start eating on the growth; stealing a dishrag, wiping the warts with it, and hiding the rag under the doorstep; cutting as many notches in a green stick as you have warts, and burying the stick; rubbing the warts with a piece of dry bone and putting the bone back where you found it without telling anyone; or, should any of these methods fail, you may sell the warts to a neighbor at a penny each.

The Ozarkian book of experience provides cures for almost every ailment that flesh is heir to. These remedies are not concoctions of the imagination, but gleaned from old-timers who actually tried them. They are a valuable part of our folklore.

A primitive remedy for nosebleed is to drop as many drops of blood into a bottle as you are years old. Cork the bottle tightly and hang in the chimney. It was believed that the nose would not bleed so long as the bottle remained there. A more modern treatment is that of putting a plug of salt pork in the nose.

A crude treatment for toothache, reported by a ninety-year-old woman who once tried it in her youth, is to go to the woods or fields and find the jawbone of a horse. Get down on your knees and pick up the bone with your teeth, then walk backward, keeping your hands behind you. The number of steps you take before dropping the bone indicates the number of years that will elapse before the tooth aches again.

Another toothache remedy is to go to a tree which has been struck by lightning, get a splinter from it, and pick the offending tooth until you draw blood. Get a drop of this blood on the splinter and stick it in the ground under the eaves of the house and let it remain there. "That will kill the nerve in a tooth any time."

I have a recent report on an asthma cure that tops them all. The disease was treated by tying a live frog to the afflicted man's throat and leaving it there until it died. This may have been an isolated case as I have never found it among the traditional cures of the Ozarks. It is reported that the frog "completely absorbed the disease."

The ringworm cure is to go to a teakettle of boiling water, rub your thumb in a circle the size of the ringworm on the inside of the lid, and then around the ringworm. Do the same with the forefinger, then with the thumb again. Do this with all the fingers on that hand, alternating each time with the thumb. When through, go away and do not look back at the teakettle.

To cure a sty on the eye, go to the forks of the road and say, "Sty, sty, leave my eye and catch the first one passing by." Another flaunted cure is to cut off the end of a black cat's tail and take a drop of the blood and put on the sty.

"Sheep nanny tea" was used in the old days to "break out" measles. A quantity of sheep droppings would be boiled in water, strained, sweetened with molasses, and drunk. One remedy to keep the mumps from "going down" was to take a red yarn string, saturate it in the manure of swine, and tie around the neck like a string of beads. A popular treatment for yellow jaundice was to dig some angleworms, fry them in their own grease, and give to the patient. Pokeroot was boiled in water and the solution applied externally for itch. The liquid burned like fire and the cure was probably worse than the ailment. Epilepsy was treated by feeding the patient colt's tongue.

Charm panaceas run the gamut from simple faith cures to strange practices that seem to hark back to the magic-saturated days of the ancient world. Several of them have characteristics in common which provide interesting speculation for the observer. Secrecy concerning the rites is important. Frequently there is a ban on kinship between patient and healer. There are definite rules for revealing the charm to others. There is a taboo against "looking back." One outstanding fact in connection with treatments which have psychical foundation is the denial of compensation. The healers do not accept pay for their services except in the form of voluntary donations.

There is some speculation as to the extent of this charm-cure practice in the Ozarks. It is my opinion that practically all the first settlers were familiar with these remedies, but only a small portion actually used them. Most of the people relied upon herbs for relief from suffering. Household remedies were gradually superseded by commercial products in the form of patent medicines. Country doctors, with saddlebags loaded with blue mass pills and other medical essentials, pushed back the wilderness horizon and established themselves at strategic points throughout the hill country. These practitioners have been a Gibraltar against the common enemies of superstition and disease.

CHAPTER XII

Wind and Smoke

. . . .

Snakes Alive!

Hite Lindsey's favorite byword was "snakes alive." He could give this expletive a lazy drawl that seemed to stretch it a full arm's length whenever his vague mind reached the point of actual surprise. It seemed to fit his emotional urge as a barlow fitted his hand. "Snakes alive, feller, you all can't mean that," he would say when a perfunctory remark penetrated the realm of his leisurely understanding. It was interesting to hear him tell a story punctuated with hillbilly candor and retarded quips of Elizabethan grace. He liked to brag about the prowess and ingenuity of his kinfolks and his tall tales concerning them were extravaganza without apology. He was a Bob Burns and Woodville was his Van Buren.

We had talked and whittled and swapped tobacco through the long summer afternoon and now that the day had dismissed the sun and the chickens were settling to roost in the old persimmon tree back of the smokehouse, I itched for a story. The purple shadows settling over the pinery indicated that it would soon be time to set our feet under the table and take our filling of cornpone, fatback, and grease gravy. Lindsey's bedtime always followed closely upon the heels of supper. I must capture a story now or wait another day.

"Hite," I began casually, "what was the strangest adventure your father ever had?"

The hillsman puffed his pipe thoughtfully for a few moments, closed his mammoth barlow, and carefully placed it in his pants pocket. A soft reminiscent light played in his eyes and I knew I had struck pay dirt. He knocked the ashes from his pipe and laid it on the windowsill. I took a fresh chew of tobacco, passed the plug, and waited. One needs to prime for a good story and I am willing to go a long ways for priming water. Storytellers are born, not made, and the machine age with all its sputter and smoke has not increased the birth rate of this rare species. And, too, it takes mellow moods and good tobacco to foster tall tales in the Ozarks.

"As I recollect," began Hite, "pap's strangest 'sperience happened right over thar in Greasy Holler. Musto' been nigh sixty year ago. He took his ax one day an' went up thar t' cut a morsel o' firewood. Th' trees an' bresh had been cleared off on each side o' th' valley up two or three hunderd feet. Th' banks wus slick as owl grease an' so steep that pap had a hard time gittin' up th' side t' whar they wus some tall trees. He got thar though an' picked out a big hick'ry that stuck up way 'bove th' other trees. Pap wus th' best chopper in th' hills an' bracin' hisself careful, he begin makin' chips fly like that thar Paul Bunyan feller what owned a blue ox. Three-four licks from pap's ax an' th' tree come smashin' down."

P-futt went a stream of tobacco juice at a knot in the pine tree in front of us. Hite adjusted his chaw and continued.

"Pap jumped back an' th' tree started rollin' down th' steep hill. Down it went, breakin' off all th' limbs and gainin' speed ever' second. When hit got t' th' bed o' th' valley, it didn't stop atall, but rolled right up th' other bank clean t' th' timberline. Then hit started back like a freight train comin' outa hell. Down it come into th' valley an' right up th' hill t' whar pap stood. Hit struck th' timber an' bounced like a bull calf on a stampede. Back down it went, faster 'an ever.

"Pap jist leaned on his choppin' ax an' watched th' thing roll. Down one side an' up t'other, then a big bounce an' down agin. All th' bark wus wore off by now an' pap said hit looked like a greased pig at a picnic. He watched it roll fer a good two hours an' then give up an' follered th' ridge home."

P-futt! P-flu-futt! I passed the plug and the storyteller took a fresh chew.

"Next day pap went back up th' ridge t' see what had happened t' th' hick'ry an', snakes alive, th' log wus still rollin'! Pap come back home 'thout no firewood.

"Right after that my ole man wus drafted into th' Civil War an' took his rifle gun an' went away. After 'bout a year he come back on one o' them thar furloughs. Th' fust thing he thought of when he got home wus that blamed log in Greasy Holler. Couldn't hardly wait t' git up thar.

"Wal, hit wus still a-rollin'. But it was jist 'bout petered out. Hit had wore down so much that pap picked it up an' brung it home an' used hit fer a ramrod durin' th' rest o' th' war."

"Snakes alive!" was all I could think to say as Hite concluded his dramatic story.

It seemed to me a fine coincidence that Hite Lindsey's favorite byword reflected his favorite hobby. Hite was an authority on snakes, if knowledge plus experience begets authority. He knew more about the reptilian family, *Ophidia*, than any other man in the hills. Of course, his knowledge was not scientific and his facts were badly mixed with fable. But to me he was an unspoiled paragon of the hills and his lore was excellent grist for my mill.

Hite told me many things about snakes and their habits. He explained that all snakes lay eggs but do not hatch them in the same manner. The harmless bull snake deposits her eggs in the sand and leaves them there for the sun to do the hatching. The rattlesnake, according to the old woodsman, lays eggs but immediately swallows them. These eggs are hatched in a special compartment of the snake's body and the young are discharged through the mouth. Lindsey said that a poisonous snake will sometimes swallow her young as a protective measure and disgorge them when the danger is over. He believed that snakes have power to charm birds and small animals, and even human beings. Naturally I took this lore with a few grains of salt, but that did not lessen my interest.

When I first entered the Ozarks I heard many stories about children being charmed by snakes. The technique of the serpent was always the same. It caught the eye of its subject and cast a charm which could not be broken until sundown. A Woodville woman claimed that she had been charmed in this manner when she was a child. Here is her story:

> I was out walking with my mother and ran ahead down a woodland trail. A large rattlesnake caught my eye and cast its spell. When my mother discovered me, I was sitting in the road entranced with the coiled serpent weaving its head back and forth in front of my face. My mother grabbed me away at the risk of being bitten by the poisonous reptile, but it did not strike. She carried me home and put me to bed and at sundown the spell broke. I suffered no ill effects from the ordeal but to this day I can sense the presence of a snake near me without seeing it.

A man of the community related an even more terrifying experience. When he was a lad of eight or nine years he wandered into the woods and sat down upon a log to rest. A large rattler cast a spell over him and coiled around his body. The father of the boy was out hunting and came upon his young son in this condition. The youth had a short stick in his hand which he was waving back and forth in methodical fashion. The snake was moving its head in front of the boy's face in cadence with the moving stick, but it made no attempt to strike. The father was a good marksman and his first thought was to shoot the reptile through the head. Then he realized that to do so might prove fatal to the boy. It would be impossible to break the spell if the snake were killed. The only alternative was to wait two hours until the sun went down. The latter method was decided upon and the long vigil began. When the sun finally dropped behind the horizon the snake released its coils and glided away. The spell broke immediately and the boy was none the worse for the experience.

It was reported one day that a hoop snake had been seen by a woman who was washing clothes on the riverbank. The reptile had rolled down the hillside, barely missing the wash pot, and disappeared in the current of the stream. I had never believed that such a snake existed, but Hite enlightened me with the following anecdote.

"When I wus a kid of a boy," said Hite, "hoop snakes wus right smart common in these parts. Why, in th' hot months of summer, 'specially in dog days, a feller would sometimes see two or three of 'em rollin' 'round in that thar holler. See that ol' snag t' th' right o' that pin oak? A feller named Pod Warner wus a-diggin' sprouts thar on th' side of th' hill one day when a hoop snake took its tail in its mouth an' started rollin' toward him. Pod saw hit comin' an' jist had time t' jump out'n th' way. Hit wus comin' hell-bent-fer-'lection, Pod said, an' he had t' jump quick as a ghost when a rooster crows. I guess th' snake had its eyes on Pod fer when it missed him, it hit slabdab into that thar tree. Hit rammed its pizen stinger into it, fer th' leaves begin t' fall off an' in two-three months th' tree wus dead.

"At another time," continued Hite, "Aunt Steller Bonham wus pickin' blackberries on a bluff above Clabber Crick. She heerd a noise in th' bresh above her, an' lookin' up saw a hoop snake rollin' straight fer her. Snakes alive, she wus scairt! Hit wus as big 'round as yer arm an' made a loop th' size of a bar'l hoop. She didn't have time t' git out'n th' way, but throwed up th' bucket she had blackberries in t' keep th' thing frum hittin' her square in th' face. When she swung th' bucket, th' snake dodged an' jist ripped her dress with th' pint of hits tail. Th' ol' woman warshed her dress th' next day an' th' pizen in hit turned three tubs o' warsh water plumb green. Hoop snakes is powerful pizen."

A friend of mine who delves in science rates hoop snake lore as imaginative myth. I repeat his theory to balance the debate of folklore vs. science.

> Possibly the habit of certain snakes, like the blacksnake, of gliding at a relatively high speed over the tops of bushes gives the casual observer the idea that the reptile has formed a huge loop and is rapidly covering the ground in this fashion.
>
> The "tail end" of the myth probably arose from the fact that certain snakes, chiefly the horn snake, uses the sharply pointed and horny-tipped tail with which to explore and feel, thus giving rise to the belief that the snake has stinging properties. There is, however, no sting in the tail of such a snake. In fact, this

modified tail is not even hollow, but is a solid pointed scale that covers the tip of the tail, within which there is no poison apparatus at all.

Some years after leaving Woodville, I saw a notice in a New York paper which stated that a certain zoo in the East would pay $1,000 for a live hoop snake. I reported this offer in my column in the *Tulsa Tribune*. Two letters of inquiry reached me, both from eastern Oklahoma. One man wrote that he had captured a hoop snake and wanted to know what to feed it while contacting the zoo and getting the reward. I outlined a diet for the captive reptile and asked for more information, but I never received a reply.

Signs and Superstitions

The emotions of mankind provide interesting subjects for investigation and speculation. I like to think of the phenomenon we call desire as smoke from the fire of feeling, rising in fantastic circles, clouding the sky of the mind with strange manifestations. In the long, long ago before primitive man could reason, feeling and action were probably twins seldom parted. That was the day of picture writing on the inner walls of consciousness. Desire was the motive force of all action. When Caveman Kip saw the luring curves of beautiful Sadie as she lounged in front of her stony domicile, a picture registered on the film of his fertile imagination. All through the night it haunted his erotic dreams. With no rational restraint to check him, he quickly "made up his mind." Early morning found him heading for Sadie's abode, intent upon dragging her to his lair by the hair of the head, if necessary. But during the night she had been kidnapped by neighbor Rip and carried into the mountains.

Kip's flaming picture settled into an ugly fantasy. With heart of lead he returned to his cave to brood over his loss. But in a few days, the smoke cleared, for the simple mind soon forgets, and the film accepted a substitute picture. Of course, each vision was registered in the memory section of the caveman's mind. Gradually he began associating these impressions and it gave birth to reason. This enabled him to see through the smoke more clearly and to control his fiery impulses somewhat. But in the beginning he was a slave to his desires, and his emotions ran rampant. His conduct depended entirely upon the pictures created within him.

The superstitions of mankind were conceived in the womb of the mind when the smoke was thick in human consciousness. Folks had to have a way to explain natural phenomena which they did not understand. Real proof was impossible, so they evolved supernatural theories to explain cause and effect to their own satisfaction. Faith was sometimes based upon insufficient evidence and the result was belief in charms, omens, magic, apparitions, witchcraft, and the whole category of superstition. These strange beliefs became a part of the folkways of mankind and they have survived to the twentieth century. They are not confined to the isolated and the illiterate for we are all still primitives, more or less, painting pictures on the walls. Perhaps superstition is the protective shell of the egg from which reason is hatched.

Superstition defies geographical boundaries. It is not hedged in the backhills nor centered in urban populations. Wherever there are ladders to walk under, mirrors to break, or black cats to fear, superstition rules reaction. It is important to keep this in mind when dealing with ways of thinking in any particular region. Not all irrational belief is found in the backhills. A white Christmas means a lean graveyard in Chicago as well as in Arkansas.

The pattern of life in the Ozarks is full of the lore of signs and superstitions. These peculiar twists of belief and practice color the personality and enliven behavior. I have lived with folks who never button a new garment before it is worn, never cut a child's hair until it is a year old, never—in the light of the moon—plant crops that grow underground, never do anything unless the sign is right. Corn is planted when the first dove "hollers" in the spring. A knife is never given to a friend as a gift. It might sever the friendship. The housewife does not sing before breakfast for that means she will weep before nightfall. A visitor is careful to leave his neighbor's house by the same door through which he entered. To do otherwise might invoke a quarrel. Thunderclaps in February mean frosts in May. A corpse is never left alone overnight. A woman carries her young baby about the house so that it will be like her. A tree that has been struck by lightning is never used for firewood. A thimbleful of water is carried around the house with the baby so that the infant will not "slobber and spit" while cutting its first set of teeth. A birthmark will disappear if the child's hand is rubbed on the face of the first corpse it sees, and then on the birthmark. Should a toad be killed, accidentally or otherwise, and the cows give bloody milk in retaliation for the crime, there is just one thing to do. Get seven pebbles and throw them over your left shoulder into an open well at sundown. The milk will be all right after that.

"If" is the hinge of the door which opens to many superstitions in the backhills. If a woman's second toe is longer than her large one, she will rule her husband. If a girl awakes on three consecutive mornings with a feather in her hair, it is a sign she will marry a cripple. If the thumb knuckle itches, a visitor may be expected. If a housewife lets a dishrag fall, someone is coming who is dirtier than she. If a person is ill with fever, feathers plucked from a black hen and burned in a pan beneath the bed will drive away the disease. If a girl's shoe comes untied or her stocking falls down, she knows that her lover is thinking of her. If the baby's eyes are sore, the mother's milk is the best possible wash for them. If a pregnant woman has a craving for a certain kind of food, it should be given her, because denial of it may cause the child to be "marked." If a child is born with a veil, the membrane should be carefully dried and given to its owner when maturity is reached. If you should have a part of the body amputated, be sure that it is straightened out and properly buried. Carelessness may cause misery that medicine cannot reach. If—but we must close this door for visits in other realms of the supernatural.

Fear of the abnormal is the base of most superstitions. If a dog howled at night, it was taken as a sign of death by the primitive mind. The pioneer host never stood in the door and watched his guests depart. To do so meant that he would never see them again. In the old days mourners never left the cemetery until the last clod of dirt was in the grave. To do so was not only a breach of respect, but it was likely to bring calamity to the relatives of the deceased. Hundreds of such beliefs continue to guard the folks of the backhills. Some of them have specific penalties for disobedience, others portend good or bad luck of a more general nature. A general atmosphere of bad luck surrounds those who thoughtlessly remove rings from their friends' fingers, close gates which they find open, or move cats and brooms. No specific calamity may follow, but general misfortune is certain to prevail.

Many people in the Ozarks, as elsewhere, believe in warnings through dreams. To dream of muddy water means trouble, but of an indefinite nature. A dream of snakes means that the dreamer has made enemies as dangerous as the reptile he dreams of. A dream told before breakfast, or one dreamed on Friday night and told on Saturday, is sure to come true. There is a widespread belief that people at the point of death are endowed with unusual gifts such as foretelling the future of friends and relatives, or glimpsing the land of no return which they are about to enter. The curse of a dying man is greatly feared, but his blessing is eagerly received.

A taboo exists in the hills against transplanting cedars. This beautiful tree is clothed with an old superstition which causes the Ozarker to shudder when he observes summer residents beautifying their homes with it. In the back of his mind is an indelible picture of the Grim Reaper. It is his belief that when the tree reaches a height sufficient to cast a shadow long enough to cover the grave of the person who transplanted it, that person will die. A Missouri woman tells me that she can remember when transplanting a cedar in some person's yard caused great confusion. The length of time it would require for it to grow high enough to cast a shadow sufficient to cover a spot as large as a grave would be computed, and some old person would be requested to set the cedar in the hole. For an aged person the risk was minimized. But sometimes this person would persist in living far beyond his normal allotment and this caused many hours of uneasiness. Some thought that cutting down the tree would appease the Grim Reaper. Sometimes an old-timer tried to outwit the supernatural by putting a flat rock in the hole before the tree was set. "That thar keeps a person frum dyin' as soon as th' tree gits big enough t' shade his grave, or hit 'most always does."

Signs of spring are legion in the Ozarks. Some hillsmen think that the arrival of the turkey buzzard in the hill country is the best sign that crop time is near at hand. Others hold to the frog theory. It is believed that frogs come from hibernation early enough to be frozen and retarded twice before their third and permanent appearance. But with most hillfolks, Groundhog Day provides the most reliable sign of spring. According to this theory, the groundhog comes from its den on February 2 (some say February 14). If it is cloudy on this ominous day, to the extent that the little animal cannot see its shadow, the groundhog stays out and spring is near. But if the sun shines, the shy creature takes fright at its shadow, returns to its den, and winter continues for a period of six weeks.

Superstitions die hard in the backhills. To erase the supernatural from the commonplace things of life is to eradicate fear and that is about as futile as attempting to put a muzzle on a milk snake. You must have something to tie it to.

As far as I am concerned, these peculiar beliefs need no apology. If a man wishes to look at the new moon with silver in his pocket or carry the left hind foot of a rabbit (killed at midnight in a graveyard) and interpret them as signs or charms of good luck, it is undeniably his right to do so. Perhaps few of these practices are trustworthy, but I prefer to allow the horse breeder to continue the traditional practice of holding a colored cloth in front of the mare at breeding time in order to color the colt to suit his fancy even if he gets a sorrel when he expects a bay. The colts of science and politics are not always colored as men would have them. I never question my neighbor's sincerity if he ties a yarn string around a persimmon tree to cure the chills or closes his windows at night because "night air is poisonous." If he prefers to sit in the cold rather than put certain kinds of wood on the fire, it is satisfactory with me, providing I am not required to sit with him.

CHAPTER XIII

Stormy Roads

. . . .

Seat of Justice

Court week in a sleepy little backhill town. For six days all is hustle and bustle in the country metropolis. We halt our checker game at the barber shop to investigate the stir. Lawyers stepping lively, briefcases in hand; sheriff and deputies on the alert; cafés taking on new help; hotel lobbies (both of them) filled with pungent cigar smoke; filling station attendants jumping like Mexican beans as cars squeak to a stop for service; plaintiffs, defendants, witnesses, jurymen—all adjusting themselves to the program of the week; the judge, with dignity, leaving the hotel for the courtroom; the editor of the county paper conditioning the Washington handpress to give the four pages of the weekly *Herald* a legal countenance; merchants dusting shelves, tossing attractive wares into show windows, and spreading reams of flypaper. The old county seat town takes on a new complexion.

The courtroom is a stage upon which the dramas of the hills are acted. With the criminal docket a heavy one, folks have driven long distances to see the emotional fireworks. They have come in buggies and wagons, on horseback and in automobiles bringing lunches, babies, and dogs with them. The dispensing of justice, or injustice, is a matter of great concern to hillsmen. Some have relatives involved, others have been called as witnesses or jurymen, many come through curiosity, or to meet friends, swap horses, and enjoy themselves in general.

The hillsman who made liquor to keep the wolf from the door, parades his emotions, unreservedly, in every word he speaks. He might as well plead guilty and have it over. The hardened Ben Stutts, who killed a neighbor's hog and sold the meat, accepts his two-year sentence stoically. Folkways are sometimes darkened with malicious conduct and it is the duty of the prosecuting attorney to delve into the darkness and bring forth the evidence. The defense lawyers, primed for action, with plenty of tobacco to loosen the vocal cords, battle for their clients, guilty or not guilty.

Twelve hillsmen, good and true men, sitting on a jury, compose a still convoy of justice. Judges in the hills become expert psychologists, for nowhere on earth is mother wit put to better advantage to outwit the law. To the evildoer, prosecution is a thorn in the flesh of his freedom and he resents it.

I mingle with hillfolks on the courthouse lawn and the public square, shaking hands with an old Civil War veteran from the Posey neighborhood, stopping to chat with Tobe Mullins from Woodville, talking politics with a prospective justice of the peace from Buckbrush township. Plenty of excitement and entertainment on the grounds. First, a real dogfight when a dignified Airedale takes issue with a quarrelsome bulldog. It took half the Clabber Creek community to pull the bulldog off. Then music in the air, for what is court week without some old-time fiddling and a few ballads.

The Foster brothers, all three of them, are here from Bug Tussle with fiddle in poke and guitar and mandolin carefully wrapped to keep out the dust and hold the melody. Talk about devil's ditties! "Just crowd in there by Bob's café and get an earful of it."

After a few old breakdowns, a ballet is in order. Boy Foster leads out with an old-time love song which the crowd accepts seriously. Young lovers on the ragged edge of the crowd move close together as bass, baritone, and tenor tell the old, old story of "Lovely Jane."

The time draws near, my dearest dear, when you and I must part.
But little you think of the pain and woe in my poor aching heart.
Goodbye, sweet girl, I hate to leave, I hate to say goodbye,
But I'll return to you again, unless your Willie dies.
We fought them hard the first four years, the next four just the same.
I loaded my trunk with golden ore and started back to Jane.
We sailed along for about six weeks, along the foamy deep;
One night we thought we all were lost; our captain was asleep.
And then we came in sight of land, in sight of our native town;
Our good old captain gave command to take the rigging down;
And then a crowd of pretty girls came running to the ship,
And Jane was there with all her curls; my heart began to wilt.
Then hand in hand, we walked along 'til we came to her father's door;
The crowd did look so very neat while standing on the floor.
The parson read the marriage law which bound us both for life,
Now Jane is mine without a doubt, my own dear wedded wife.

The ballad ends, the singers rest and smoke makin'-cigarettes while
the crowd mills around in anticipation of more old-time singing. The
jury, grave and silent, files by as the sheriff leads them to the Busy Bee
café for supper. A group of men in front of the drugstore discuss the day's
proceedings. Young Jimmie Winters got thirty days in the county jail for
disturbing a religious assembly—tossing a hornet's nest into the arbor
while the parson was praying. Lem Keeter got a change of venue in the
dog-killing case. "A man sure can't get justice in his home county." Luke
Walters has his case continued for the third time. His "continuation lawyer" knows human nature. The Potts boys plead guilty to a misdemeanor
and get a suspended sentence. The big murder trial will start first thing
in the morning and all is expectancy for the event. The prosecutor will
ask for the death penalty, but the best criminal lawyer in the district will
handle the defense. It will be eye for eye and tooth for tooth and folks
will talk about it until it becomes a tradition.

To realize the vital part the courts have in folk life, one must be present at a session of circuit court. It is a revelation of— But, listen, the Foster

boys are tuning up again. I wonder how Nate Watkins, with ten years to do, would feel if he could hear the words over there in the jailhouse.

> Down in the valley, valley so low,
> Late in the evening, hear the train blow.
> The train, love, hear the train blow;
> Late in the evening, hear the train blow.

> Go build me a mansion, build it so high
> So I can see my true love go by,
> See her go by, love, see her go by,
> So I can see my true love go by.

> Go write me a letter, send it by mail,
> Date it and stamp it to Birmingham jail.
> Birmingham jail, love, Birmingham jail,
> Date it and stamp it to Birmingham jail.

> Roses are red, love, violets are blue.
> Angels in heaven know I love you,
> Know I love you, dear, know I love you,
> Angels in heaven know I love you.

Gallant Outlawry

The classical gang of freebooters known as the James Boys operated in Kansas, Missouri, and Arkansas following the Civil War. Outstanding members of the gang were Jesse James, his brother Frank, Cole Younger, and Clell Miller. Numerous small fry worked with these desperadoes but they seldom made the headlines. Some of the robberies and escapades of the James gang took place in the Ozarks, it is said, but this is merely popular opinion and has never been proved in court. The crimes and pranks of these daring robbers were frequently marked with gallant

action in the manner of Robin Hood and Dick Turpin. But it must be
remembered that time twists historical fact into romantic legend. Even
a gallant outlaw is hardly a fit subject for hero worship.

The robbery of a stagecoach between Malvern and Hot Springs
National Park in January 1874 is usually attributed to the James Boys.
This was before the railroads were built into Hot Springs and many
wealthy visitors left the train at Malvern and rode the stage twenty-five
miles through the hills to the spa. The coach carried fourteen passengers
and was loaded to capacity on the day of the robbery. Money, watches,
and jewelry worth three or four thousand dollars were taken from these
passengers. The mail pouches provided a much larger haul and it is estimated that the gang secured a total of more than $30,000 in the holdup.

This robbery was conducted in the usual James manner with the
five freebooters cracking jokes and parading their wit without reserve.
They did not neglect to include the usual display of chivalry. One man
was given five dollars to permit him to send a message to his relatives.
Another victim of the holdup was a man with a southern accent. He was
asked if he had served the Confederacy during the Civil War. He said
that he had, naming his regiment and command. His money and valuables were promptly returned. The James gang boasted that they never
robbed a man who fought the Yanks.

Many theories have been expounded concerning the disposition
of the booty secured from this stagecoach robbery. One story is that
the gang was hotly pursued by United States officers and that they hid
the loot, valued at $32,000, in the Ouachita Mountains of Yell County,
Arkansas, and never returned for it. Many expeditions have searched for
this treasure but, if found, it has never been reported.

The late B. W. Rice of Caldwell, Idaho, knew the James brothers
personally when he lived in Missouri. He told me the following story:

> A few weeks before Jesse James was killed at St. Joseph, he was
> at the house of a friend of mine in Mexico, Missouri. Croquet
> parties were popular in those days and my friend was host to a
> group on his spacious lawn. Jesse was present but he remained
> in the house.

One of the events at the party was a contest in pistol shooting. A few of the men had made good showings when our host invited James out to take part in the sport. Only two or three of us knew the celebrated bandit.

The host placed a piece of card an inch square on a locust tree twenty paces away and everybody watched to see what the stranger would do. Jesse stood with his back to the mark a few seconds, then wheeled quickly, a pistol in each hand, working them up and down, firing eight shots. Each of the eight bullets found the mark. He did not remain at the party after the shooting, but quickly mounted his horse and rode away.

A few years ago an aged man visited Eureka Springs, Arkansas, and asked Sam A. Leath, an experienced Ozark guide, to show him to a place on the old stage trail two or three miles south of the city. Finding the spot he was looking for, just off State Highway 23, the old man told the following story:

It was in the late seventies when I resigned my parish at Ozark, Arkansas, to take over a church at Pierce City, Missouri. With four other men I traveled north on the stage, which was the only transportation available at that time. My companions were strangers but congenial fellows and I thoroughly enjoyed the ride through the Boston Mountains. At this spot, just south of Eureka Springs, we were halted by two bandits who proved to be Jesse and Frank James. They ordered us from the coach and stripped us of our money and valuables. Placing the loot in his hat, one of the highwaymen called me aside and asked me if I were not a minister of the gospel. I answered in the affirmative.

"Your companions are notorious gamblers," said the bandit, "and we have a special reason for robbing them. But with you it is different. We never take from preachers, widows, or orphans." With these words, he poured a generous portion of the booty into my coat pocket and warned me not to return it to the gamblers. The bandits then mounted their horses and disappeared in the woods.

There was an ominous silence among my four companions while riding into Eureka Springs. I couldn't understand it. They made no complaint about being robbed and gave no indication of reporting the incident to the law. Even the driver of the stage seemed unconcerned about the affair.

Arriving in town, I secured a room at a hotel for the night. As I was about to retire, I heard two men talking in an adjoining room. I recognized the voices as belonging to the two men we had encountered on the road. They were occupying the room next to me.

"Do you suppose that man was telling the truth when he said he was a preacher?" said one of the men.

"I think so," replied the other, "but to make sure we will test him out at the breakfast table in the morning." He continued by outlining the "third degree" they would give me.

I heard every word of the plan and prepared to meet it. Far into the night, I prayed for strength to meet the ordeal. Then I fell asleep and did not awake until called for breakfast.

The brothers were waiting for me when I reached the dining room. When I took a place at the table, the one I decided was Frank sat down beside me. Immediately I felt the pressure of steel against my ribs. Jesse sat across the table in front of me. He asked me to say grace.

Never before did such a fervent prayer fall from my lips. I thanked the Lord for the food, for guidance on the journey, for the welfare of my old parish, for the people of my new pastorate, and, lastly, for the companionship of the two men who were with me. I concluded by asking that richest blessings reward them all through life.

All through the prayer I could feel the gun pressing against my side and could sense the piercing eyes of the bandit leader from across the table. When I concluded the prayer, we ate the food set before us and conversed in a congenial manner. At the conclusion of the meal, Jesse called me aside.

"You're all right, parson," he said. "Luck to you in your new parish. If you travel this way again you may depend upon our protection."

I continued my journey and took up the pastorate at Pierce City. But I never saw the James brothers again.

Gallantry is a legendary trait of numerous other bandits who had their hideouts in the backhill country. The period from 1871 to 1896 was marked by a reign of terror in that part of the Indian Territory, now eastern Oklahoma. Desperadoes flocked to this region and the federal court at Fort Smith became a world-famous tribunal for ferreting out crime. Not all the bad men and women of that period possessed the chivalry of the James gang. Belle Starr had a keen mind that she used to advantage in her romantic but sordid world. Once she broke jail by eloping with the jailer. But she was not noted for her gallantry.

Most of the famous bushwhackers who had been tutored by the infamous Quantrill were cruel killers without quake of conscience. Judge Isaac C. Parker handled 13,490 criminal cases during his twenty-one years as judge of the United States Court at Fort Smith. This court has a record of trying 28,000 criminals and suspects in twenty-five years. It was hell on the border, without mincing words.

Henry Starr was an exception to the rule of hardened banditry. He was killed while attempting to rob the People's National Bank at Harrison, Arkansas, in 1921. It is said that he would not commit murder to accomplish a robbery and that his code of honor kept him from harming innocent persons.[1] Once he was asked by a United States marshal why he followed a life of crime. He replied, "I wish I could find out. I have known men who craved liquor, drugs, and tobacco. I must have excitement. I crave it and it preys upon me until I just slip out and get into devilment of some sort."

Bully of the Town

Kingston, in Madison County, Arkansas, is the ideal village of the hills. I lived there six years, from 1924 to 1930, teaching school and dabbling in regional journalism. I have never found a community more to my liking. The majority of the people are old-line Ozarkers of a class that would complement any community in the nation, urban or rural. The pastoral life of the neighborhood may be compared with Acadia, as pictured by Longfellow in *Evangeline*. Charles J. Finger once said that the village might be set down in the midlands of England without any linguistic confusion. The people have Elizabethan grace both in speech and mannerisms. Their self-reliance is worthy of comment. Although hit hard by drought and depression in recent years, they have remained economically independent. Such a peaceful people seldom feels the teeth of the law and they fail to provide law enforcement machinery, so that, like the Acadians of old, they are sometimes the victims of strange interludes of outlawry. The rakings of the hills are not blind to opportunities afforded them. When the Kingston bank was held up a few years ago, the robbers quietly walked out of town, taking the cashier with them. I once witnessed a small feud break into a free-for-all fight on the public square with a dozen men participating. There was no one in authority to make arrests, and pandemonium resulted.

This condition of laxness prevailed during my residence in the village. The sheriff's office at the county seat was twenty miles away and phone connections were inadequate. A killing might take place and a getaway be made, with officers trailing far behind. As a rule the community life moved along in regular order from day to day. Of course, drunks were conspicuous on the town square, profanity was freely indulged in, and young men would let off steam by racing their horses through the village, whooping, and firing pistols into the air. But the townspeople tolerated these things with salutary patience. Occasionally there was an exception. Everyone remembers the time a young hillsman took possession of the village and held absolute dictatorship until removed from the scene at the points of a pistol and two shotguns.

One Sunday morning just as the sun peeped over Bradshaw Mountain, a young man on horseback rode into the village square. It was an ideal spring morning and the redbud tree in front of the hotel was a riot of color. The young man rode leisurely, singing as he rode "Show

Me the Bully of the Town." In the middle of the little square stood the town pump with its broken handle. The bully, looking for the town bully, rode up to the pump, dismounted and hitched his horse, still singing the ditty in a loud voice. It was discovered later that the gay young blade had attended a Saturday night dance in a nearby settlement and had imbibed an excessive amount of corn liquor. After breaking up the dance in the early hours of the morning, he decided to ride into Kingston and take charge of the town. So, with plenty of volume to advertise his prowess, he sang his challenge to all who might hear, at the same time polishing a large horse pistol with a pocket handkerchief.

It was not long until the newly arrived bully had a customer. A high school youth who lived in the country had spent the night with relatives in their apartment over the garage. Seeing the fellow stop at the pump, he decided to go down and chat with him. So he ambled down the stairs at the end of the building to greet the visitor. He could hardly believe his eyes when he found himself looking down the barrel of a mammoth pistol.

"I'm the bully of the town," said the outlaw. "Get back up them steps in a hurry." The youth needed no second instruction. It was a little early to start the day's loafing anyway.

The second intruder into the bully's domain was the town druggist. The merchant had started to his store on the northeast corner of the square and had reached the front door before the outlaw noticed him. Immediately the gun took the direction of the drugstore and the druggist was ordered to shake the dust from the cuffs of his trousers. The merchant was fumbling with his keys when the order came and he first thought it was meant as a joke. A second order and a look at the gun convinced him that the man really meant business. He had the correct key in his hand, but to save his life he could not find the keyhole. He quickly retired to the rear of the building to watch developments through a knothole in the board fence.

By this time, people were moving freely about the village and the outlaw was as busy as a chicken in a bread tray, clearing the square of intruders. The commands were received with surprise and frequently taken as a joke. But the young man at the pump made it plain that he was not to be misunderstood. One look at the large pistol he handled so recklessly gave sufficient cause for immediate retreat. At times the outlaw would issue his challenge in song, "Show me the bully of the town." He was enjoying the situation immensely.

After an hour of this unconventional procedure, word had spread throughout the neighborhood that an outlaw had taken possession of the town square and would let no one pass. The nearest officer was a deputy sheriff who lived three or four miles out in the hills. He was hastily called and permitted to view the situation from a side door of the garage. A plan of attack was quickly outlined and agreed upon. Two citizens were deputized to assist in making the arrest. The deputy was to step into the open, gun in hand, and ask him to surrender. The two deputized citizens were to walk in at right angles with pointed shotguns. They would get their man, dead or alive.

The deputy was a man who never knew fear. He stepped from the garage with the gun leveled at the bully's heart and gave his order. But it had no effect. Instead, the outlaw leveled his gun at the deputy and waited developments. The men approaching at right angles kept shouting at the man to drop his gun, threatening to blow his brains out if he pulled the trigger. But the outlaw sat tight. The deputy moved steadily toward his antagonist with his trigger finger crooked for quick action. It was a tense moment and anything might happen. The line tightened like a hangman's noose as the three men closed in at the same time. The bully handed over his gun and submitted to arrest.

An immediate trial was held at the home of the justice of the peace. The defendant pleaded not guilty, claiming he meant no harm, but "just wanted to have a little fun." He was fined one hundred dollars and costs. Not having any cash with him, he requested that the deputy ride with him to his home in the hills and get the money. He did so, collecting the fine. As they rode over the mountain toward the setting sun, the bully's voice rose in song, "Show me the bully of the town."

CHAPTER XIV

Lore and Legend

. . . .

The Fighting Parson

The fighting parson is a legendary figure who still stalks the hills after two generations have been laid under the sod. His courageous spirit continues to chill the wayward and warm the righteous. A record of the hill country would be incomplete without a glimpse of Brother Smithers and his hard-shell philosophy. Loma Ball told me the story of his arrival in the hills, which I repeat here with her special permission.

Ed Sinkler was the bully of the neighborhood. He was tall and muscular, with deep-set black eyes and dark curly hair which, because of infrequent combings, was bushy and unruly. He was known throughout the community as a good and willing fighter. Nobody had ever seen him fight, nor had anybody ever known anybody who had seen him in action, but the idea persisted that he could, and would, whip any man who happened to incur his displeasure.

Ed was a garrulous fellow, given to boasting, and he advertised the fact that he could hold a kicking mule with his bare hands, that he had once twisted the barrel off a rifle gun, and that he could draw nails out of a board with his teeth. Despite lack of proof of these claims, belief in them grew. Ed Sinkler's prodigious strength became a byword in the community. A man was "as strong as Ed Sinkler" or could "lift as much as Ed Sinkler."

Old Squire Greenup and the new preacher sat on the squire's porch talking. The preacher was a shrewd-looking fellow in his middle thirties who wore his long-tailed black coat with self-conscious dignity. Ed Sinkler ambled up the road and stopped before the gate.

"Howdy, Squar," he said.

"Evenin', Ed. Won't you come up an' take a chur." Ed came up and the squire introduced him to the new preacher.

"Reckon I ain't got time t' set, Squar," said Ed, assuming a business-like tone. "I jist come down t' see Brother Smithers hyar. I hearn as how he had driv up t' see you'ens."

"Anything private?" asked the squire. "If'n 'tis, I'll go in th' house an' let you fellers talk by yerselves."

"Jist keep yer chur," Ed assured him. "'Tain't nothin' private atall. Th' chances air that hit'll be knowed from hyar t' yander 'fore nightfall anyhow." He cleared his throat and turned to the preacher. "Hit's come t' my yurs, Brother Smithers, that you've been a-makin' some slurrin' remarks 'bout me, an' I've come down t' ast you 'bout it."

Slowly the preacher rose to his feet. His face indicated no emotion. He was fully five inches taller than Ed, and when he straightened up his head rustled the strings of beans and dried apples that the squire's wife had festooned from rafter to rafter. "I ain't sayin' nothin' one way er 'nuther," the preacher replied quietly. "Until I know whut I've been quoted as sayin', I ain't admittin' nothin' ner denyin' nothin'."

Ed struck an antagonistic pose. "I hearn that you said that ef I'd come into th' meetin'house while meetin' was goin' on 'stead o' settin' outside with my arm 'round some gal, I'd be a more useful citizen t' th' community. Did you say that?"

"Do you do that, Brother Sinkler?" The preacher's eyes twinkled.

"That ain't th' pint," Ed insisted. "I ast you, did you say it?"

"You answer my question fust."

"All right, I'll answer you. 'Tain't none o' yer business. Preachin's yer business, not mindin' my courtin' transactions. Take off yer coat an'

come out hyar in th' road. We'll settle this thing right now. Yer guilty, an'
I don't want t' mess up Mis Greenup's flower beds a-thrashin' you hyar
in th' yard."

"Ed, Ed." Squire Greenup pleaded for peace. "You ain't goin' t' do
nuthin' rash, air ye? Ca'm yerselves, fellers, ca'm yerselves." Neither of the
men appeared to hear him and the little squire, his dignity insulted, drew
himself up pompously. "Gentlemen," he said in his best magisterial voice,
"ef ye fight I'll have t' deal with you accordin' t' th' law."

By this time the preacher had removed his coat, loosened his collar,
and rolled up his sleeves. His arms were sinewy, and his shirt, clinging
damply to his body, disclosed ridges of fine, pliant muscles upon his
shoulders and back.

"May I pray?" he asked quietly of his adversary.

"Pray ef ye want to. In fack, I'd advise it."

The preacher knelt at the edge of the porch. "O Lord," he prayed
in a loud voice, "thou knowest that when I kilt Bill Thompson an' Clate
Jennings that I done it in self-defense. Thou knowest, too, Lord, that
when I splattered th' brains uv Kemp Staples all over his co'n patch that
hit wus forced upon me. An' now, O Lord, when I am jist on th' verge o'
puttin' this hyar poor wretch in his grave, I'm askin' ye t' have mercy on
his soul. Amen."

The preacher arose, took a long-bladed knife from his pocket and
began whetting it on the sole of his shoe. Dismally, plaintively, his voice
rose in song.

> Hark from the tomb the doleful sound,
> Mine ears attend th' cry.

Now Ed Sinkler was nothing if not resourceful. Living in compar-
ative comfort for thirty years without having engaged in any gainful
occupation had sharpened his wits to a remarkable degree. He burst out
laughing loudly. The preacher, surprised, stopped whetting his knife. Ed
laughed because he had a reputation at stake. To run would be ruinous to
that reputation. To fight would be equally ruinous. He had to stand his
ground and craftily he chose his course of action. Striding up to the porch

he held out his hand. "Yer all right, parson," he said. "I wus jist a-testin' out yer mettle. When I hearn that you'd ariv 'mongst us I says t' myself, 'I'm goin' down t' see what kind o' goods that feller's made of fer no feller that ain't got no backbone has got any business in these hyar parts.'"

By this time the preacher had recovered from his surprise. Wrath overcame him. "I want ye t' know I made that thar remark you mentioned. What air ye goin' t' do 'bout it?"

"Nuthin' atall, Brother Smithers. Surposin' you did say it. I reckon th' only way you could feel that way 'bout it is because you ain't never done no sparkin' settin' outside a meetin'house. Ef you had ever tried it onct, you'd never say nary word agin it. Hit's th' most satisfactory courtin' . . . "

Abruptly the preacher donned his coat. Casually he pulled his chair up beside the one on which the squire had collapsed. "As I wus a-sayin', Brother Greenup," he said, as if no interruption had occurred, "thar's baptizin' by sprinklin' an' by pourin', an' thar's baptizin' by dippin', but thar's only one uv 'em that's right."

Treasure Trove

The fabled cities of gold which lured Coronado and his conquistadors into sunbaked deserts had no more romantic appeal to the Spanish imagination than the "lost mines" of the Ozarks to the treasure hunters of the present generation. All through the year picks are sunk into Ozark earth with fervid hope. The lure of hidden treasure creates a fantasy not easily erased from the minds of men.

I once traveled with a lone prospector into the backhills of Madison County, Arkansas, and viewed with my own eyes the intricate signs of Spanish occupation, and traced the green serpentine lines in the rock that were gold in the prospector's eyes. I went, I saw, I concurred. But I returned with pockets as empty as the proverbial sack that will not stand upright.

We left the village of Kingston one fine morning "an hour by sun," in quest of the mountain of gold. The compass of our fancy pointed to a range of ragged hills to the southward. "There's gold over there," said the prospector and, being a novice at gold hunting, I could only take his word for it. For three hours we rode in a jolt-wagon, crossing a turbulent stream a dozen times. Coming to the end of the wagon trail, we faced an untrod wilderness of hills and canyons. We abandoned the wagon and team and, footloose and free, followed what my companion called the Old Spanish Trail to the legendary mine. For two or three miles I tagged the heels of the eager prospector through canyons, over ridges, into pocket-like valleys.

It was a glorious October day. The hills were sweethearts of the sun, flinging their red-gold tresses invitingly. Birds and other creatures of the wilderness sat mute to watch our invasion into their domain. The all-pervading presence of the day took hold of me and I forgot, for the moment, the lure of yellow gold and flashing jewels, and the jingle of Spanish pieces of eight. But my companion, schooled in mineral lore, heard nothing, felt nothing but the magnetic pull of the lavish wealth in the ragged pockets of the hills.

Arriving at the mine, I focused my Kodak upon the shaggy cliffs and numerous points of scenic and legendary interest pointed out to me. I heard the story, old as the hills themselves, of the smelter and the lost mine. Under a giant ledge of rock, I saw what appeared to be an ancient dumping ground. From all appearances, the canyon had been a busy workshop of man in the dim, distant past.

In the rock of the creek bed ran green lines which seemed to disappear into the walls of the canyon. To me, they were merely colored threads of nature's tapestry in stone, but to the old prospector they were infallible lines of treasure trove. My companion admitted that he had not found the lost mine but felt that he was near it. Shining nuggets, handpicked from the canyon's wall, were produced as evidence. A faded paper from his pocket showed the record of an assay made by a government mint.

With pick in hand and dreams of gold in pocket, I dug into a layer of soft rock where the green lines twisted themselves into hiding. I dug diligently for an hour, then panned the dirt in the water of the tumbling brook. But no glittering particles rewarded my efforts. I tried again but with the same negligible results. The gods of fortune refused to smile. Homeward we made our way with lagging footsteps.

"Gold in them thar hills"? Yes, abundant gold for the spade of the imagination. Each bubbling spring is a radiant jewel on nature's breast. The crystal streams are ribbons of silver daringly knotted at the throats of the hills. The setting sun from Penitentiary Mountain is a ball of gold for the poet's eye. That is treasure aplenty, treasure worth prospecting for. But the Ozark earth has not yielded up the yellow gold that is grist for the mills of trade. Perhaps it is there, as my friend the prospector believes. Perhaps . . . but as for me, I seek the other treasure.

Indian Footprints

Fourteen tribes of Indians lived in the Ozark region between 1541 and 1837, according to certain historians.[1] Only two of these tribes, however, were what we would call legal landowners—the Osages who were in possession of the region when the first white men arrived, and the Eastern Cherokees who were settled by treaty in 1817. The Osage claim consisted of about fifty million acres extending from the Mississippi to the Verdigris. It included all of the Ozark region bounded on the north by the Missouri and on the south by the Arkansas. The southern portion of this region, consisting of a little more than 2,000,000 acres, was assigned to the Eastern Cherokees in exchange for a tract of equal size east of the Mississippi. Shawnees, Delawares, Dakotas, Sac and Fox, Northern and Southern Cherokees, and a few other tribes occupied portions of the Ozark region, but they had no permanent claims. Nomadic tribes visited the highlands on hunting expeditions or made pilgrimage to the healing springs with which the region abounds, but they did not attempt to possess the land. Because of its central location and the abundance of game and water, this region was the redman's mecca for several hundred years preceding the arrival of the white settlers. The piecemeal occupation of

these highlands by the aborigines offers a challenge to the archaeologist
and historian.

The removal of the Osages began about the time of the Cherokee
immigration, but it was many years before the transfer was completed.
Remnants of this vigorous tribe continued to roam the hills until 1875.
The forced migration of the Cherokees from their homelands east of
the Mississippi, beginning in 1817, is a pathetic chapter of our history.
Thousands of them died while en route to the western lands the United
States government had assigned them. The hardships along the Trail of
Tears has become a Cherokee tradition.

The treaty with the Cherokees carried a guarantee of permanency,
but the rapid settlement of the country by white settlers soon caused the
government to change its policy. In 1828, the headmen of the Cherokee
tribe were called to Washington to sign a new treaty. The Indians at first
refused to sign a violation of the former pact, but during the latter part
of the year it was forced upon them. In the early part of 1829, the government began the removal of all Indians from Arkansas. The emigration
continued for about ten years. In the latter part of 1837, only a few roving
parties and scattered mixed-breeds remained in the state. In 1846 several
hundred Cherokees returned from the Indian Territory, now Oklahoma,
and petitioned the government for citizenship papers and for the right
to settle in northwest Arkansas, but United States soldiers forced them
to return to the land that had been assigned to them.

The Ouachita region, south of the Arkansas River, was occupied by
the Caddos, Quapaws, Choctaws, Creeks, and Seminoles from 1541 to
1828. They were removed to the Territory early in the nineteenth century
to make way for the white settlers. The name Arkansas comes from the
Quapaws by way of the French under Marquette. The original meaning
of the word is "handsome man."[2]

Indian legends abound in the Ozarks as a result of the redman's long
residence in the region. Almost every stream, spring, cave, and promontory has legendary footprints. These Indians were deeply religious and
they interpreted natural phenomena with a supernatural slant. A typical

legend is that concerning the origin of Mammoth Spring in Fulton County, Arkansas:

> A great many moons ago, according to the Indians, there was only a great meadow at the site of Mammoth Spring. A tribe headed by Chief Red Cloud occupied this region. The chief's daughter, Natalitia, had been married to a tribesman by name of Towakanee and Red Cloud proclaimed a festival of many weeks' duration. In the midst of the festivities there fell upon the land a terrible drought and the people began to suffer for want of water. Selecting a number of warriors, the chief sent them to the Big Water [Mississippi River] to bring back rain to his people.
>
> The warriors were so long in making the journey that many people perished, among them Natalitia. Crazed by grief, Towakanee committed suicide by dashing his head against a rock. When the warriors finally returned, Red Cloud, in a rage, had them put to death and buried in a common grave in the great meadow.
>
> When the grave was closed a mighty rumbling noise was heard within the ground and a great stream of water burst forth to form a giant spring.

When night falls at Mammoth Spring, a hissing sound is heard to come from the water. Scientists explain that this is caused by the escaping of carbonic gas that has been held in solution. But according to the legend, it is the gasping of the spirits of the dead warriors.

Sam A. Leath, who probably knows more Ozark Indian lore than any other person living today, tells the colorful story of the famous Hiawatha's visit to the Magic Healing Springs, now Eureka Springs, Arkansas.[3] Here is Leath's version of the legend:

> It is an Ojibway tradition that Hiawatha, immortalized in Longfellow's poem, once visited the healing springs. He came from the land of the lakes to treat with the Dakota chief, Newadaha, for his daughter, Laughing Water. A remnant of the Dakotas, headed by Newadaha, had sought refuge in the Ozarks

when they were defeated by their archenemies, the Ojibways. Hiawatha offered to establish peace between his people and the Dakotas if the chief would accept him as a son-in-law. It was agreed that the girl would return with him to the camps of the Ojibways in the Great Lakes region as evidence of the peace pact.

The young couple started immediately upon their journey without revealing their plans to the other Dakotas. Just as they reached the cliff in what is now called Happy Hollow, they were seen by Newadaha's pickets. They thought Hiawatha was kidnapping the girl and laid hands upon him. But the Indian girl plunged a knife into the heart of one of her own tribesmen in order that her lover might escape. They continued their journey, reached the shores of the northern waters, and spent their lives together in the land of the Ojibways.

Happy Hollow with its charming scenery and cool springs was the legendary wooing ground of Hiawatha and Laughing Water. This cove is now filled with beautiful homes, among them being the residence and studio of Cora Pinkley Call, Ozark writer, and the palatial lodge of Wilbur Bancroft, where Ozarkian writers and artists are royally entertained each year during the third week of June.

Breadtray Mountain is located at the junction of the James with the White River in Stone County, Missouri. The name was applied by early pioneers because of the peculiar topography of the promontory. Breadtray has a legendary reputation seldom paralleled. It is a landmark of strange incident and hillfolks carefully avoid it. Of the many stories connected with it, four are outstanding.

Long ago there lived a band of Chickasaw Indians in the vicinity of Breadtray Mountain. They had discovered deposits of silver and they manufactured crude jewelry which they used as a medium of exchange. These ornaments became so popular that they decided to use the cave under the mountain as a workshop, and as a place of safe storage for their silver. They continued this work for many years, but finally were overcome by an enemy tribe and forced out of the region. Before leaving, they hid their treasure in a secret passage of the cave and sealed the entrance.

Legend declares that they never returned and that behind some wall in the bowels of Breadtray there lies the vast treasure of the Chickasaws.

Another legend says that an Indian village was located on the top of Breadtray Mountain. The tribe was haunted by starvation and ill fortune. One day a beautiful girl from a neighboring tribe came to them with the startling information that the Great Spirit would bring them peace and plenty if she became the bride of the chief's son. The wedding took place and the tribe's misfortunes came to an end. The girl was greatly respected by everyone except the medicine man who had profited by the people's misfortunes. He cursed the young woman and she immediately left the village, saying that the Great Spirit would banish the tribe from the face of the earth. Legend says this prediction was carried out and that the curse even extended to the land on the top of Breadtray Mountain. That is the reason nothing grows on the top of the mountain to this day.

One of the most popular Breadtray legends has a Spanish origin. The conquistadors mined silver in the vicinity and hid it in a fort on the mountaintop. They enslaved the Indians and forced them to work in the mines. When a large quantity of the ore had been mined, the Spaniards decided to leave the country and take fifty Indian girls with them. But the redmen thwarted their plan and killed all but three of the Spaniards, who escaped into the hills. These men returned to look for the treasure, but they were killed by sentries. Since that time many adventurers have sought the lost hoard, which was supposed to be secreted in sealed vaults below the site of the fort, but no trace of it has been found.

The fourth legend has its setting in the latter part of the nineteenth century. The notorious Bald Knobber gang operated in Stone and Taney Counties in the eighties. It is thought that they used the cave under Breadtray as a base for their operations and that they cached their loot there. In 1889 the entire gang was captured and executed except one man. He escaped from the jail at Ozark, Missouri, and fled the country. Old-timers think that he returned to the cave later and recovered the loot.

For many years an incessant search has been carried on in the vicinity of St. Joe, Arkansas, for a fabled silver mine. The fantastic story of this treasure carries some earmarks of truth and many diggings have been made in quest of it.

An Indian by the name of Woodward was said to be the original owner of the mine. He talked about his mine freely and boasted that if white men had enough sense to locate it they could shoe their horses with silver. To prove the existence of the treasure, he offered to conduct two men to the mine, providing they would permit him to blindfold them during the trip. This was done and the visitors were led to the mine. When the blindfolds were removed they were stunned by what they saw. The ore existed in almost unbelievable quantities. They were conducted out of the cave in the same fashion by which they entered and the location remained as much a mystery as ever.

The story goes that the crafty Indian sold shares in his mine, promising to reveal the location when the deal was completed. He collected the money and then skipped to the Indian Territory. Years later he returned to St. Joe, but old landmarks had been obliterated and he could not find the coveted treasure. He returned to Oklahoma and died shortly afterwards.

It has been four hundred years since Hernando de Soto crossed the Mississippi River (June 18, 1541) and met the chiefs of five different tribes of Indians assembled on the western bank. He was in constant association with the redmen during his long trek through Arkansas. Many of these aborigines were friendly and it is said that they helped the Spaniards build the boat that carried them away—down the Ouachita River. But there were exceptions to this spirit of fraternalism. At Caddo Gap, in Montgomery County, stands a monument that attests a bitter struggle between the whites and the reds. Carved in the stone of the monument is this inscription:

> Here De Soto reached his most westward point in the United States. Here was the capitol of the warlike Tula tribe of Indians who fiercely fought De Soto and his men. Relics found in this vicinity suggest the romance of past centuries about which history will ever be meager and incomplete.

Following de Soto came the Frenchman, Du Tisne, in the seventeenth century. Tradition says that the first log house in America was built by this explorer, assisted by friendly Indians. But the redmen did not always welcome the French with open arms. On one occasion the Osages decided to give Du Tisne a passport to the happy hunting ground. But he shocked them by pulling off his wig and showing his shaved head. Perhaps it was the first time in Indian history that the redmen had observed a man scalp himself. To further astonish his dusky companions, he drew a sunglass from his pocket and set fire to a bunch of dry leaves. Then he mixed brandy with water and set it on fire. The Osages were big men, some of them seven feet tall, and their bravery was unquestioned, but they could not decipher the Frenchman's magic and he was permitted to live.

The early Anglo-Saxon settlers had many interesting experiences with the Indians. When the Bass family moved into the Springfield (Missouri) area in 1829, the Kickapoos would not let them stop because they had a plow tied on the side of the wagon. The redskins were no fools and had already learned that the white man's civilization follows the plow.

Fact and Fable

If the evening star has a spot of blood on it, look out for war! So say the old folks of the Ozarks. Or the warning may come on the shell of a chicken egg. At a time of national stress, eggs are frequently reported with miraculous imprints on them. The signs may be strange symbols with ominous meanings, or actual words of warning worked into the shell. These things are given credence by many people. But, according to the seers of the hills, the most reliable sign of impending war is the appearance of the black eagle in the Jacks Fork country.

Jacks Fork is a tumbling branch of Current River which threads and loops its way through the hills of Texas and Shannon Counties, Missouri. This rugged section was settled by mountaineers from Virginia, Kentucky, and Tennessee and, in moving to the Ozarks, they brought their legends and superstitions with them. Here we find survivals of the black eagle legend.

One of the early settlers on Jacks Fork was Jim Hill. He came with his family in 1860 and settled in the valley of the little river where the land was exceedingly rich and wild game abundant. The Hill family had a tradition of patriotic service dating from the American Revolution. The War of 1812, the struggle with Mexico, and numerous Indian wars found them in the ranks, serving their country.

The Civil War broke out soon after Jim Hill, with his wife and five sons, reached the Ozarks. The Hills were in sympathy with the North and Jim's father, who was left behind in Virginia, was killed by a Confederate during the early days of the outbreak. The war had been going on several weeks but no word of it had reached Jim Hill. But soon after the death of his father, the legend says that an enormous black eagle with the dismal color of death appeared in the Jacks Fork country.

The Hills recognized the bird as a sign that war had broken out between the North and South, and it was interpreted as a call to the colors. The father and his three older sons immediately joined the forces of the Union. Two of the boys were killed in the war but the father and one son returned to the hills at the close of the struggle. There is no record of the appearance of the ominous bird during the war with Spain or the first World War, but the belief persists that it will again appear, if necessary, to call the descendants of the fighting clan of Jim Hill.

. . . . . .

Ghost stories are an intricate part of the lore of the backhills and each community has its favorites. The vampire superstition common to the peasants of southeastern Europe is unknown here, but ghosts of Anglo-Saxon lineage, correspondent to the shade of the immortal Banquo, set their reversed feet in the Ozarkian imagination. A ghost or shade differs from a vampire in that it is a purely psychical phenomenon and may flit through closed doors and walls without difficulty. Vampires are restricted by physical limitations and fear a second death. A ghost is a departed soul returned to earth and is not perceptible to touch. It takes fantastic sizes and shapes and may hide in a peanut shell or slip through the eye of a needle. It seems to be at its best (or worst) at the hour of midnight, and it frequents graveyards, or unholy places where foul deeds have been committed. But even a ghost has certain limitations that are strictly adhered to. One of them, given frequent mention in the old ballads, is the daylight taboo. When the cock crows to herald the approach of dawn, the specter must depart for the nether regions without delay.

In the southern Missouri hills there exists, for some of the people, a specter that occasionally takes the form of a headless man. Natives report seeing it and hearing its groans on dark, drizzly nights. One night it took a position on the horse behind a young swain who was returning home from a sparking escapade. Its cold breath on the back of his neck was a chilling experience. Strange behavior for an apparition without a head and minus physical qualities. But the strange hitchhiker departed as suddenly as it appeared, without noise or ceremony. The victim of the adventure is sincere in his statements and has tried to find an explanation for this strange phenomenon. But this ghost defies analysis. Its antics are as varied as Arkansas weather. Once it appeared in the road with its head in its arms and glided along as if coasting on roller skates. At another time it lay concealed in a brush pile and moaned so loudly that a team of mules on the near highway took fright and ran away. A marvelous apparition for a modern age! Perhaps it is one of the fallen archangels of mythology that had parachute trouble and landed in the wrong world.

The lore of the Ozarks is filled with legends that spread a magic carpet for the imagination. In this egg-shaped empire with its 60,000 square miles of territory, there are thousands of romantic tales that act as interludes in the solemn dramas of folk life. One outstanding tradition which lingers in the spotlight is that of the Lost Louisiana Treasure. The search for a legitimate tracer to the fabulous wealth of this cache has been a favorite pastime with treasure hunters for many years.

The location of this hidden wealth is, of course, a matter of conjecture. The legend is common to all parts of the Southwest, but the details have variations of local color. In Arkansas, the lodestar may shift from the Mulberry River Cliffs in the Ozarks to the peaks and canyons of the Ouachitas. Two or three counties have been named as likely locations of the treasure.

The story has its original setting in Mexico in the days following the Cortez conquest of the Aztecs. The mines were fabulously rich and many ships, laden with gold and silver, sailed for the Spanish homeland. On one occasion, pirates tried to thwart this shipment. Hard pressed, the sailors turned their galleons into the Mississippi River and took shelter in protective coves of the Big Waters. While in hiding, they contacted Indians who excited them with rumors of rich mines in the region farther north. The lure was irresistible and they disbanded their ships, loaded their cargoes on rafts, and poled up the Mississippi and Arkansas Rivers.

The legend states that they found crude mines worked by Indians near the mouth of the Mulberry River, but these supplied scant gold. The Spaniards prospected for several months in the surrounding country, but found nothing of value. Harassed by the redmen, they buried the treasure they had brought from Mexico in the deep shaft of a mine, sealed it securely, and departed, expecting to return and recover it at some later time. The territory was taken over by France soon afterwards and eventually became the property of the United States by the purchase of 1803. The Spanish adventurers never returned for their treasure and the story ends with the usual legendary speculations.

. . . . . .

An interesting story of the Ouachita Mountains is that of the Giant of the Hills. This wild man, seven feet tall, was reported seen many times in the backhills of Saline County during the years following the Civil War. He was of the white race, wore no clothing, and his body was covered with long, thick hair. He made his home in caves, for the most part, but at times was seen in the canebrakes along the Saline River.

While he had never been known to harm anyone, the giant was greatly feared and shunned by all the settlers for miles around. He had never been heard to utter a sound and that enhanced the mystery. Eventually it was decided that he should be captured and a party was organized for the hunt. A daring young man led the group with a pack of deerhounds. The wild man was tracked to a cave and lassoed with a rope. When the lariat noose fell over his shoulders he emitted a strange sound like that of a trapped animal. He was taken to Benton and lodged in jail—a small building made of logs. He immediately tore from his body the clothing provided by his captors and escaped from the flimsy jail, only to be recaptured, this time in the canebrakes.

Just what became of the wild man no one seems to know. Old-timers say he disappeared and was never seen in the country again. The following story ties in nicely as a sequel to this.

Soon after the giant escaped, the young man who had led the first hunt rushed into the cabin home of his parents, grabbed his gun and called to his mother, "Ma, don't look for me till you see me comin'; it may be a day, it may be a year." He had found giant footprints and wanted to get started while the trail was hot.

These tracks were fourteen inches long and four feet apart. The place was Saline County, not far from the county seat of Benton. According to the story, the young man followed the tracks successfully across southern Arkansas and into Texas. Along the way he came upon nine other men who had discovered the big tracks and were following them. In this company, he traveled across the Lone Star State, subsisting almost entirely upon raw meat killed along the way.

It was almost a year before the Arkansan returned home with the disappointing news that not one of the trailing party had caught a glimpse of the giant who made the tracks, although they did find several persons who claimed they had seen him, always traveling in the darkness of night.

The climax of tall tales in the Ozarks is found in the romantic legend of Grand Gulf. This story is seasoned with some archaeological approval but it is my opinion that actual proof is as far away as the millennium. It is interesting folklore, but not to be taken too seriously. I summarize the tale as reported in the *Thayer* (Missouri) *News* eight or nine years ago.

Grand Gulf begins with a canyon a few miles north of the Missouri–Arkansas line in Oregon County, Missouri, which carries a fair-sized stream of water. The stream disappears into a subterranean cavern. A few miles below in Arkansas is the famous Mammoth Spring which is a small river rising from the bowels of the earth. It is an established fact that the gulf and the spring are connected. Tests have been made by emptying sacks of oats into the stream in the canyon and observing the grains emerge in the spring. A lost river, born in Missouri, reborn in Arkansas.

The fantastic part of this narrative is the legend associated with Grand Gulf. Someone at some time conceived the idea that Job and his herdsmen pitched their tents and fattened their herds in the vicinity of the lost river. This was the land of Uz spoken of in the Old Testament. Job's eldest son lived near him and had his habitation destroyed by the first tornado mentioned in the Bible (Job 1:19).

Years after Job recovered from his boils, the land of Uz gained a remarkable civilization. They had fields and livestock and were not nomadic like the American Indians. The legend asserts that they traveled by boat up and down the stream in Grand Gulf which connected two important villages. (The legend doesn't explain how they emerged at the spring end of the route.)

After a long time, the inhabitants of pastoral Uz were attacked by powerful bands of savages from the far north. It was a massacre, with village after village being destroyed. Several people escaped immediate death by taking refuge in Grand Gulf, but the savages discovered their hiding place and rolled stones into the outlet at the spring, flooding the great cavern. Only a few escaped this horrible catastrophe. It is claimed that ancient hieroglyphics have been found, carved in copper and stone, telling the story of this great conflict.

About thirty years ago two Missourians tried to explore the underground river in Grand Gulf, but failed. They traveled by boat down the long canyon to the mouth of the cavern where the river sinks. They made their way underground for some distance, but turned back when passage became impossible. They found an old landing place in perfect condition and brought back an earthen jar estimated to be three thousand years old. The site of what is thought to be an ancient village has been found not far from Grand Gulf. These recent discoveries will probably spur the archaeologists on to greater action, but I cannot accept this land of Uz business.

CHAPTER XV

Men of the Mountains

. . . .

Backhill Hermit

The hermit was sitting by an open fire in the yawning mouth of a cave on White River. I had left the Freeman place near the ferry at dawn to do some fishing in the vicinity of White Rock Bluff. The stream was ideal for floating and my boat drifted several miles in the clear water as I tempted the sporting bass with the lure of live minnows. But luck seemed to be against me. No strikes rewarded my efforts. I was about ready to turn my boat and start poling upstream when the sight of the old man, and the picturesque setting of the cave, caused me to rest my paddle. The scene impressed me as a picture from the gallery of "life's other side." The high bluff on the eastern side of the stream screened the sun from view. Mauve shadows lay in the transparent waves of the churning water. Near the foot of the cliff, about forty feet above the waterline, the opening of the cavern gaped wide. The hermit was cooking breakfast over a wood fire. He sat on a rock, pipe in his mouth, gun across his knees, as he watched the flames eat into the dry wood.

It was early October, the time of the "moon of painted leaves," and the oaks, elms, and maples were dressed like Joseph of old, in a coat of many colors. Except for the roar of the tumbling water and the occasional bark of a squirrel in the woods across the stream, all was quiet. For several minutes I sat glued to the boat, transfixed by the charm of the scene before me. When the old man saw me, he motioned greeting and I joined him on the spacious porch of his curious home. I had read much of hermits of old, but this was my first contact with a man who had joined forces with nature in the solitude of the Ozark hills.

The hermit, whom I came to know as Joe Miller, had a typical Anglo-Saxon appearance. He did not present an uncouth mien such as one might expect from this way of life. His beard was trimmed and the gray locks of his long hair curled gracefully over his jacket collar. He wore a broad-brimmed hat which he seldom removed from his head during waking hours. His clothing was conventional cloth from the country store—blue denim overalls, cotton shirt, and woolen jacket. His shoes were rough brogans, hand-sewed and pegged for rough usage.

The old man had lived many years on White River, moving up and down the stream as prompted by the supply of game and fish. He hunted, trapped, fished, and gathered roots and herbs. Except for occasional trips to the country store or the county seat, he seldom left his wilderness home. The wooded hills supplied squirrel, quail, turkey, and an occasional deer, and he could fish without going more than ten steps from his cave. Wild fruits grew in abundance along the stream and nut-bearing trees were everywhere. If he needed sweetening, he could course a bee, chop the tree, and collect the honey. With such inviting natural surroundings, the hermit had little need for the pension check sent to him by the government as a reward for his services during the Civil War.

Joe Miller had one discrepancy which excited my interest. He had a dread of snakes. He explained that this fear was caused by being bitten by a rattler in his youth. Snakes seldom enter the damp caves of the Ozarks, but the hermit took no chances. He had constructed a snake-proof "bedroom" which was a marvel of ingenuity. He had secured an old metal water tank at a nearby mill, cut out the ends, and hinged them to open and close at will. With the help of neighboring woodsmen he had suspended it with chains from the limb of a large oak tree near the entrance of the cavern. He had feathered his nest with straw and sacks and old quilts and had comfortable sleeping quarters even in winter. The tank swung ten feet above the ground and was accessible by means of a rope ladder which he drew up after him. The contraption was partially sheltered from wind and rain by the overhanging cliff.

In viewing the hermit's domicile, I noticed a number of bottles and fruit jars anchored with rocks and pegs around the entrance of the cave. Miller explained that snakes will not crawl in the vicinity of glass and that these objects were used as a precaution to keep the reptiles away. I have never investigated this theory, but assume the old man knew what he was doing.

A small spring gushed from the rocks at the entrance to the cave. This gave him a plentiful supply of water for drinking, cooking, and laundry. An aperture just inside the cavern served as a supply room for clothing, toilet articles, cooking utensils, and firewood. There was neither rent nor taxes to disturb the hermit in his independent way of life.

I visited Joe Miller many times during the months that followed. He was a congenial companion, had a keen mind, and possessed a wide knowledge of nature lore. Here are a few nuggets from the hermit's cave of knowledge. Some of them are scientifically correct; others are not. It is not my business to draw the line between fact and fallacy. I report as Joe told them to me:

Dragonflies sting.
Moles are blind.
Frogs drink through their skins.
Ants smell with their feet.
Snakes hear through the tongue.
Horsehairs left in water will turn into hair snakes.
Warts are caused by handling toads.
The tarantula's bite is fatal to man.
No snake dies until the sun goes down.
Dogs' tails and walnut trees draw lightning.
Thunder sours milk and kills the chickens in setting eggs.
The age of a rattlesnake is determined by the number of rattles
    in its tail.
Water may be found by witching with a green stick.

The black widow spider is more deadly than the rattlesnake.

Teeth should never be pulled in the afternoon or when the zodiac sign is about the head. To do so may cause profuse bleeding.

The best whetstone rock is always found on the north side of a mountain at an angle of forty-five degrees.

A live snake placed in a barrel of cider will keep it sweet.

Pigs castrated when the zodiac sign is in the heart will die.

Transplanted trees should always be set out in the same relative positions as when dug from the ground.

The seventh son of a seventh son is endowed with miraculous powers.

The growth of vegetables is affected by the moon.

The joint snake breaks in pieces and goes back together again.

Snakes will not enter a garden where gourds grow.

Hens will not lay in a field where there are potatoes.

Smoking a pipe will keep off epileptic fits.

If you look straight into a fire that is being kindled, it will not burn brightly.

Telling a lie may cause a blister on the tongue.

Horses have an instinctive fear of ghosts.

To sleep in the moonlight may cause insanity.

Scrambled owl's eggs cure drunkenness.

A cow that loses her cud should be given a rag to replace it.

There is danger of baldness if the hair is cut in the dark of the moon.

To cure chicken pox, lay down in the chicken house door and permit a black hen to fly over you.

To take out fire from a burn, repeat to yourself: "Two little angels came from heaven. One brought fire and the other frost. Go out fire and come in frost." Blow on the burn as you say the last word of these lines. Keep repeating until you are sure the fire is drawn out.

Hideaway Bent

No one will accept the theory that man is the victim of modern life. Man is captain of his own soul and, in a great measure, the maker of his own destiny. He towers over circumstances, and though crushed to earth will rise again. Man is a fighter. True he has destroyed his fellowmen, for he has often had to fight or perish, but as long as he fights for constructive things—he is a noble fighter. But when he tramps under his feet justice and mercy, and employs brute force, these things are not the measure of a man.

Man is a thinker. But the fact alone that man is a thinking animal does not make him great. What is the measure of a man? The true worth of a man is unselfishness; the way he lives his life among his fellowmen, judged by the standards of loyalty, honesty, and decency.

The man whose memory we honor today lived the simple life he loved among the hills. He led no great armies to victory. He was no great captain of industry. He did not write his name across the stars, but he wrote it in the hearts of his fellow man with his simple life in the hills. He preferred this life. He was born in Maine and educated at Bowdoin College, a personal friend of Longfellow and Hawthorne, with an active mind and a keen intellect, yet he loved the simple life. The actualness of reality. These are the things that make a man.

These lines I have taken from an address delivered by Dewey J. Short, member of Congress from Missouri, at the grave of Levi Morrill ("Uncle Ike" of *The Shepherd of the Hills*) in Evergreen Cemetery at Notch, Missouri, October 20, 1929.

· · · · · ·

I once had an idea that I might pass a very pleasant life, providing I could wean myself from the comforts of civilization, by living in a cozy rock shelter on James River which I had found while exploring the backhills. The shelter is on a hillside overlooking a spacious valley and the river runs close by. In the distance extends a range of hills as far as the eye can see. It is a solitary place, far from the haunts of man, and one might sing and laugh or weep and moan, according to mood and conscience, without being criticized or disturbed. I sat in this snug shelter and watched a harvest moon rise over the hills and put the stars to flight. The thought came to me that I might attain qualities and even possessions denied me in the world of trade if I made the hills my permanent home and courted nature instead of books. A few years behind my whiskers in this shelter on the hillside might help me regain the spirit I had lost while mingling with men.

I had about decided to check out of civilization and migrate to the rock shelter in the Ozarks when the United States entered the first World War. This made an abrupt change in my plans. I joined the National Guard at Kansas City and was soon inducted into the regular army. The rock shelter and the forty acres of land I had bought on White River earlier in the year, were left to look out for themselves.

Two years later I returned from France and reentered the hills. Hideaway Lodge was built in a grove of cedars on a hill by the river. For three years I lived as a thoroughgoing individualist. During the summer season I cooked over an open fire and washed the utensils in a spring near the cabin door. I occasionally slipped out of my solitude to clerk in the country store or substitute for the teacher in the district school. But most of my time was spent in the woods. Like Thoreau, I preferred to sit on a pumpkin and have it all to myself rather than be crowded on a velvet cushion. On the average, I worked one day and rested six, which was good for both body and soul. But such an experience was too good to last. Three years later I tied a knot in the latchstring at Hideaway Lodge and took a job teaching school at Kingston, Arkansas.[1]

There are thousands of men and women with hideaway tendencies who have found the Ozarks a pleasant refuge. Many of them are people with creative bent who enjoy the nourishment of solitude. Some come to regain health of mind and body and get a new look at life. Fountains of health in the form of bubbling springs continue to entice pilgrims from far and near as they did the pioneer who left his name with McFadden's

Three Sisters Springs in the Ouachita Mountains. Harold Bell Wright turned to the hills for health and inspiration and found a pot of gold. His novels of the Ozarks have been read by millions of people. It has been more than thirty years since Wright pitched his tent by Old Matt's cabin above Mutton Hollow, but he still holds the record as the best press agent the Ozarks have ever had.

Levi Morrill was a graduate of Bowdoin College, but he spent the major portion of his life as postmaster in a tiny office at Notch, Missouri. Harold Bell Wright made his home near the forks of the road which gave Notch its name. He and Morrill became great friends. When *The Shepherd of the Hills* came from the press, the old postmaster had stepped into literature as Uncle Ike. He was known to thousands of people by this name until his death in 1929.

William Henry Lynch was a pioneer of the Ozark awakening. He was a man with an international mind, born in Quebec, Canada. He was a scientist, lecturer, and traveler. He became interested in Marvel Cave in Stone County, Missouri, and helped explore the twenty-two passages and three rivers of the mammoth cavern. In 1889 he bought the cave property and devoted a large part of the remaining thirty-eight years of his life to it.

Lynch possessed a strange passion for his cave. Its vast interior was a challenge to his genius. He was a poet, and subterranean beauty was his theme. He traveled widely, lecturing at home and abroad, but the lost rivers and strange formations of Marvel Cave always called him back to the Ozark hills.[2]

William Hope "Coin" Harvey selected Monte Ne in Benton County, Arkansas, as the site for his Pyramid of Civilization. Early in the present century he began building a structure to house evidences of our modern civilization. Harvey opposed our present financial system and was firm in his opinion that civilization would fall and chaotic conditions follow. His pyramid was planned to preserve the achievements in literature, art, and science for a future age. His immediate purpose was to attract the attention of the world to the inequities of our present monetary systems.

Harvey planned to build a concrete structure with a base or pedestal sixty feet square. On top of this was to be the pyramid proper. It was to be a shaft-like formation, 130 feet high, ending in a summit six feet square. It would contain several thousand square feet of room space and cost $100,000.

The pyramid was to be a storehouse of civilization. Volumes on science, history, religion, and industry, and the literary masterpieces of the ages, would be placed in containers, hermetically sealed. All types of articles used in domestic and industrial life, from pins to automobiles and airplanes, would be stored to record our industrial achievement.

Work began on the foundation of the pyramid in the late twenties and in August 1931, the national convention of the newly organized American Liberty Party was held in a stadium adjacent to the project. Harvey founded the party and was honored with the nomination as its presidential candidate.

Coin Harvey attracted attention on the lecture platform. He would invariably close his talks with a lengthy catechism. He would state a question and its answer and then have the audience repeat it with him. I have heard him bore a sleepy audience almost to distraction with his monetary theories.

William Hope Harvey did not live to build his Pyramid of Civilization, but should you visit Monte Ne you will see the foundation stones of his vast dream. It is a monument to the strange, bizarre passion of this unusual man.[3]

A man is usually known by his achievements. Beethoven lives in his sonatas and symphonies; Shakespeare in his immortal dramas; Raphael in the frescoes he painted on the walls of the Vatican. In a tiny but still important orbit, Elmer J. Bouher lives in the community church he built at Kingston-in-the-Ozarks.

Kingston's reputation as a cultural and educational center is partially due to its rural isolation. Had the village been located on a railroad, or even a main motor highway, it is highly probable that the people would have been contented with their lot and made no effort to better conditions. But Kingston is thirty miles from a railroad and off the beaten path of motor traffic. Until recent years, it was hemmed in by a turbulent mountain stream without bridge or ferry.

A year or two before the first World War, the Board of Missions of the Presbyterian Church sent the Reverend Elmer J. Bouher into the hills of Madison County, Arkansas, to make a social survey. At Kingston, Bouher found a solid, God-fearing, law-abiding people. They had schools and churches, but the visiting preacher thought them inadequate to the social needs of the community. He saw hundreds of sterling young people growing into manhood and womanhood without adequate educational advantages. In his report to the board of missions, Bouher stressed the cultural need of the people and the unusual opportunity for service. Concrete action followed this report. Bouher was assigned to shepherd the flock at Kingston.

The building program began soon after the World War. Bouher's first thought was for a church, a place of solemn assembly where the people might worship. It took four years to build what is considered to be one of the most beautiful church buildings in rural Arkansas. Almost everyone in the community helped in the building program, quarrying stone for the foundation, cutting logs in the forest and transporting them to the community sawmill, and assisting in the construction of the building. The board of missions assisted by supplying funds for foreign building material. The church was formally dedicated in June 1926.

The atmosphere of the sanctuary, as intended by the minister-architect, is one that leads to worship. The chancel is painted white. The wine-colored pipe organ in the background adds the necessary contrast to harmonize the scene. On the speaker's platform in front of the organ are comfortable oak chairs and a beautifully hand-carved pulpit stand. Choir stalls for twenty-four singers are set in at the sides of the platform.

The auditorium has a seating capacity for four hundred people and the pews are of solid oak, spacious and comfortable. The minister established an orderly method of seating the congregation—the old New England method in which a pew is assigned to each family. The minister's pew, two seats back, is labeled with a silver plate. The floor is of finest hardwood from the neighboring forest. With the exception of the doors and windows, practically the entire building was constructed of native materials.

The place of worship, or church proper, is only a part of the project on Community Hill at Kingston. The community building contains twenty rooms which include an auditorium, classrooms for school purposes, and a library of 5,000 volumes. It is a center for community meetings and activities of all kinds.[4]

In 1929, the Sky Pilot, as the minister was called, retired from this work after fifteen years of devoted service. He came to the hills with a dream which lengthened into a vast reality. Other workers now carry on the activities of the project, but it will always be recognized as the lengthened shadow of one man—Elmer J. Bouher.

Rose Wilder Lane's statement that the valleys grow corn, but the hills grow men is aging into a proverb. Out of the solitudes of the hills come individuals to carve their names in the halls of civilization. Thomas Elmore Lucy, the old trooper, is an example of this class whose first social nourishment was in a stern pioneer environment.

Thomas Elmore Lucy is a member of a North Carolina family who followed wilderness trails to the Ozarks many years ago and settled in Pope County, Arkansas. Thomas Elmore stretched into six feet of manhood in the sylvan hills near Russellville. His talent asserted itself even in his barefoot days and his fingers were dabbled with printer's ink by the time his feet were imprisoned in shoes. He developed into an artistic printer and a forceful writer. He studied elocution and dramatics and became an outstanding impersonator of historical characters. It is in this role that he has circled the globe and gained the reputation of Arkansas's most widely traveled man. Seven books and hundreds of miscellaneous poems and articles have come from his facile pen. He has the upward vision of the pioneer, the sinew of the native tiller of the soil, and the grace of his Elizabethan ancestors. He is "a hijacker of happiness on the world's hikeway."

. . . . . .

Through the obscure history of the Ozark and Ouachita Mountains stalks the shadow of the illustrious Albert Pike, soldier-poet, philosopher, and Masonic authority. He was a native of Massachusetts, but came to Arkansas in 1832 to write his name in song and story throughout the Middle West. His first job was that of a schoolmaster in the Boston Mountains, with half of his meager salary paid in pigs. He was famous as a soldier, serving as a captain in the Mexican War and heading an Indian regiment in the service of the Confederacy in the sixties. He lived at the border town of Fort Smith for a number of years.

Pike's sojourn in the Ouachita Mountains of Montgomery County, Arkansas, is one of the strange interludes of history. His Masonic associates, and even his relatives, ridicule the idea that he ever lived in this wilderness region, but the tradition is firmly established in the minds of the people of Montgomery County. Ira C. Hopper, onetime secretary of state for Arkansas, grew to manhood at Caddo Gap, which is about eighteen miles from the site of Pike's mountain retreat. He makes this statement:

> Among the mountains of a certain secluded and almost unknown region of Arkansas may be seen today the place where Albert Pike lived and worked during the unknown period of his life. Old settlers of the neighborhood remember the time when he lived in their midst, and how he conducted himself, wrote and studied, and the story has been handed down as a tradition of the settlement.

This obscure neighborhood is Greasy Cove in the southwestern part of Montgomery County. It is thought that Pike entered this section from the Indian Territory in 1862. He came to do some creative writing and the solitude of the place appealed to him. It is said that he wrote three books during the two years spent at Greasy Cove, one of them being the famous *Morals and Dogma*.

Pike's entry into the hills is vividly described by Ida Sublette Cobb in *The Silver Shuttle*. She has given me permission to use the following extract from her story of the illustrious Mason:

General Albert Pike arrived in Caddo Gap like a monarch, in a
beautiful shiny buggy, his white hair falling over his shoulders,
his snowy beard billowing over his chest. To the buggy were harnessed two of the most superb white horses the mountain people
had ever beheld. In front of the horses marched the vanguard of
twenty Negroes. Behind the buggy came a heavily loaded wagon
of the prairie schooner type. To this wagon were hitched four
prancing horses. Following in the wake of the wagon, their eyes
whitely rolling, marched twenty solemn stalwarts forming a rear
guard. It being wartime made the incident far more interesting
than it would have been in time of peace.

Pike bought forty acres of land from John Berry Vaught, paying
him four hundred dollars in gold for it. In 1863, he erected a beautiful
log house and brought furniture from Little Rock. He lived in style and
comfort on the banks of the Little Missouri River in backhill seclusion.
But his arcadian experiment soon came to an end. Marauding jayhawkers
discovered his retreat and laid plans to destroy it. The destruction came
in 1864 when they burned his house and threw his books into the river.
According to the story, he escaped ahead of the freebooters with his
trunk of gold and a few personal belongings, and never came back to the
Ouachita Mountains.[5]

"Bring me men to match my mountains," chants the poet and the
call is filled with volunteers of unquestioned integrity. Granville Jones
was a man of the mountains who wrote the golden rule upon the table
of his heart. He had vision and intellect consistent with great leadership
and might have been a statesman with a powerful influence. But if he had
political ambitions, he kept them to himself. His mission was to inform
and inspire the general public from the lecture platform and his work was
stamped with a trademark of completeness.

Granville Jones grew to manhood in a pocket of the Ouachita hills
at Caddo Gap. He was a self-made man with a talent for oratory. The
Chautauqua platform was the medium through which he reached the
people. The patriotic vision of this man of the mountains is revealed in a

lecture he gave at Chickasha, Oklahoma, in October 1922. One pertinent
paragraph shows his faith in American democracy:

> I hear men talk of dangers that surround us, of the difficul-
> ties that confront us like mountains, of the problems that over-
> shadow us like dark storms; but, ladies and gentlemen, I am
> an American. Our fathers had problems and they solved them;
> they had enemies and they met them breast to breast and put
> them to flight; they had difficulties that rose before them like
> mountains, but they scaled their mountains of difficulty. We are
> the sons of our fathers with the same old fighting blood, and
> the same old fighting spirit. I say tonight that Americans under
> God can do anything that ought to be done. We can meet our
> enemies and put them to flight; we can face our problems and
> solve them; we can come to our difficulties and surmount them.
> Some people may have lost faith in this Republic, in what the
> flag stands for. I am not among those. I not only believe in the
> history of my country, but I believe in its present, and I believe
> in my country's future.

My residence in Ozark land has been rewarded by personal acquaintance with hundreds of stalwart men of the mountains, men who knew
the privations of oxcart days, but lived to herald the new age of the
twentieth century. They have not had great roles in the world's affairs,
but they have played the part of the common man in the drama of living,
and played it well. The older ones have passed on, but a few remain with
us as bulwarks of integrity in a restless age. I think the Ozark region
has been greatly enriched by the lives of such Missourians as William
Edward Howard, A. M. Haswell, W. S. Strong, George W. Clark, B. W.
Rice, Truman Powell, B. F. Carney, and W. S. White. Arkansas has produced many mountain men who have spent their lives memorably in the
Ozark and Ouachita hills as teachers, preachers, statesmen, business-
men, and farmers. A few of them are: Fountain Lycurgus White, Charles
Henry Buerklin, Thomas Smith Evans, Sam Leath, Hamp Williams,
Claude L. Jones, W. T. Martin, Joe Caldwell, Andy Johnson, Roy Milum,

Joel Bunch, and Payne McCracken. Some of these men are not known beyond the borders of their respective communities; others spread their influence throughout their state; each one gave or is giving himself in service in a large way to his fellow men.

Most of the honor for pioneering in the Ozarks is given to men. The pioneer mothers are revered in the memory of their descendants, but their names are not so well known as are those of the fathers, husbands, and sons. But this does not lessen the importance of the women who stood by their men through a crucial period of history. When the complete story of the Ozarks is written, the names and deeds of many illustrious women will be included. One of them will be Elizabeth Pettigrew Robberson for whom Robberson Prairie, ten miles north of Springfield, Missouri, was named.

Elizabeth Robberson was a true pioneer mother—a courageous widow who brought her fourteen children over wilderness roads from Tennessee in 1830. Her husband had died the year before and she decided to go west to permit her children to grow up with the country. A few of the older ones had already married and they with their families joined the trek. The Robberson wagon train passed through Springfield a year after the first log cabin was built and drove on to the broad open prairie which now bears their name. Large tracts of land were settled by these immigrants and a community started. The pioneer woman who led the way died in 1868. Her grave is marked by a weather-beaten monument in Robberson Cemetery, named for her, and not far from her original home in the Ozarks.

CHAPTER XVI

Traits and Trends

. . . .

The Woman Who Waits

A casual observer might conclude that sentiment is dead in the Woodville neighborhood, but close scrutiny would convince him that romance still lives on the granite ridges and gully-washed farms of this backhill Ozark community. Especially would it be so if he were lucky enough to see Ludie, "the dream girl," walking from the spring with a bucket of water.

It is a tradition with the lovelorn that the words of Mercury are harsh to the feminine ear after the songs of Apollo. Perhaps that is the reason Ludie Evans spends so much time by the old signal oak, trysting place of yesteryears, dreaming the hours away.

I first saw this mountain maid a year before our country entered the maelstrom of the first World War. I was idling away my time fishing in the river near the big spring above the village. Bruce Evans had built his gristmill by the spring thirty years before. The Evans clan was a race of millers who liked to set wheels turning in new lands. Bruce's grandfather had moved into the Missouri Ozarks from Tennessee in 1840, bringing his milling machinery with him. Bruce had a good location for business and prosperity blessed his efforts. Folks would ride or drive from the Bug Tussle neighborhood on the north and from Sassafras Pone on the south to have their grinding done at the Evans mill.

It was a bright June morning in the James River Ozarks, the fog having lifted on a glorious day of mellow sunshine. I had caught a string of smallmouth bass and goggle-eye in the vicinity of the mill and was resting on a rock by the spring, smoking my pipe. The laziness of the hour spread satisfaction such as defies pursuit but often comes in moments of relaxation. The world looked rosy as I tied a handsome spinner on my line for a cast. Suddenly, without the slightest warning, the reflection of a pretty girl appeared in the clear water of the spring at my elbow. When I turned my head and saw the maiden in flesh and blood, I had to blink my eyes before reality asserted itself.

I answered the girl's smile with a cordial greeting and continued my fishing. She filled the bucket she carried with cool water from the spring and then followed the path up and over the hill toward a wreath of smoke that emerged from a clump of maples. It was Ludie Evans, known as Woodville's dream girl. A week later I met her in a more formal way at a community play party. I also made the acquaintance of her dashing lover, Wade Spillman.

At that time, pretty girls were quite easily numbered at Woodville. The party revealed that fact to me. Few of them had the comely grace of Emily Freeman of White River and Joyce Delmar of the Posey neighborhood. There was Millie Adams, cheeks painted like a barn door; Drusilla Bullock, giggling her unattractiveness; and a dozen more girls neatly dressed in ginghams and percales, swinging in the whirl of "Tideo." It took but a single glance to see that Ludie Evans was queen of the circle. Young Spillman seemed proud of her, too, and when they started playing "Skip t' My Lou," and he was the skipper, he didn't hesitate to show his favoritism, but promptly skipped to Ludie and led her to his place in the ring.

A dark, handsome youth, whom I later learned to know as John Denby, also took an interest in Woodville's dream girl. He was a strapping fellow from the Bull Creek neighborhood, hill-bred but graceful, and it looked as though anything might happen if he and Wade should tangle. But we were locked in the maze of "Old Dan Tucker" at the moment.

Old Dan Tucker is a fine old man,
Washed his face in a fryin' pan,
Combed his hair with a wagon wheel,
An' died with th' toothache in his heel.

Away, away for old Dan Tucker,
He's too late t' get his supper;
Supper's over, breakfast a-cookin',
Old Dan Tucker standin' a-lookin'.

Gaily sang the crowd of husky youths and buxom maidens as they followed the turns and twists of the old party game. Ludie's mother looked on with approval as her charming daughter bowed and swung gracefully in turn. It was a high moment in the social life of the community; old and young forgot dull care and joined in the happy rhythm of the song.

All went well until the "cheating" started in "Pig in the Parlor." Young Denby beat Wade's time by a margin and a look passed between them that was not in harmony with the festive occasion. It was a mere spark of passion's fire, but with power to flame and destroy. That night, after Spillman had carried Ludie home on his horse, there was a meeting of the young men at the crossroads near the Devil's Eyebrow. Hot words were exchanged and a fight followed. That was the beginning of a period of community warfare which cast a long shadow over Woodville and the adjacent country for several months. It led to battle royal in which friends and relatives took part. Luckily, there were no casualties, but bitter hate had come to poison the heart of this arcadian land, and an actual feud between the Spillman and Denby clans was imminent.

Then came the excitement of our entry into the great World War and the lesser struggle was forgotten. Both Wade and John were drafted into the army during the first months of the war, and went to France. Denby returned the next year, shell-shocked—a total physical and mental wreck. Spillman was listed as missing in the Meuse–Argonne offensive and, at the end of the war, his machine-gun outfit returned without him.

Ludie did not marry although her chances were legion. Spring came to the hills with its lavish spread of beauty. Summer returned with its mild zephyrs carrying fragrance and memories. Winter's loneliness iced her features, but left her heart warm with expectancy. But Wade Spillman failed to make his appearance.

Five years after the war closed, I revisited the Woodville community and spent a week fishing on the river near the Evans mill. Ludie was a woman now, possessed with the quiet dignity of her people. She had retained much of her youthful beauty even while stepping in the lonely treadmill that life had bequeathed her. For hours at a time she would stand by the signal oak, looking longingly into the valley that leads to the level land. "He will come, he *must* come," she would sob as she rekindled the fire of hope which time had never quenched.

Twenty-three years have passed since the World War and the Ozark Country has taken on many modern improvements. The old ferry on White River has been eliminated and a steel bridge now spans the stream. Graveled highways have been constructed to serve practically the entire county. Tart Tuttle has put in a filling station adjoining his store and is thinking of opening a tourist camp. The old log schoolhouse at Bug Tussle has been torn down and the district consolidated with the school at the county seat. Millie Adams is the mother of five boys with no time to paint her face or curl her hair. Drusilla Bullock has married a hard-shell preacher and lost her giggle. John Denby sleeps in the Antioch Cemetery on Paw-Paw Ridge. But Ludie Evans, now a woman of middle age, remains true to the sweetheart of her youth. Her constancy is unshaken.

Economic Drift

Folklore, formerly known by the awkward name "popular antiquities," is concerned with what might be called the organic age. This epoch began long before the dawn of history seven thousand years ago. Primitive man showed shrewdness in selecting and taming animals best adapted to domestic use, and plants which responded best to cultivation. Science has been unable to find wild plants comparable in value to the staple varieties such as wheat, oats, rye, and rice—plants selected and tamed by man in prehistoric times. And the same may be said of animals. Long before the invention of written language, the dog, horse, cow, sheep, and goat had been domesticated. But in the inorganic world, in fields of physics and chemistry, ancient man did not explore. The adventure with molecules and atoms was reserved for the historic age. Steam and electricity, and all their modernistic trappings, are products of the machine age. Folklore is part and parcel of pastoral life. With the coming of science, it folds its tent and sulks away.

When social workers first entered the Ozarks a few years ago and made surveys of rural condition they found the natives, for the most part, satisfied with things as they existed. "Leave us alone and we will scrape up a living some way," was the answer given when relief was offered. Any assistance bordering on charity was spurned except by the class recognized as social deadwood. The average hillsman craved neither work nor luxuries. His fierce pride resented being told what to do and how to do it. His greatest wish was to be left alone.

The social workers soon realized that instinctive caution is deeply seated in the hillsman's nature. It is an accredited folkway to outwit changing conditions cautiously like a cat playing with a mouse. Belief and practice in the backhills may have strange imprints of inconsistency. A man may jokingly refer to some household superstition, but you don't find him burning sassafras wood in the fireplace or ignoring a chain letter. His creed may be as antique as his walnut furniture but he clings to it like a tenderfoot riding a raft.

This inconsistency in behavior is probably responsible for the apparent break in the traditional morale of the hillsman in recent years. He saw the handwriting on the wall and realized that his way of life must go. He decided to crush pride with the heel of necessity and accept government aid. He adjusted his logic as best he could and tried to save face by accepting employment on federal projects. He had come to the end of his primitive trail of freedom, and necessity forced him onto the regimented high road.

The Ozarks without the independent spirit of the hillsman will be as drab as Shakespeare's *Romeo and Juliet* with Juliet left out. But it is useless to butt heads against the wall of the inevitable. The economic drift is toward regimentation and all the king's horses and all the king's men cannot put the old freedom into the hills again. The very thing the hillsman feared ten years ago is rapidly coming to pass. Perhaps the Ozarker is in the same position as the stranger who stopped at a mountain cabin to inquire for the location of a hillbilly's still. The wildcatter's son offered to direct the man to the still for a quarter, but asked payment in advance. "I'll pay you when I get back," said the stranger. "But," said the boy, "*you ain't comin' back.*"

The following agencies now render aid to farmers in the hill country: Civilian Conservation Corps, Soil Conservation Service, Farm Security Administration, National Youth Administration, Vocational Agriculture, Farm Credit Bureau, Protective Credit Association, and the National Forestry Service. These agencies do not overlap and each has its place in modernized rural life. It has taken several years to prove to Ozark farmers that these agencies are at their disposal to aid them in keeping the soil that the soil may keep them.

The social workers say that during the Depression, especially from 1930 to 1933, conditions in some parts of the Ozarks were pitiful, but that in the last few years the government agencies have penetrated each rural community and that the economic level has been greatly raised. They hold that many of the people living in the underprivileged sections will always have to be helped by someone: their neighbors, the community, the state, or the federal government. At present they are being assisted by the United States government through employment on projects of the Works Progress Administration or by direct relief.

The Ozarkian desire for freedom still lives in the hearts of thousands of the people and I believe this feeling will continue as long as the blood stays pure Ozarkian. But the machine age has brought a new order of life to the backhills and the Elizabethan remnants are in the melting pot. No one knows what the outcome will be.

NOTES TO THE TEXT

The following notes, all written by the editor of this reissue, are not intended as an exhaustive annotation. They are meant to clarify the meaning of obscure vernacular words and phrases, to provide historical context or correction, and to suggest further reading on certain subjects that have been submitted to scholarly examination since the first publication of this book.

CHAPTER I

1. Anyone who writes about the Ozarks must settle on a definition of the region. In *Ozark Country* Rayburn uses what might be called a broad cultural definition of the Ozarks, albeit one that quickly fell out of use in the years after the book's publication. Geographers continue to classify both the Ozarks and the Ouachitas as parts of the US Interior Highlands, but most scholarly studies concentrate on one region or the other. It was only in the early twentieth century that professional geographers such as Curtis Fletcher Marbut and Carl O. Sauer began differentiating between the geologically distinct Ouachita Mountains south of the Arkansas River and the Ozark Uplift north of the river. But the more widely recognized "Ozark" label continued to be applied to some places south of the Arkansas River. Some promotional materials for Hot Springs, Arkansas, continued to advertise the resort town's location in the Ozarks into the post–World War I era. The Ozark National Forest still contains a section, the Mount Magazine District, that is located south of the Arkansas. Like Rayburn, folklorist Vance Randolph also used examples from both the Ouachitas and the Ozarks in his early books, but the practice mostly disappeared after World War II. See Marbut, *Soil Reconnaissance of the Ozark Region of Missouri and Arkansas* (Washington, DC: US Government Printing Office, 1914) and Sauer, *Geography of the Ozark Highland of Missouri* (New York: Greenwood Press, [1920] 1968).

2. There have been almost as many explanations for the etymology of the word "Ozarks" as there have been chroniclers of the region. The most widely accepted explanation today suggests that the regional term is related to the roots of the word Arkansas. French explorers of the Mississippi Valley adopted the Illini word for the Native Americans now known as the Quapaw, calling them the "Arcansas." At the Arkansas Post in the eighteenth century, French officials began signing their letters with the abbreviated *aux arc* or *aux arcs*, meaning "at the land of the Arkansas." This new geographical designator gradually made its way up the Arkansas and White Rivers, and British and English-speaking American settlers anglicized it as Ozark or Ozarks. Lynn Morrow, "Ozark/Ozarks: Establishing a Regional Term," *White River Valley Historical Quarterly* 36 (Fall 1996): 4, 5.

3. The most commonly accepted explanation for the etymology of the word "Ouachita" is quite similar to Rayburn's final example. According to the *Encyclopedia of Oklahoma History and Culture*, "the Ouachita name came from the French spelling of the Indian word *washita*, meaning 'good hunting ground.'" Shayne R. Cole and Richard A. Marston, "Ouachita Mountains," *Encyclopedia of Oklahoma History and Culture*, https://www.okhistory.org/publications/enc.php?entry=OU001.

4. Though still treasured by many, the account of Schoolcraft's journey is not as rare as it was in Rayburn's day. See Henry Rowe Schoolcraft, *Rude Pursuits and Rugged Peaks: Schoolcraft's Ozark Journal, 1818–1819*, introduction, maps, and appendix by Milton D. Rafferty (Fayetteville: University of Arkansas Press, 1996). See also Schoolcraft, *A View of the Lead Mines of Missouri* (New York: Charles Wiley & Co., 1819).

5. For an updated and more accurate rendition of this story, see Lynn Morrow, "The Yocum Silver Dollar," *White River Valley Historical Quarterly* 8 (Spring 1985): 3–10.

6. Basic information on most of the people Rayburn mentions can easily be found in online encyclopedias, including Wikipedia. Exceptions are Nancy Clemens, May Kennedy McCord, Mary Elizabeth Mahnkey, and "Mirandy." Nancy Clemens was one of several pen names used by Ozarks native Fern Nance (1910–2003), a one-time Springfield, Missouri, reporter who published a number of books and magazine articles in the 1930s. As Fern Shumate, she returned to regional prominence in the 1980s as a regular columnist in the *Ozarks Mountaineer* magazine. May Kennedy McCord (1880–1979), the self-styled "Queen of the Hillbillies," was a southwestern Missouri native who became a noted newspaper columnist, radio personality, and amateur folklorist in Springfield. Her life and columns are the subjects of *Queen of the Hillbillies: Writings of May Kennedy McCord*, Chronicles of the Ozarks, edited by Patti McCord and Kristene Sutliff (Fayetteville: University of Arkansas

Press, 2021). Born in Harrison, Arkansas, but a resident of Taney County, Missouri, most of her life, Mary Elizabeth Mahnkey (1877–1948) was a rural storekeeper and postmistress who, for more than half a century, contributed community news, reminiscences, and poetry to newspapers in southwestern Missouri. Mahnkey became something of a regional celebrity in 1936 when a New York publishing company named her the nation's outstanding country correspondent and publicized her trip to the city. Rayburn's reference to "Mirandy" most likely signifies the radio character from "Uncle Luke and Aunt Mirandy of Persimmon Holler," a regular skit featured on *The National Farm and Home Hour*, which was broadcast to a nationwide audience out of Chicago in the late 1920s and early 1930s. Mirandy was voiced by Marian Driscoll Jordan (1898–1961), a native of Peoria, Illinois, who had no known connection to the Ozarks and who later went on to fame as Molly in the long-running and beloved radio program *Fibber McGee and Molly*.

CHAPTER II

1. Rayburn's celebration of the "Anglo-Saxonism" of the Ozarks and the region's "Elizabethan culture" was common among chroniclers of the Ozarks and Appalachia in the first half of the twentieth century. Motivated by xenophobic fears of the "new immigration" of the late 1800s and early 1900s, imperial racial theories, and Jim Crow–era racism, many white Americans of Protestant, northern European lineage romanticized the southern highlands as the country's last bastion of white racial purity. This romanticization also downplayed the racial and ethnic diversity that existed in parts of the highlands. See Henry D. Shapiro, *Appalachia on Our Mind: The Southern Mountains and Mountaineers in the American Consciousness, 1870–1920* (Chapel Hill: University of North Carolina Press, 1978); David E. Whisnant, *All That Is Native and Fine: The Politics of Culture in an American Region* (Chapel Hill: University of North Carolina Press, 1983); and Ian C. Hartman, *In the Shadow of Boone and Crockett: Race, Culture, and the Politics of Representation in the Upland South* (Knoxville: University of Tennessee Press, 2015).
2. See Arthur H. Estabrook, "The Population of the Ozarks," *Mountain Life and Work* 5 (1929): 7–12.

CHAPTER V

1. For more information on play parties and play-party music, see Alan L. Spurgeon, *Waltz the Hall: The American Play Party* (Jackson: University Press of Mississippi, 2005).

CHAPTER VI

1. "Whetting a banter" (or banner) was a phrase indicating a reaper's boastful challenge to fellow reapers. Technically it refers to loudly scraping or sharpening a scythe with a whetstone. See Vance Randolph and George P. Wilson, *Down in the Holler: A Gallery of Ozark Folk Speech* (Norman: University of Oklahoma Press, 1953), 298.
2. "Sowbelly with the buttons on" was once a common phrase associated with the consumption of salted fat pork from the belly of a pig, called sowbelly. The word "buttons" likely refers to the animal's teats, since sowbelly was routinely eaten with the skin left on the cut of meat.
3. The phrase "took bread and had bread" indicated that someone at the table took another piece of bread before finishing the one on their plate, an omen that a hungry person was sure to visit.

CHAPTER VII

1. In old Ozarks vernacular, to "hone for" something was to desire or crave it.
2. The most common monster in Ozarks tall tales and folklore, the gowrow was a giant, tusked reptile with sharp blades on its tail. It was reported to live in caves or under rock ledges and feed on large mammals, perhaps even humans. See Vance Randolph, "Fabulous Monsters in the Ozarks," *Arkansas Historical Quarterly* 9 (Summer 1950): 55–65.
3. The razorback made a bold comeback in the Ozarks in the early twenty-first century. At the current time, feral pigs are a major issue for the region's farmers, and a number of government agencies (the Missouri Department of Conservation, the Arkansas Game and Fish Commission, the National Park Service) continue to develop methods for reducing the population of an invasive species that was once almost eradicated.
4. The term "jack salmon" refers to the walleye. Until a generation or so ago, walleye fishermen in the region commonly used the abbreviated term "jack salmon" or "jack" to refer to this game fish. "Redhorse" in the next line refers to one species of suckerfish, which were commonly gigged, grabbed, or netted during their annual spring spawning run. The town of Nixa, Missouri, has celebrated Sucker Day since 1957.

CHAPTER IX

1. There are numerous works on the traditional music of the Ozarks, but nothing is more fundamental than Vance Randolph's four-volume *Ozark Folksongs*, published between 1946 and 1950 by the State Historical Society of Missouri. Twenty-first-century students and fans of the region's traditional music have

access to a wealth of original recordings and other materials through three online collections: the *Max Hunter Folk Song Collection* (https://maxhunter.missouristate.edu/), the *John Quincy Wolf Folklore Collection* (web.lyon.edu/wolfcollection/), and the *Ozark Folksong Collection* (digitalcollections.uark.edu/cdm/landingpage/collection/OzarkFolkSong).

2. For a discussion of singing schools (past and present), see Brooks Blevins, "Where Everything New Is Old Again: Southern Gospel Singing Schools," *Southern Cultures* 22 (Winter 2016): 135–149.

CHAPTER X

1. For a comprehensive look at death and burial customs in the Ozarks, see Abby Burnett, *Gone to the Grave: Burial Customs of the Arkansas Ozarks, 1850–1950* (Jackson: University Press of Mississippi, 2014).

CHAPTER XI

1. "Thrash" or "thresh" was the common Ozarks pronunciation of the infant infection known as thrush.

CHAPTER XIII

1. It may have been said "that he would not commit murder to accomplish a robbery," but Henry Starr was apparently willing to take a life to avoid being captured, killing a deputy marshal who attempted to detain him in 1892. Jon D. May, "Starr, Henry," *Encyclopedia of Oklahoma History and Culture*, https://www.okhistory.org/publications/enc.php?entry=ST060.

CHAPTER XIV

1. Rayburn was often on shaky ground when attempting to write straight history, and nowhere was this more evident than in this section on Native Americans. Furthermore, his mixture of heroic idealization and demeaning language ("redmen," "mixed-breeds") reflected the ambiguous and othered status of natives in popular narratives of the era. For a recent examination of the roles of various American Indian nations in Ozarks history, see the second and third chapters of Brooks Blevins, *A History of the Ozarks, Volume 1: The Old Ozarks* (Urbana: University of Illinois Press, 2018).

2. The most commonly accepted etymology for the word Quapaw is that it is a derivation of the Illini word "Arcansas," which French explorers adopted and applied to the natives who occupied the area around the mouth of the

Arkansas River. Joseph Key, "Quapaw," *Encyclopedia of Arkansas History & Culture*, www.encyclopediaofarkansas.net/.

3. It may have been more accurate had Rayburn claimed that Sam A. Leath *created* "more Indian lore than any other person living today." A longtime Eureka Springs tourism promoter and director of chambers of commerce in Eureka Springs, Harrison, and Paragould, Arkansas, Leath (1877–1966) was among a stable of early twentieth-century whites who created and perpetuated romantic tales of heroic, noble, and usually doomed Native Americans. Leath likely concocted such stories to entertain trail-riding tourists in Eureka Springs. His penchant for storytelling seems to have impacted his own legacy. A 1955 *Arkansas Historical Quarterly* piece on Leath (which he coauthored) also contains apparent errors and exaggerations of his life. For instance, he claims that his father, a noted Baptist evangelist, died in a blizzard in Washington state in 1888, though Rev. D. W. Leath actually died in Alabama in 1912. Not surprisingly, heroic and noble American Indians figure prominently in Leath's version of his own life story. F. P. Rose and Sam A. Leath, "The Story of Sam A. Leath," *Arkansas Historical Quarterly* 14 (Summer 1955): 120–127; "Rev. D. W. Leath," *Sabbath Recorder*, December 30, 1912, 891.

CHAPTER XV

1. According to his autobiography, Rayburn's life as a "thoroughgoing individualist" in the immediate postwar years was limited to the summer months, as he made his living by teaching school in Kansas during the academic year. Rayburn, *Forty Years in the Ozarks: An Autobiography* (Eureka Springs, AR: Ozark Guide Press, 1957), 19.

2. In the late nineteenth century, Marvel Cave would have still been known as Marble Cave. It was renamed Marvel Cave in the 1920s.

3. Today Harvey's unfinished pyramid and most of the remnants of Monte Ne lie submerged beneath the waters of Beaver Lake, created in the 1960s when the Army Corps of Engineers built a final dam on the White River. Gaye Bland, "'Coin' Harvey," *Encyclopedia of Arkansas History & Culture*, www.encyclopediaofarkansas.net/.

4. The grand Kingston Church was eventually converted into a health clinic before being dismantled in the early 1950s. Abby Burnett, *When the Presbyterians Came to Kingston: Kingston Community Church, 1917–1951* (Kingston, AR: Bradshaw Mountain Publishers, 2000).

5. For more information on Pike, see Walter L. Brown, *A Life of Albert Pike* (Fayetteville: University of Arkansas Press, 1997).